Identity and Ecclesiology

Identity and Ecclesiology

Their Relationship among Select African Theologians

Stephanie A. Lowery

FOREWORD BY
Daniel J. Treier

PICKWICK *Publications* • Eugene, Oregon

IDENTITY AND ECCLESIOLOGY
Their Relationship among Select African Theologians

Copyright © 2017 Stephanie A. Lowery. All rights reserved. Except for brief quotations in critical publications or reviews, no part of this book may be reproduced in any manner without prior written permission from the publisher. Write: Permissions, Wipf and Stock Publishers, 199 W. 8th Ave., Suite 3, Eugene, OR 97401.

Pickwick Publications
An Imprint of Wipf and Stock Publishers
199 W. 8th Ave., Suite 3
Eugene, OR 97401

www.wipfandstock.com

PAPERBACK ISBN: 978-1-4982-9845-2
HARDCOVER ISBN: 978-1-4982-4892-1
EBOOK ISBN: 978-1-4982-9846-9

Cataloguing-in-Publication data:

Names: Lowery, Stephanie A. | foreword by Treier, Daniel J.

Title: Identity and ecclesiology : their relationship among select African theologians / Stephanie A. Lowery.

Description: Eugene, OR: Pickwick Publications, 2017 | Includes bibliographical references.

Identifiers: ISBN 978-1-4982-9845-2 (paperback) | ISBN 978-1-4982-4892-1 (hardcover) | ISBN 978-1-4982-9846-9 (ebook)

Subjects: LCSH: Church. | Christianity—Africa. | Theology, Doctrinal—Africa. | Church and social problems—Africa.

Classification: LCC BV600.3 L6 2017 (print) | LCC BV600.3 (ebook)

Manufactured in the U.S.A.   04/24/17

To my professors (in chronological order: Paul R. Schaefer, James Bibza, R. Todd Mangum, John R. Franke, and Daniel J. Treier) who model godly lives,

To my Grandma Voreis, and Grandpa and Grandma Lowery, who are my examples of faithful prayer warriors,

To my father, who taught me about joy, laughter, and courage,

And most of all to my mother, who taught me what unconditional love looks like:

Ninakupenda!

Contents

Foreword by Daniel J. Treier | ix
Acknowledgments | xi
Introduction | xiii
List of Abbreviations | xv

1. The Context of Theology in Africa | 1
2. Theology in Africa | 11
3. Identities in Africa | 46
4. Communal Identity in Scripture | 83
5. Ecclesiology in Africa | 128
6. Christian Social Identity in Africa and Beyond | 195

Bibliography | 221

Foreword

The need for this English-language monograph addressing African ecclesiology may be surprising, but it is genuine. In the first place, there are surprisingly few monographs addressing African ecclesiology in any language. The major academic survey of the subject, from Charles Nyamiti, is now relatively old; it was much briefer than the present work, and narrower in focusing coverage on a more select stream. So the present work by Dr. Lowery is already distinctive in treating both earlier and more contemporary sources, as well as both Catholic and Protestant figures and works. Dr. Lowery herself was raised in Africa and has done thorough reconnaissance on the academic resources in English and French as well as other material and perspectives. She is careful to listen and learn, to ask questions, to indicate issues, but not to tell Africans how to think. She seeks to avoid imposing alien constructs on the material even as she ponders how to bring the African conversation to the attention of other contexts.

Yet beyond the need simply for a monograph addressing African ecclesiologies, we need an English-language work of this type in order to help "the West" listen to African brothers and sisters in Christ. This listening should involve several components, most likely in phases. First, most basically, the present book has value in providing orientation to African theology in general, about which most of us Westerners remain woefully ignorant. Second, Dr. Lowery helpfully dispels a fairly common myth about the history of African theology, according to which its first generation focused on defending the legitimacy of "inculturation" while now its subsequent generation has moved on to other subjects. In point of fact, the concern for inculturation remains, even if sometimes transposed into new keys. Third, more specifically, the present book helps the church around the world to learn of African ecclesiological challenges so as to be in prayer and solidarity with brothers and sisters in Christ.

Fourth, and quite fundamentally, Dr. Lowery's work introduces Christians around the world to distinctive resources arising from a particular ecclesiological culture and history. From our African brothers and sisters we hear a compelling reminder of the Bible's own distinctive emphasis upon community and shared Christian identity. Furthermore, in hearing this reminder from our African brothers and sisters we encounter a compelling case study: How do we discern the distinctiveness of the Christian gospel, with its implications for the reality we call "church," vis-à-vis its rootedness in particular cultures? When do such local communities help us to see more clearly how God made people to be the church, whatever their context? When do such local communities hinder us from being authentically Christian, whether in moments of individualism on the one hand or tribalism on the other? And when are the practices and perspectives of such local communities simply different, attesting in that diversity to the plurality of God's gifts, the freedom of the gospel, and the multiplicity inherent within Christian love and unity? In wrestling with more socially versus more personally formed identities as we compare "African" and "Western" tendencies, we face an instructive instance of the challenge of biblical inculturation.

After reading Dr. Lowery's work, and encountering the thinkers whom she engages, I have not discerned all the answers to this set of questions. But I have been challenged to engage such questions more deeply, to see the wide range of their implications, and to appreciate the potential resources that are available when I begin to pay more attention to my sisters and brothers in a faraway part of the world.

—Daniel J. Treier

Acknowledgments

A well-known African proverb teaches that "if you want to go fast, go alone; if you want to go far, go together." The road of the dissertation, and what led up to it, have been possible only because of those who have set my feet on the road and walked with me through portions of this journey. I am forever indebted to the godly scholars who first introduced me to biblical and theological studies (James Bibza and Paul R. Schaefer), changing the path of my life. Thank you to my seminary mentors (R. Todd Mangum and John R. Franke, the latter who gave me the first opportunity for in-depth exploration of theologies in Africa), and to my doctoral advisor (Daniel J. Treier) who encouraged and sharpened my thinking and writing. Thanks to Tite Tiénou and Victor I. Ezigbo for sharpening the final product. I am also grateful to Jeffrey Greenman and Gene Green for their passion for global theology. I also would not have made it this far without the support of my cohort at Wheaton, my home churches (Life Church and EUM), and my family and friends, especially those from Ghana, Kenya, Rwanda, Tanzania, and Uganda.

In a larger sense this all began when my parents chose to be missionaries in Africa, bequeathing me a love for Africa and wonderful memories of growing up there. My parents believed in me most and were my first teachers—thank you.

—Stephanie A. Lowery

Introduction

Ecclesiology should naturally be a prominent doctrine in Africa because of the cultural emphasis on communal identity. Yet there are few scholarly studies of African ecclesiology. The present work starts to fill that gap, thus offering its contribution to African theology.

To begin with, contested notions of 'African' identity are addressed before five characteristic themes of African theology are proposed: identity, inculturation, liberation, life, and community. 'Identity' is the crucial concern that integrates the other characteristic themes, so the work demonstrates the prominence of concern for identity among theologians through particular attention to Mulago gwa Cikala Musharhamina, Kwame Bediako, and Mercy Amba Oduyoye.

Having laid this groundwork, the book examines biblical texts that have been particularly important in African theological treatments of identity and ecclesiologies. Then five ecclesiology proposals in Africa are profiled in chronological order, from Elochukwu E. Uzukwu, Agbonkhianmeghe E. Orobator, Augustin Ramazani Bishwende, Paul Mbandi, and Georges Titre Ande.

These African ecclesiologies share a deep concern over the nature of ecclesial solidarity: Does it respect and integrate diversity, and treat all members as equals? The theologians base their understanding of ecclesial unity especially on Trinitarian theology of the Incarnation, and relational views of God and humanity. Their ecclesiologies demonstrate that 'identity' is not a passé concern of first-generation African Christian theologians, but continues to integrate several major concerns of African theologies. The concern with communal identity—African and Christian—responds to biblical, distinctively Christian priorities that become more apparent in the African pursuit of a healthy, dignified identity.

African ecclesiologies repeatedly stress including all persons as equals in interdependent community. The issue of whether church should be described as 'family' is debated, precisely because of a shared commitment to deep Christian solidarity alongside worries over conflict produced by pre- or extra-Christian identities. The unity among God's people is not to come at the expense of God-given diversity yet it overcomes previous barriers to solidarity in Christ (whether ethnicity, gender, role, language, etc.).

Finally, the social identity approach provides a language with which these culturally prompted, biblically based insights can be heard by non-African readers. The notion of a 'superordinate' identity, which relativizes but does not remove secondary identities, can be especially helpful in articulating the African ecclesiological aspirations regarding unity in Christ over against ethnic conflict.

List of Abbreviations

AFER	African Ecclesial Review
ATJ	Africa Theological Journal
BECNT	Baker Exegetical Commentary on the New Testament
CBQ	Catholic Biblical Quarterly
IJST	International Journal of Systematic Theology
Int	Interpretation
JBL	Journal of Biblical Literature
JETS	Journal of the Evangelical Theological Society
JSOT	Journal for the Study of the Old Testament
JSOT Sup	Journal for the Study of the Old Testament Supplement
JTSA	Journal of Theology for Southern Africa
LNTS	Library of New Testament Studies
NICOT	New International Commentary on the Old Testament
NovTSup	Supplements to Novum Testamentum
SBL	Society of Biblical Literature
SBLDS	Society of Biblical Literature Dissertation Series
THOTC	Two Horizons Old Testament Commentary
WUNT	Wissenschaftliche Untersuchungen zum Neuen Testament
VT	Vetus Testamentum

Chapter 1

The Context of Theology in Africa

Modern African self-theologizing is now over a half century old. Christian theology in Africa is a complex mixture of formal and informal engagement with Africa's strengths and struggles, including encounters between Christianity and African religions and encounters with Western powers.[1] As this work will show, it is natural for Christian theologies in Africa to be preoccupied with questions of identity that arise amid these varied encounters.

One characteristic feature of African theologies that draws periodic attention is their communal focus, hence the focus here on ecclesiology. For example, this communal emphasis surfaced when the Anglican Communion drew upon African concepts to organize its 2008 international Lambeth meeting. "I belong; therefore I am," a well-known saying asserts. But full-length analytic studies of African ecclesiology per se scarcely exist, a deficit this work seeks to remedy.

As Charles Nyamiti notes, there is undoubtedly concern with and writing about African ecclesiology.[2] However, in-depth surveys of ecclesiologies are lacking: Nyamiti's is one of the few available. *Contemporary*

---

1. I am here distinguishing between African religions—commonly referred to as 'African traditional religions' or 'indigenous religions'—and Christianity. The focus here is on the particular religion's origin; the phrasing does not imply that Christianity has not become inculturated in Africa. There are many terms used for this particular region of the world: the West, the Global North, the North Atlantic, the First Third world as opposed to the Two Thirds world, etc. To be more specific, in this work the phrase generally refers to North America and Western Europe. The term 'Western' has been chosen here because it is the most widely used and recognizable term worldwide and has common parlance in African literature.

2. Nyamiti, *Some Contemporary Models*, ix.

Models of African Ecclesiology opens with biblical material regarding God's people, including one page on "adumbrations" of the church in the OT, then explores ecclesiology in the Catholic church's catechism as well as providing the text "Letters to Bishops on Some Aspects of Church Understood as Communion." In part 2, Nyamiti surveys some contemporary models of ecclesiology in Africa from both the inculturation and liberation streams of theology, most by Catholic theologians, then gives closer examination to two particular models and responding to criticism of his own theology. So theologians such as E. Uzukwu, Bénézet Bujo, and Manas Buthelezi receive 1–2 pages each, while Nyamiti devotes more attention to his criticism of A. E. Orobator (60 pages) and his response to Orobator's criticism of Nyamiti's theology (nearly 20 pages).

Nyamiti's survey, then, is valuable in providing a brief overview of several ecclesiologies, but his work is mainly one of ground-clearing: he is prompted by concerns of deficiencies in African ecclesiologies, and wants to address these before laying out his own ecclesiology in full in a later book.[3] He concludes that ecclesiologies in Africa often fall into the traps of secularism, reductionism, superficiality, and an 'earthly' focus; he hopes for more "serious philosophical and theological speculation."[4] My contribution will lie in extending the work of surveying African ecclesiologies to include other voices and deeper analysis, filling in areas that Nyamiti touches on only lightly: more biblical exploration, links with major concerns in African theology as a whole, and deeper exploration of some ecclesiologies.

A historical-theological analysis of general trends in African ecclesiology, developed through careful attention to representative and influential formal African ecclesiologies along with broader attention to the pervasively communal sense of identity, might aid scholars in appropriating latent riches. Near the end of this historical-theological analysis, the social identity approach aids in sharpening the articulation of these ecclesiological trends and identifying pressure points for future theologians to address more fully.

No more than a brief historical introduction is required to explain why questions of communal identity—African identities generally and Christian identities in Africa specifically—have been prominent concerns in African philosophy, literature, and theology.[5] While portions of northern Africa were introduced to Christianity quite early, the majority of the continent, particularly the interior, heard the Gospel much later. It was not until the

---

3. Ibid., ix–x, 231–32.

4. Ibid., 231.

5. Nils E. Bloch-Hoell notes that unfortunately, 'Africa' and 'African' are terms frequently "taken for granted" ("African Identity," 98–100).

middle and end of the nineteenth century that European missionaries began to have noticeable effects. Around the same time, at the Berlin Conference of 1884–85, Europe allocated the continent of Africa. Desire for power and conquest, for resources and the glory of making great discoveries led these 'civilized' countries toward Africa, a vast, mysterious continent. To avoid problems amongst themselves, the European powers divided up the continent, to have clarity over who claimed and controlled each region. Among the countries represented were England, Italy, Belgium, France, Germany, Portugal, and Spain. How Africans felt about having arbitrary boundaries laid out, new nations formed, and their land put under the authority of foreign governments, was seemingly irrelevant.[6]

In the late 1950s, as European countries began taking steps toward relinquishing control of their respective African colonies, African churches likewise considered their own roles as independent congregations with indigenous leadership. Contemporary written African theologies emerged in 1956.[7] When freedom came in the mid-1900s, Africa was far from unchanged: in the relatively short time Europeans held power, they drastically affected the face of society, economics, politics, education, and religious beliefs, dismantling much of traditional culture, while 'improving' Africa by introducing European education, technology, and Christianity.

The result of many changes in so brief a time was nothing short of an identity crisis for African cultures. Catapulted into the modern world, ripped from their traditional cultures yet not deeply rooted in the new, foreign soil, many Africans uncomfortably straddled two worlds. In addition, some African intellectuals perceived Christianity as an alien faith, while Western theologians seemed to doubt the legitimacy of and need for African theologies.[8] These pressures understandably led many early African theologians to take a defensive, apologetic approach to their work. It is in this context that theologizing in Africa began, and for this reason a major question of African theologies was and is that of identity: How shall we define ourselves?[9] How do we root ourselves and find our voice and place

6. Ungar, *Africa*, 44.

7. Tiénou, "Evangelical Theology," 216–17.

8. For instance, atheist Ugandan poet Okot p'Bitek referred to the Christian God as "the new God of Christianity" and in Mugambi's assessment, "Okot notices that there are some African values which differ very much from those of Christianity, therefore, it is impossible to encourage the establishment of Christianity among Africans without at the same time forcing them to abandon their cultural and religious heritage" (Mugambi, "Okot p'Bitek," 94). P'Bitek therefore castigated Christian theologians (such as John Mbiti) who described African religions as 'progressive revelation' or *praeparatio evangelica* for the Christian gospel.

9. To say 'African theology' in the singular can be misleading: it is reductionistic.

in the world?[10] What form(s) should Christianity take in Africa, and how does it relate to African religions? How do oppressed people, their history and heritage dismissed as negligible at best, thrust unprepared into Western forms of modernity, find firm ground upon which to stand?[11]

Every culture and every generation struggles with identity questions at some point. A person or group of people desires to clarify what makes them like and unlike others, or to delineate what they stand for: "Identity is constructed at the boundary of sameness and difference."[12] Identity incorporates the labels others place on a person, as well as the self-perceptions and labels the person or group chooses.[13] Human identity has both individual and communal aspects.[14] So a person may identify themselves in part by achievements or further elements that make them distinct from others: being the daughter of X and Y, having achieved a particular social honor at a certain age, cultivating a specific skill, and so forth. An individual's identity also incorporates their communal or social identities, their membership in

---

The term 'African theologies' is more precise, because there is no single homogenous theology presented by African theologians. However, numerous theologians and anthropologists agree that there are common denominators that allow one to speak of 'Africa' as a unity in some sense. Accordingly, one may speak of 'African theology' as a category or field within which are found various theologies. Throughout this work, theology refers specifically to African Christian theologies, never to theologies from African religions or Islam.

10. There are various 'voices' or streams within the theological conversation on the continent—Black theology (mostly from South Africa), liberation theology, reconstruction theology, womanist theology, and inculturation theology (also referred to as African theology), which focuses particularly on issues of contextualizing the Christian faith. The majority of theologians writing about ecclesiology are in inculturation, liberation, or reconstruction streams, so there is less from womanist theologians here. I have excluded Black theology for reasons mentioned elsewhere.

11. The idea is not to promote nationalistic or ethnic theologies, but to realize that differing contexts bring up different emphases in theological constructions, all the while seeking to remain faithful to the Christian gospel. For recent examples of North American evangelical theologians addressing the issue of global theologies and contextualization, see Keener and Carroll R., *Global Voices*; Vanhoozer, "One Rule?," 85–126; Rah, *The Next Evangelicalism*; Tennent, *Theology in the Context of World Christianity*; also, Grenz and Franke, *Beyond Foundationalism*.

12. Pachuau, "Ethnic Identity," 54, cf. 57.

13. Anyidoho, "Identity and Knowledge Production," 167 n. 1; Jenkins, *Social Identity*, 20–21, 76–77, 142; Tajfel, "Interindividual Behaviour," 37; Tajfel and Turner, "The Social Identity Theory," 284.

14. Barentsen, *Emerging Leadership*, 38; Gilroy, "Diaspora," 301; Haslam and Ellemers, "Social Identity," 41; Haslam, *Psychology in Organizations*, x, xiv, 22, 31, 44, 46; Jenkins, *Social Identity*, 3–4, 19–20; Okure, "Christian Identity," 171; Worchel et al., "A Multidimensional Model," 17.

various social groups.[15] These may include religious affiliation, social status, occupational guild, sports team affiliation, and the like. The question is, What is the nature of Christian communal identity, and what resources does ecclesiology offer in these identity struggles?

From where or what do identity crises in Africa arise?[16] For Stan Chu Ilo, the root of African identity questions is clear. He isolates

> two factors: the historical factors which have created the political structures of African nations, and continue to influence African economy, social integration or social dislocation in most of these countries. The cultural crisis which touches on identity, worldview, status, equality, gender issues, family life and traditions, the social capital, the common good, and the bases for living and working together among various ethnic nationalities and diverse cultural and religious communities in Africa. Both the cultural and historical factors raise similar but related perplexities with regard to African identity and Christianity's role in identity formation.[17]

Ilo terms this confusion "homelessness," the search for foundations, transcendence, fulfillment and meaning.[18] 'Identity' can be used in seemingly endless ways; here, as in social psychology broadly speaking, 'identity' and 'self-definition' are synonyms referring to the ways in which a person describes herself. The predominant way(s) of referring to oneself—whether it is by one's occupation or membership in a group or some other identifier—offers insight into what is most important to the person's self-concept in that particular context and time. In this work, the concern is with the relationship of two particular social identities: African and Christian.

Identity has been a concern in Africa for various reasons.[19] However, while identity is often discussed or implicitly a concern, it is not fully defined in African theology.[20] Thus one contribution of the present work is

---

15. Gaertner et al., "The Common Ingroup Identity Model," 134.

16. See Appiah, "The Quest of African Identity," 62; Dedji, *Reconstruction and Renewal*, 229, quoting Jean Marc Ela; Niang, *Faith and Freedom*, 28; Maluleke, "Identity and Integrity," 26, 28, 39; idem, "In Search of 'The True Character,'" 217; Mbaka, "Self-Realization and Self-Esteem," 2, 6; Mudimbe, *The Invention of Africa*, 59; Onyemelukwe, "Search for Lost Identity," 35–47; Peter Bisem, quoted in Stinton, *Jesus of Africa*, 37–38.

17. Ilo, *The Church and Development in Africa*, 114.

18. Ibid., 115, cf. 114–22.

19. See Maluleke, "In Search of 'The True Character,'" 217.

20. Kwame Bediako's magnum opus *Theology and Identity* spans over four hundred pages, defending the theological relevance of identity, showing historical precedents, etc. but amidst the work he does not offer an in-depth, explicit definition of the term

to make explicit the concept's usage by theologians in Africa, as well as exploring how the identity of 'people of God' faces the challenges of social crises and rapidly changing cultures on the continent. Multiple fields are employed to analyze the nature of this identity, specifically its response to difference in unity, and to highlight its prominence for ecclesiologies in Africa. The identity 'African' continues to be debated, raising questions about the 'in Christ' identity in that context. To what extent have ecclesiological constructs provided a firm theological basis for an African Christian identity, or where might the Christian identity need adjustment, in light of current cultural emphases and issues? Given that most African cultures have historically valued community and solidarity, presumably ecclesiological loyalties could play a major role in the Christian's identity search. Where ecclesiology engages the issue of identity, the characteristics associated with a flourishing, healthy Christian identity can be examined.

A Brief History of Research

Hence anyone studying theologies in Africa will quickly detect recurrent concerns: a defense of African theology's necessity and the importance of a visible, culturally understandable and relevant form of Christianity. An early conference of African theologians and biblical scholars concluded that it was imperative "to discover in what way the Christian faith could best be presented, interpreted, and inculcated in Africa so that Africans will hear God in Jesus Christ addressing Himself immediately to them in their own native situation and particular circumstances."[21] These scholars believed that Christians in Africa ought to be able to know God directly,

---

'identity.' For example, he refers to "forging" a Christian identity in the second century BCE, the "process of Christian self-definition," and a "Christian self-consciousness" (xii; xv; 31, 32). He also discusses the Christian search for a "clearly defined identity" (quoting Robert Wilken) and the need for a Christian identity "in terms relevant and meaningful" in the cultural context (41, 48). Yet since his purpose is primarily apologetic, he argues more for the necessity of an integrated, contextually relevant Christian identity than for a particular understanding of identity itself, or for biblical bases for the Christian communal identity. In terms of the character of Christian identities in Africa, one of Bediako's primary concerns is that an African Christian identity produce a unified, rather than divided, self, an integration of past heritage with present faith and culture. However, he does not explore much about the character of Christian identity and its links with life, solidarity in community, etc. This critique is not intended to belittle his work, but to suggest that his method and focus precluded and generated many of the questions asked here. Indeed, African Christian identity looks not just to the past, but also addresses the present and points to the future.

21. Idowu, "Introduction," 16.

and express this knowledge in their own languages and thought forms.[22] Despite deep concerns about universalistic tendencies and a loss of fidelity to scriptural authority, Nigerian Byang H. Kato affirms that "an indigenous theology [in Africa] is a necessity."[23] Likewise, fellow Nigerian Tokunboh Adeyemo declares that while Christ's uniqueness must be protected, God's general self-revelation in the world and thus to all cultures must be upheld. Adeyemo then compares the view of salvation in African religions with a biblical view of salvation, which would indicate that general revelation in African cultures has value, despite its limits.[24] Ghanaian John S. Pobee in *Toward an Africa Theology* notes that theology fails to communicate if it is not contextualized, and proceeds to say that

> acknowledging the need for African theology is easy, but it is only the beginning of the study and of problems. The fundamental problem is, What is man? Who is *homo sapiens*? Who is *homo Africanus*? There is no prototype[25]

and hence no glib answer.

While none of these quotations specifically employs the term 'identity,' the concept is clearly present from theologians like Adeyemo and Kato to Idowu and Pobee. They were all wrestling with what it means to be African, what forms Christianity can and should take in Africa, and therefore with the mien of African Christians. The context must be well known in order to faithfully contextualize the message. Once the context has been studied, what are the most appropriate or fitting ways in which Christianity could or should be expressed? In short, theologians in Africa have been greatly concerned with identity in the past. As this work will show, their approaches to ecclesiology continue to wrestle with identity today.[26]

Community and solidarity are frequent themes in African theology, and indeed, the question of identity is not just about what sets a person apart, but also about group membership and the group's identity. Communal identity has also been linked with corporate solidarity (a phrase more commonly used in OT/HB studies), segueing naturally to ecclesiology. Once we arrive in the realm of ecclesiology, however, we are surprised to find a dearth of large-scale studies of African ecclesiology per se such as this work seeks to provide, and we are even surprised to find a relative shortage

---

22. Ibid., 9.
23. Kato, *Theological Pitfalls*, 16.
24. Adeyemo, *Salvation in African Tradition*, 14, 17, 19, 24–25.
25. Pobee, *Toward an African Theology*, 40.
26. For example, see Niang, *Faith and Freedom*.

of explicit African ecclesiologies developed in detail. Yet these relatively few ecclesiological works are the focus of the present project: What insights do these selected theologies in Africa offer with regard to a Christian's identity as a member of God's people? This form of the question becomes prominent because in African ecclesiologies—perhaps contrary to expectations based on some other recent trends—the theme of identity remains prominent.

The Approach of This Study

The scope of theology in Africa is broad: it covers biblical studies, systematic theology, ethics, politics, and more. Despite a common theme of community that surfaces repeatedly in African theologies of various types, ecclesiology has not historically been one of the more prominent foci. While, given the level of interest in community and solidarity, one would think that ecclesiology would be pertinent for Christians in Africa, the amount of formal ecclesiological texts is fairly manageable for a project in historical theology. The focus here will be on descriptive analysis, with biblical interaction providing a context for what African theologians themselves have done, as well as an exploration of how these texts from Scripture are brought to bear on Christian identity and ecclesiologies. While the majority of formal ecclesiologies written on the continent are Roman Catholic, serious effort has secured some works by Protestant theologians as well.

This study spans from the 1950s to the present: the nearly sixty-five years that comprise modern, indigenous African theologizing. The 1950s signaled the final breaths of colonialism and the beginning of published African theology. In the intervening years between then and now, African countries have gained political independence, and experienced approximately half a century of self-rule.[27] The focus of this study will rest upon the mission-instituted churches in Nigeria, the Democratic Republic of Congo, and Kenya. On one hand, South Africa is excluded because the particularities of apartheid have given Black theology a unique shape.[28] On the other hand, North Africa had less theological output in this time span, and may also be excluded because Christians in this region are generally from much

---

27. For example, Kenya celebrated fifty years of independence on December 12, 2013.

28. Proponents of theologies in South Africa include Allan A. Boesak, John W. de Gruchy, and Desmond Tutu. For examples, see Boesak, *Farewell to Innocence*; de Gruchy's, *The Church Struggle in South Africa*; *Bonhoeffer and South Africa*; and *Liberating Reformed Theology*; Tutu, *No Future without Forgiveness*.

older churches (the Coptic church, for example) as opposed to the mission-instituted churches examined here.[29]

The next chapter, then, begins by defining the term 'Africa' because the debate on this topic illustrates the complexity of the identity question, and why identity has been a major concern of theologies in Africa. Five core concerns in such African theology can be described: identity, inculturation, liberation, life, and community. These themes are interwoven, and in fact the latter ones aid in understanding the question and shape of identity. However, despite the fact that identity is commonly mentioned, it is rarely explicitly defined, a point this work begins to address.

Accordingly, the third chapter compares identity conceptions in African theology from earlier and later eras, with a threefold purpose. First, the chapter argues that identity is still a relevant topic in theology. Increasing modernization and globalization on the continent have not removed the interest in identity as some expected, but if anything may have heightened the concern. Second, the chapter further defines the nature of the identity in question. Third, the chapter begins to ascertain if specific conceptions of identity are more likely to provide African identities that can survive, even thrive, amidst the forces of rapid change on the continent.

The fourth chapter investigates communal identity in biblical passages theologians in Africa appropriate in order to support their claims. The biblical survey allows deeper exploration of the distinctive character of the identity of God's people, particularly the relationship of diversity and unity. There is a recurring concern that differences within the church be valued, yet not be given so great a priority that they negate equality or overwhelm the most important self-identifier, that of unity with God and other people 'in Christ.'

The fifth chapter finally narrows the focus strictly to the formal ecclesiologies, arranged chronologically, of Nigerian Elochukwu E. Uzukwu, Nigerian Agbonkhianmeghe E. Orobator, Congolese Augustin Ramazani Bishwende, Congolese Georges Titre Ande, and Kenyan Paul Mbandi, theologians with a spectrum of theological commitments and church affiliations whose ecclesiologies nevertheless share certain emphases. As a result of this interaction, the chapter can synthesize the desired character of the Christian identity among African theologians: the traits they believe are necessary for the church's flourishing and witness, the traits central to its identity.

---

29. African-initiated or African-instituted churches constitute a significant force on the continent, but for reasons of availability and scholarly responsibility here the focus is on academic, written theology published by theologians from mission-established churches, such as the Roman Catholic, Anglican, Presbyterian, and Africa Inland Church.

Concluding the book, the sixth chapter offers a brief summary, and introduces the social identity approach as a possible language with which African insights can be confirmed, sharpened, and mediated to non-African audiences. The most basic goal of this work is to offer descriptive historical-theological analysis of select African ecclesiologies, since African ecclesiology in general has garnered little study. The more particular goal of comparing and integrating insights from biblical studies, systematic theology, and the social sciences in undertaking this task is first and foremost to provide a deeper account of how 'identity' is being employed in African theologies, and to demonstrate its continuing relevance even in more recent ecclesiology. Another resulting contribution is analysis of ecclesiologies in this region with regard to their understanding of unity and diversity within the church, in other words, an analysis of the nature of Christian identity and solidarity. A final contribution is to suggest that elements of the social identity approach can enrich the claims of African ecclesiologies, expand on their discussions of the Christian identity in general, and strengthen Christian identities in Africa.

Chapter 2

Theology in Africa

This chapter grounds the remainder of the work, first defining the contested term 'Africa,' an example that details the complicated nature of communal identity discussions on the continent and highlights the value of ecclesiological input. I also define 'theology in Africa,' then isolate five major themes in African theological literature. Identity, inculturation, liberation, life, and community are all prominent and interdependent foci; the latter four shape the understanding of (communal) identity. While these themes occur in other theologies, in African theologies they mutually reinforce each other in unique ways, partly due to the historical and social context. These prominent values can be employed in formulating a more theologically based definition of 'Africa' and African identities as well as for ecclesiology, as we shall eventually see.

With modernization, urbanization, and globalization, traditional communal identities—based on clan, ethnicity, and more recently on geography/nationality, hence inherently limited and exclusive in nature—are in flux, raising the question of how to describe African identities in a postcolonial era. "Popular concern about identity is, in large part perhaps, a reflection of the uncertainty produced by rapid change and cultural contact: our social maps no longer fit our social landscapes."[1] The concern is understandable; the problem is that theologies in Africa tend to employ the term or concept of 'identity' without much or any definition of the term: it implicitly indicates a person's self-perception, yet the term is highly malleable, both in popular and scholarly discussions.[2] In this work, 'identity'

---

1. Jenkins, *Social Identity*, 9.
2. Ibid., 8–9.

indicates a "people's sense of who they are, as their subjective self-concept. This definition interprets identity as a subjective psychological experience."[3] Jack Barentsen distinguishes between personal identity (that which makes a person unique or different) and social identity (a person's sense of belonging to a particular group), and describes some ways in which adopting a Christian social identity can transform people.[4] Identifying that the concept is primarily employed by African theologies to describe the communal aspect of identity, as in this work, can suggest further ways to develop the notion once it is tied in more explicitly with ecclesiologies.[5]

Clarifying the Category "Theologies in Africa"

Theology

Human thoughts on the Bible and its implications for life always involve translation and interpretation. They are shaped to some degree by the translator's context. Revelation 21:24–26 indicates that YHWH delights in the unique, varied contributions of the world's cultures. Thus, there are—or ought to be—some differences in perspective between a Christian theology developed in the United States of America and one originating from Kenya. Different viewpoints within Christian theology are both unavoidable and potentially beneficial, surfacing new perspectives that might otherwise have been misunderstood, downplayed, or entirely overlooked. Can we speak, then, of perspectives categorized as 'African theology'?[6]

---

3. Barentsen, *Emerging Leadership*, 38.

4. Ibid. This usage parallels that of Hogg et al., who in speaking of identity refer to a person's self-definition and self-concept, which includes the social categories or groups to which one belongs ("A Tale of Two Theories," 259).

5. S. Alexander Haslam argues that "people's sense of self can be determined both by *personal identity* (their sense of themselves as unique individuals) and by *social identity* (their sense of themselves as group members who share goals, values and interests with others). Moreover . . . many of the most significant organizational phenomena—from leadership and motivation to communication and commitment to change—are dependent upon this ability to define and promote the self in a way that is inclusive of other people" (*Psychology in Organizations*, xiv). Groups "are not only external features of the world, they are also internalized so that they contribute to a person's sense of self" (Haslam and Ellemers, "Social Identity," 41).

6. African theologizing takes place both orally and in writing. Songs, conversations, and stories convey theology in a different, but certainly not lesser, way than written, and more specifically academic, theological works. As important as all the varied forms of theology are, the present work focuses on gaining a larger hearing for formal, written ecclesiologies from Africa.

John Pobee defines African theology as an "attempt to use African concepts and African ethos as vehicles for the communication of the gospel in an African context."[7] In other words, African theology consciously draws from its context in order to express the gospel message: the context shapes the gospel's audience, and also contributes means through which to best communicate the message in that same context. Pobee's definition highlights the important role of context in theologizing, which is affirmed by other theologians in Africa. In this work, the terms 'African' and 'theologies in Africa' refer exclusively to Christian theologies and theologians, relying primarily on works directly produced by African thinkers and only secondarily on descriptions of African theologies by non-Africans. The focus involves conveying theology in African terms and ideas and addressing African realities. Yet there is a question that must be addressed before proceeding any further: What exactly is meant by 'Africa'?

Africa

The debate over the term 'Africa' forefronts the question of identity, as a brief overview will show. Some scholars decry the notion of 'Africa' entirely. Others propose various ways of defining the essence or heart of what it means to be African.[8] Entire books have been devoted to the topic of 'Africa' and arguing about whether or not it has any true referent other than the geographical. One prominent author is V. Y. Mudimbe, author of *The Invention of Africa* and *The Idea of Africa*.[9] Along with Mudimbe, theologian Emmanuel Katongole agrees that "Africa was to a large extent the way it was (is) as imagined by Europe, with concepts like 'chaos,' 'tribe,' and 'primitive' integral to that imagination—if only as a way to confirm the European imagination of Europe as civilized and developed."[10] In 1754 David Hume wrote that he was "apt to suspect the Negroes and in general all other species of men . . . to be naturally inferior to the whites. There never was a civilized nation of any other complexion than white, nor even any individual eminent either in action or speculation."[11] Seven decades later, in 1822, G. W. F.

---

7. Pobee, *Toward an African Theology*, 39.

8. The definition of 'Africa', whether or not it can be considered a unity, the question of if 'Africa' is entirely a European conceptual construct, etc., could take up an entire book. Here I offer a basic, broad engagement with the topic for the purposes of illustrating the ongoing pertinence of identity, particularly the communal identity 'African', to set up the ecclesiological background.

9. Mudimbe, *The Invention of Africa*; idem, *The Idea of Africa*.

10. Katongole, *The Sacrifice of Africa*, 8.

11. Hume, *The Philosophical Works*, quoted in Eze, *Achieving Our Humanity*, 22.

Hegel described "Africa proper" as "the land of childhood, removed from the light of self-conscious history and wrapped in the dark mantle of night. . . . There is no subjectivity, but merely a series of subjects who destroy one another." Furthermore, "All our observations of African man shows him as living in a state of savagery and barbarism, and he remains in this state to the present day. . . . [A]nd nothing consonant with humanity is to be found in his character. . . . We cannot properly feel ourselves into his nature, no more than into a dog."[12]

Indeed, the very term 'Africa' arises from some confusion. Mudimbe's *The Idea of Africa* studies how the concept of Africa came about, particularly through various European influences, but in his preface discussing the term itself, a prior puzzle is noted:

> Let us note that the very name of the continent is itself a major problem. The Greeks named it Libya and used to call any black person an *Aithiops*. The confusion begins with the Romans. They had a province in their empire known as Africa, and their intellectuals used the same word for the "tertia orbis terrarium pars" (e.g., Sallustius, *Iug.* 17, 3), that is, the continent as we know it, being the third, after Europe and Asia. With the European "discovery" of the continent in the fifteenth century, the confusion becomes complete.[13]

Did 'Africa' refer to a province, a people with a particular skin color, or an entire continent? And would the people categorized have claimed that a unity or similarity existed between them?

Further problems arose with the negative characterization of Africa. Malvern Van wyk Smith explores the early European image of Africa from Greek antiquity up to the Renaissance period. Homer's *Odyssey* provides the notion that there are two Ethiopias. One Ethiopia was the Kushite empire of Meroe on the Nubian Nile, admirable people, who were sharply contrasted with "the nomadic tribes of the Sahara and sub-Saharan regions who became the 'other Ethiopians' . . . and were frequently presented as savage, bestial, and treacherous. This division came to control numerous subsequent descriptions of Africa, from Herodotus in the fifth century BC to as late as the *Nuremburg Chronicle* of 1493."[14] A more recent work of Van

---

12. Hegel, "Geographical Basis of World History," quoted in Eze, *Achieving Our Humanity*, 24.

13. Mudimbe, *The Idea of Africa*, xi. Cf. Bloch-Hoell, "African Identity," 98–107. For a book-length argument about the racial definition of 'Africa,' and the possibility of moving beyond racialized views of human beings, see Emmanuel Chukwudi Eze's *Achieving Our Humanity*.

14. Van Wyk Smith, "'Waters Flowing From Darkness,'" 67.

Wyk Smith's, *The First Ethiopians: The Image of Africa and Africans in the Early Mediterranean World*, continues in this vein of study and argues that the roots of Western racism are actually in late New-Kingdom Egypt, which desired to disassociate Egyptians from the rest of Africa.[15] In short, the term 'Africa' was problematic from the beginning, first being loosely defined, and then negatively defined: hardly a promising start.

In the first half of the twentieth century, Africans who had been in Europe often developed a different view of Africa than their fellow citizens back home. Appiah states that "what the postwar generation of British Africans took from their time in Europe . . . was a sense that they, as Africans, had a great deal in common: they took it for granted, along with everybody else, that this common feeling was connected with their shared 'African-ness,' and they largely accepted the European view that this meant their shared race."[16] Before the most recent centuries, Appiah believes, a sense of 'African-ness' or African unity was largely absent on the continent. Alexander Crummell, one of the 'fathers' of African nationalism, affirmed the idea that Africa was defined by being the 'home' of the black race, and Kwame Nkrumah, Aimé Césaire, and Leopold Senghor shared a Euro-American view of race—indeed, it was the basis of Pan-Africanism and Négritude.[17] Appiah contrasts this nineteenth-century development with the OT view that "what is distinctive about peoples is not so much appearance and custom as their relationship, through a common ancestor, to God" and "what *essentially* differentiates [other peoples] from the Hebrews is that they do not have the special relationship to Jehovah."[18]

In nineteenth-century colonialism, Mudimbe locates a firm basis for—and spread of—"the concept of *deviation* as the best symbol of the idea of Africa."[19] Not only was African unity conceived by Europeans as having a primarily racial basis, but the Africa imagined was a place of alterity. Mudimbe observes that this alterity was a negative category, implying that those in the category were not merely strange but inferior beings: "The African has become not only the Other who is everyone else except me, but rather the key which, in its abnormal differences, specifies the identity

---

15. Van Wyk Smith, *The First Ethiopians*.

16. Appiah, *In My Father's House*, 9. He continues by saying that for francophone Africans, "a different situation led to the same results." For more discussion of race and moving beyond definitions of humanity linked to race, see Eze, *Achieving Our Humanity*.

17. Appiah, *In My Father's House*, 3–10.

18. Ibid., 11–12.

19. Mudimbe, *Idea of Africa*, xii; emphasis mine.

of the Same."[20] The study of others served simply to bolster the identity of Europeans, who viewed themselves as the standard for other cultures and persons. In the Enlightenment desire to classify and categorize, Africa and its inhabitants were labeled savage, mentally retarded, a lower level of beings; if there were valuable aspects in their cultures, they were attributed to a non-African origin.[21] Lest one assume that such ways of thinking are long past, Mudimbe provides an example of a 1983 work by Carl Sagan that demonstrates the same tendency.[22]

Many European and American thinkers in the past negatively linked Africa with the black race, which was then characterized as backward or ignorant.[23] Yet thinkers like Césaire and Senghor built the philosophy of Négritude on the idea of racial solidarity, claiming for Africans across the continent a unity based on biological race. Rather than denigrate blackness, they sought to exult in its difference from whiteness. Yet in so doing, they accepted the label forced upon them by non-Africans, acquiescing to the storyline and dualistic view that came with that label.

Noting dangers of defining Africa racially, Kwame Anthony Appiah rejects all forms of racism and ethnocentrism, and seeks another basis for Pan-African solidarity.[24] Edward Blyden, an early promoter of a "racial authenticity" and "racial integrity," referred to an African "personality," as if it were one identifiable essence.[25] He rejected certain negative connotations then attached to the black 'race', but had no desire to reject racial understandings of peoples; rather, he embraced and relied upon race for his vision of Africa's future. Blyden is just one example among many of his era whose thoughts centered on race in a biological sense. Mudimbe notes that Africa and Africans were "perceived, experienced, and promoted as the sign of the absolute otherness," associated with "folly,"[26] and even in the 1950s "still concerned with questions of African humanity, intellectual capabilities, and moral evolution."[27] One striking aspect of *The Invention of Africa* is the continual juxtaposition of segments from *Planet of the Apes* with the subject matter. One particular section opens with these lines from the novel:

20. Mudimbe, *Invention of Africa*, 12.
21. Ibid., 13.
22. Ibid., 13–15, citing Carl Sagan, *Broca's Brain: Reflections on the Romance of Science*.
23. Appiah, *In My Father's House*, 5, 21.
24. Ibid., 20.
25. Mudimbe, *Invention of Africa*, 117, 131, 133.
26. Mudimbe, *Idea of Africa*, 38–39.
27. Mudimbe, *Invention of Africa*, 39.

"Rational men? Men endowed with a mind? Men inspired by intelligence? No, that's not possible."²⁸ Sadly enough, Mudimbe, Appiah, and many others agree that the general image of Africa and Africans in the nineteenth century was predominantly negative.

African nationalism of the twentieth century possessed "a semblance of ideological unity," but actually this unity was only due to a common commitment to "ending white colonial oppression; seizure of political power by the African elite; and nationalist re-imagination of nationhood."²⁹ It was a reaction against these external colonial forces and their control of African futures, but once the African nations achieved political independence, their unity dissolved as their internal ideological differences divided them again. Ndlovu-Gatsheni observes that "African nationalism, that initially assumed the character of developmentalism and a civic conception of the nation, is gradually falling into cultural nationalism, Afro-radicalism and nativism," which Kwame Appiah condemns.³⁰

One particular point of Simon Kofi Appiah's article "The Quest of African Identity" provides a poignant summary of the entire discussion. He concludes,

> It becomes clear that Africans find themselves in a vicious circle whenever the question of 'being-African' (Africanness) is raised. The crisis of cultural narrative leads to the loss of identity and the latter leads again to the search for cultural roots or 'original' traditions. Yet since this search begins from a crisis of narrative, Africans find themselves filling the vacuum with an ideology of pre-colonial tradition, which outwardly pretends to solve the identity crisis, but inwardly sets forth its effect on the people. Thus Africans often become the victims of the burden of their own actions as a result of a yet-to-be-resolved crisis of identity.³¹

The identity predicament strikes on various levels: national, cultural, and personal. The question, "What is Africa?" cannot be treated lightly, but neither can it be avoided: it demands to be faced and dealt with. Ngindu Mushete highlights that for Africa, dialogues about modernity are not discussions "between Africa's past and its tormented present with a view to its future. Rather, it takes place between Africa's present and the Western present as well as the Western past."³² The dialogue is complicated by adding

---

28. Ibid., 153.
29. Ndlovu-Gatsheni, "Africa for Africans," 64.
30. Ibid., 67.
31. Appiah, "The Quest of African Identity," 62.
32. Mushete, "Modernity in Africa," 144.

cross-cultural elements into the discussion, as well as two voices—instead of just one—from the present. This dialogue, according to Mushete, also loses its future focus. Concluding his article, he wonders if Christians in Africa will know how to respond to the many cries of fellow human beings, and stand with them in solidarity, bringing freedom from their heavy burden of a mangled past and distressing present.[33]

If one rejects both nationalism and common 'race' as possible bases of African solidarity, where then can unity be located? Kwame Appiah firmly states that there is no collective African culture, no "common stock of cultural knowledge" or "central body of ideas" shared by black Africans.[34] Mudimbe reiterates this rejection of a supposed cultural unity, a cultural unity that he indicts John Mbiti's works for promoting.[35] Furthermore, cultural nationalism in Africa has only enforced "the imaginary identities to which Europeans subjected us."[36] Having rejected these commonalities, 'Africa,' it seems, has become a symbol carrying very little weight, or at least none in a positive sense: it carries only negative connotations.

Kwame Appiah therefore acknowledges the "constructed nature of the modern African identity (like all identities)," and suggests that this construction deserves further study.[37] If modern African identities are constructed from various sources, and the present idea of Africa is a European invention and imposition, one must invariably ask if Africa is anything more than a geographical reality and what substance African identities possess. Mercy Amba Oduyoye, in discussing the church's future in Africa, proposes that, in part, Africans share this distressing historical relationship with the European colonial powers, which provides a "unifying thread" through the diverse realities in the continent.[38]

Kwame Appiah affirms that Africa possesses distinctive traits; his own concern is philosophy. Thus he proposes that a specifically African philosophy focus not on blackness but on addressing philosophical problems crucially or uniquely raised in African contexts, critically drawing on its own traditions.[39] In the transition from traditional to modern worldviews, the 'African identity' is simply one identity an African bears, and it is an identity

---

33. Ibid., 151.
34. Appiah, *In My Father's House*, 80, 95.
35. Mudimbe, *Invention of Africa*, 79.
36. Appiah, *In My Father's House*, 62.
37. Ibid., 61.
38. Oduyoye, "The Church of the Future," 495.
39. Appiah, *In My Father's House*, 90–92, 103. He also discusses whether African philosophy will have a distinct methodology.

not static but dynamic, being shaped and re-formed in the present and on into the future.⁴⁰ In other words, the former conception of Africa centering on 'race' and negative connotations, the image created by Europeans, can be changed and re-made so that 'Africa' will carry a different connotation and image when people hear it.

Defining Africa by 'race' is dangerous, since the notion of 'race' is precarious, being rejected by some intellectuals; hence, we discard this notion. If Africa is not defined by 'race', what could define and unite it? Nils E. Bloch-Hoell addresses the question of African unity, proposing it arises not from common race, but from a common view of life. Bloch-Hoell reflects on the Arab influence on the North, and on that basis distinguishes between North and sub-Saharan Africa. He concludes that there are at least two unifying traits common to the latter region: viewing religion as integrated in all aspects of life, and refusing to distinguish between the sacred and secular.⁴¹ Another contributor on this topic, Nigerian Agbonkhianmeghe E. Orobator, believes that despite great plurality on the continent, one can speak of unity and commonality in Africa based on the "pressing socioeconomic and political issues" present-day African nations face: severe poverty, AIDS, neo-colonialism, and the anthropological poverty brought about by Western destruction of African cultures and history.⁴²

Admitting the complexity of this discussion, we should nevertheless reject racialized definitions of Africa. Moreover, we should also move beyond Bloch-Hoell's suggestion, and instead agree with Orobator on the position that at least one mutual—though negative—factor in Africa is a shared history of colonialism and common problems resulting from that history. Within this work, the phrase 'Africa' designates a unity based not on race but partly on the factors noted above by Orobator: this portion of the continent's shared experience of colonialism and its persisting influence. It is vital to note that the challenges facing the church in this region are simply that: problems it faces, which affect but most certainly fall far short of fully defining its identity. The church in Africa faces challenges, as the church does in every area and era; the African church also draws upon strengths and resources from its context, such as its vibrant worship and deep commitment to obeying the Bible. For this work, South Africa is excluded because the far-reaching effects of apartheid have given that region a markedly distinct context and different experience of colonialism. Africans in West, Central, and East Africa, then, share some common ground within which

---

40. Ibid., 107, 177.
41. Bloch-Hoell, "African Identity," 101–2.
42. Orobator, *The Church as Family*, 29–31.

one can meaningfully compare and contrast ecclesiological models. Even if the concept of Africa was originally an invention of outsiders who defined it negatively, it is a concept with meaning today, geographically, historically, and culturally. Here 'African', then, most simply means a person of any skin color born and/or raised primarily in Africa. The history of the term's usage, however, continues to influence perceptions of Africa and theology in Africa today, as will become evident. For example, unfortunately Orobator does not stress that these challenges do not *define* Africa; thus, he fails to provide a positive image of Africa, one that emphasizes the many strengths of the continent, not just its challenges. The foundational themes later in this chapter suggest a way in which Africa can be defined by theological commitments, not just by the challenges it faces.

Theology in Africa

African Christian theology, as a broad category containing multiple types of theologies, seeks to make the Christian faith relevant and understandable in African cultures.[43] If the Christian Scriptures, and the theologies related to and dialoguing with them, are not based in a person's own language and thought forms, addressing issues in their context, how much of the Christian message will a community truly grasp and to what degree will it be internalized? Scripture is given to God's people, and each one within their culture must struggle with it. Even American Richard J. Gehman affirms that cultural "context is the medium through which God communicates and by which we respond."[44]

---

43. The question of the place of African theology famously arose in the January 1960 debate between T. Tshibangu and A. Vanneste. Elochukwu E. Uzukwu firmly declares, "African theology has reached adulthood. The debate about its right to exist is over.... In 1960 Professor A. Vanneste told his student, T. Tshibangu, and the Kinshasa audience that an African theology would be second class; universal (European) theology was preferable." Yet "in 1989 during the theology week of the same Faculty of Kinshasa African theology was assessed. Curiously, Vanneste and Bishop Tshibangu ... were preoccupied about the direction African theology should follow. The right of doing theology from the African perspective was calmly accepted" (Uzukwu, "Trends in African Theology," 100–101). Augustin Ramazani Bishwende refers to this same debate, and Vanneste's position that "Il faudrait que les théologiens africains ... acceptant d'être des théologiens de seconde zone en contribuant par là au modèle unique et universel de la théologie occidentale." Bishwende too notes that Vanneste's later work attests to a change of position on his part, to the point of agreement with Bishop Tshibangu, his former student (Bishwende, *Église-Famille de Dieu*, 39–40).

44. Gehman, *Doing African Christian Theology*, 80, 83.

Another way one might argue this point is by examining the nature of Christianity as a historical religion. The Christian story claims that God has acted in this concrete world, in specific times and places. Christianity claims historical roots, and will wither and die if cut off from those roots.[45] Being a historical religion, Christianity therefore has struggled through the ages to ask, 'What should Christian faith look like in this context (as opposed to some other)?' If contextualizing the faith was not an issue, the NT would not record conflicts between the Jewish and Gentile Christians over how to live out their faith, coming as they did from different backgrounds with different mores. In Mario I. Aguilar's words, "Theology has a living historical character, so that all theology is culturally and socially positioned."[46] For Christianity to truly take root in Africa it must be expressed "in African ways" and "address African questions" such as polygamy, the spirit world, poverty, and so forth.[47] It must be demonstrably relevant to cultural concerns if it is to be embraced and put forth deep roots.

John Pobee's argument for the necessity of doing theology in Africa is that since God's revelation was historical in nature—rooted in a particular time and place—then as such the very "nature of revelation implies a pluralistic situation."[48] The importance of context is why the qualifier 'African' is added to the aforementioned theologies. Far too often Euro-American theologians still do not refer to their works as 'contextual theology' but simply 'theology.'[49] Yet scholars have increasingly realized that all humans are inescapably influenced by their cultures: they are limited, particular beings with specific viewpoints. So there is no pure, a-contextual theology, and intellectual honesty requires admitting that as a consequence, all theology is and should be local and contextual to some extent.[50] Catholic theologians across the African continent seized upon the Pope's address to Ugandan bishops in 1969, where he expressly said, "The language and mode of manifesting the one faith, may be manifold, suited to the style, the character, the

---

45. 1 Cor 15:1–19, New International Version.

46. Aguilar, "Postcolonial African Theology," 309.

47. Gehman, *Doing African Christian Theology*, 182.

48. Pobee, *Toward an African Theology*, 19. Another iteration of this thought is as follows: "For most of us it is difficult enough to respect those with whom we might disagree, to say nothing of those who might be different from us in culture, language, and tradition. For all of us pluralism can be a rock of stumbling, but for God it is the cornerstone of the universal design" (Sanneh, *Translating the Message*, 27).

49. As mentioned previously, the term 'Western' has been chosen because it is the most widely used and recognizable term worldwide, and a common term in African literature.

50. E.g., Schreiter's *Constructing Local Theologies* or Bevans and Schroeder, *Constants in Context*.

genius and the culture of the one who professes the one Faith; you may, and you must, have an African theology."[51] It is clear that African theologians are not alone or aberrant in calling for a theology that is fitted to their context.

The first contemporary written theologies in Africa by Africans were published in 1956, shortly before many colonies gained independence in the following decade.[52] As mentioned previously, fighting for respect and recognition of the validity of such an endeavor, early writers expended a great deal of time and energy providing reasons why truly African theologies were necessary.[53]

Theologies in Africa can be categorized into various streams, the number of which is debatable. Some thinkers discern approximately five: womanist theology, liberation theology, Black theology of South Africa (sometimes grouped under liberation theology), reconstruction theology, and inculturation theology, also known simply as African theology.[54] Another recent focus of the field is postcolonial theology, which Edward Antonia links to inculturation theology.[55] Others discern two main streams: inculturation and liberation (socio-political) theologies.[56] Unsurprisingly,

---

51. Cited in Parratt, *Reinventing Christianity*, 16.

52. Oral theologies are indeed valuable, particularly as reflections of grassroots theologies, and as indicators of the extent to which formal theology has or has not moved from academic circles to a more informal, less academic level. However, they are beyond the purview of this work. *Des prêtres noirs s'interrogent* and P. D. Fueter's article "Theological Education in Africa" were published in 1956. The former "marks the birth of the quest for conscious self-theologizing by Africans" (Tiénou, "Evangelical Theology in African Contexts," 216).

53. For example, Osadolor Imasogie in his closing paragraphs states that "it is only as the Word becomes flesh in every cultural human situation that the 'unsearchable riches of God' in Christ can be approximated, as much as it is humanly possible under the mediation of the Holy Spirit" (*Guidelines for Christian Theology in Africa*, 86).

54. Some suggest that Black theology should constitute its own category, in part due to its 'militant' nature. For example, John S. Pobee distinguishes Black theology, though he qualifies that by saying that African theology (or inculturation theology) does share the concern for liberation, but places priority on finding appropriate African concepts to convey the gospel to Africans (*Toward an African Theology*, 38–39). Thus the difference is one of degree. Because I am simply painting the background with broad brushstrokes at this point, I have located South African Black theology as a subset of liberation theology since Black theology, womanist theology, and other liberation theologies all share a common orienting concern; namely, the freedom of oppressed, less-powerful groups within a society.

55. Antonio, "Inculturation and Postcolonial Discourse," 1.

56. Ande, *Leadership and Authority*, 2; also Bujo, *African Theology in Its Social Context*, 15; Maina, *Historical and Social Dimensions*, 52; Orobator, *From Crisis to Kairos*, 28, where he refers to Adrian Hastings, and Hastings's hint, along with Orobator's agreement, that there may be a third stream or source of theologies in Africa: the living experiences of the church.

these streams are not always distinct, as themes often overlap various categories, and the categories themselves differ according to which scholar one consults. Yet despite the diversity and differing emphases, there are some common themes, such as liberation and identity.[57] For example, Mercy Amba Oduyoye sharply critiques African theologies, even liberation theologies, for failing to address issues of gender. She charges "African theologians who have used the liberation paradigm to express the church's faith" with addressing "structures of injustice, analyzing class (economics) and race (skin color); they usually ignore gender," and consequently women remain in a lesser class, despite the Bible's teaching that female and male both bear the *imago Dei*. Yet she views the work of African women theologians as liberation oriented, even if it approaches the concern from a different starting point. Some theologians even see identity issues as a sub-category within the overarching theme of emancipation, or liberation.[58] Aguilar agrees there is a common thread in all these types of theologies, "a commonality of purpose, i.e. the search for an African Christianity that could be expressed through an African liturgy and communal life."[59] More recent works hint at a possible merging or meeting of the streams, such as the work of Titre Ande in Congo. Ande notes that inculturation is vital to any theology, yet at the same time the gospel liberates people from all forms of enslavement.[60]

The concern of these theologians, then, is that Christianity can and must take form in an African context, and such a culturally appropriate and understandable form of Christianity should allow Christians in Africa to remain African, as opposed to becoming culturally Euro-American.[61] This

---

57. Oduyoye, *Daughters of Anowa*, 180–81. Oduyoye explicitly links liberation to Christ and the church in the introduction.

58. "One of the themes that characterize (*sic*) African theological reflection is the quest for emancipation. By emancipation, we refer to freedom from social and religious exploitation with the goal to achieve an African identity, which involves African self-determination, self-assertion, dignity, integrity, personality and self-assertion" (Muli, "The Contribution of African Theological Reflection," 9.

59. Aguilar, "Postcolonial African Theology," 302.

60. Ande, *Leadership and Authority*, 121, 132–33. Cf. Maina, *Historical and Social Dimensions*, 16.

61. Non-Christians have felt this identity confusion too, but since the focus is Christian theologies in Africa, a Christian example is provided here. Diane B. Stinton quotes a 1998 interview with Peter Bisem of the National Council of Churches in Kenya, where Bisem comments that "it is now plainly understood that the style of mission and approach, that is, the missionary practice of uprooting converts from their traditional environment, sometimes tended to create . . . an identity crisis in the hearer of the message. Because the presentation was as if God speaks to this person, and now, cuts him or cuts her off from his initial identity—uproots, if you like" (*Jesus of Africa*, 37–38). Certainly not all Christians in Africa experience this confusion: Agbonkhianmeghe E.

search is, in a word, a search for identity and belonging.[62] Seeking after a truly African identity is not a pursuit unique to theologians by any means; the theme appears in literature and philosophy, for example.[63]

Having laid out a basic explanation of the reason for and differences within African theologies, we can proceed to identify and examine more precisely five prominent themes within these theologies, themes that together can offer a definition of Africa which is not limited to its challenges, and themes that will point to the prominence and nature of ecclesial identity. The first of these leitmotifs is at times more implicit while the latter four are often explicit: (1) identity, (2) inculturation, (3) liberation, (4) life, and (5) community.[64] Yet I will argue that actually the issue of identity remains foundational, despite being less obvious to some. Thus I will further demonstrate that the other themes affect how the concept of 'identity' functions. Since the five themes frequently overlap, this interrelationship further indicates that they are core themes deserving attention. After examining the more explicit themes, I return again to identity to propose a basic definition that will be expanded and nuanced further in later chapters.

Orobator testifies that "since converting to Christianity I have rediscovered the richness of my African religious heritage in surprisingly new ways as I live and pray as an African Christian. Many years after my conversion, both my African religious heritage and Christian faith come together in a way that I find meaningful, enriching, and deeply satisfying. Contrary to what some writers believe about African Christians, I do not feel torn between two worlds" (*Theology Brewed in an African Pot*, x–xi).

62. For example, Tanzanian Charles Nyamiti remarked that "the African theologian is still culturally alienated; that is, in spite of his good will and efforts, he has not yet fully recaptured his African soul, feel and personality" (*The Way to Christian Theology*, 26).

63. Westerners too noticed the confusion and isolation that some Africans felt, stranded between the Western world and their African heritage—for example, Turnbull, *The Lonely African*. For the exploration of African identities in light of the colonial incursion, one need look no further than the novels of Chinua Achebe often referred to as 'the African trilogy': *Things Fall Apart*; *No Longer at Ease*; and *Arrow of God*. This identity search is the subject of the next chapter. In the discipline of philosophy, Léopold Sédar Senghor, later president of Senegal, was one of the three 'fathers' of the Négritude movement in the early half of the twentieth century, which promoted a distinct and proud black identity over against a Western, Caucasian imperialist identity.

64. For example, Jean-Claude Loba-Mkole states that the church's mission in Africa "is specifically apprehended as inculturation, liberation, Church-as-family, innovation, reconstruction or life promotion" (4). Thus, inculturation, liberation, and life are among the major issues he believes the church must address. The theme of community arises in his mention of "Church-as-family," and inculturation, innovation, and reconstruction as part of the church's mission touch on reconstructing self-identity of individuals and people groups, presumably ("Paul and Africa?").

Foundational Themes

Identity

As already noted, the initial theme of identity can be a difficult concept because of the vagueness and elasticity of the term. Defining it can be a thorny and elusive quest; a fuller exploration of identity in Africa is the focus of the next chapter. However, the other foundational pillars aid in beginning to define what sort of identity is under consideration in these African theologies: it is a focus on communal, or social, identity. An example can clarify how the themes of community and identity are interrelated.

Titre Ande's ecclesiology argues that Congolese identity bears the effects of colonialism, the missionary legacy, and nationalism. These forces contribute to ethnocentrism.[65] "Theology in Africa must be liberating in all aspects of life. This liberation concerns men and women, both at personal and social levels. Therefore, Africa needs 'practical ecclesiology' which relates not only to selfhood and identity, but also takes seriously the local socio-political situation."[66] The "Life-Community" model is based on a new, transformative identity in Christ, open to others by the Spirit, resulting in a "supra-ethnic community."[67] Ande draws upon history, ethnicity, and other social forces as shapers of identity, and argues that Christianity must offer a new identity that 'supersedes' old loyalties as it brings a person into the community of God's people.[68] At the same time, the community must be 'open' to others. An implicit presupposition in Ande's work is that multiple forces shape a person's self-perception. Identity includes all these forces of one's self-perception, while among these multiple identities one identity or more may dominate. Ande argues that as Christians are new creatures in Christ, loyalty to God must be their primary identity. Christianity is a communal faith—it creates a community—and as such it affirms African values of relationships shaping a person's identity.

In short, Ande uses 'identity' not in a highly technical sense, nor with the idea that one particular facet of identity is all there is to a person. Rather, identity arises from various forces in one's context, though one influence may, and perhaps should, dominate in one's self-perception. The question facing African thinkers is how to understand African identity given the ways in which Africa has been described by Euro-Americans, as well as its current trials in social areas, and the struggle of African ways with imposed

---

65. Ande, *Leadership and Authority*, 15, 93.
66. Ibid., 121.
67. Ibid., 144, 155, 157.
68. Ibid., 132, 133.

Western-style modernity. All these forces, along with others like ethnicity, combine into a potent and potentially explosive mixture. The question of a person's primary means of self-identification is not easily answered.

In some contexts, such as some Euro-American cultures, identity is frequently conceived of in individualistic ways. One of the first questions asked when meeting a new person is, "What do you do?" This focus on the individual vocation apart from community is not traditionally how Africans viewed the world. Though it may at times feel like it, in reality no person is, as Paul Simon sang, an island. No one is completely self-made or self-reliant; people are shaped by the culture around them, and exist in interdependent relationships with others.

Historically, bare individualism was not viewed positively in many African societies.[69] The African did not say, "I think, therefore I am." Instead, an African identity frequently derives from relationship with others: "I am in community, therefore I exist" or "We are, therefore I am."[70] There is no 'I' without 'we'; the person is always shaped by their community, and not an isolated individual. Joe M. Kapolyo illustrates this point by discussing how societal roles frequently play a part in determining a person's identity. However, when Kapolyo refers to societal roles, he has in mind not the vocational function the person performs, but rather their relationships—"We feel dignified when, upon the birth of our first child, all our relatives and acquaintances cease to address us by the use of our name and instead use the term 'father or mother of . . .'"[71] He later notes that both Euro-American and African popular definitions of the individual fail to reference God, and reiterates that all human beings ought to remember that they never independently exist, but rely on the creative and sustaining acts of God to whom they ultimately relate.[72]

One African people group, the Bemba, have a proverb that conveys the same point in a more pointed and poetic manner: *umuntu ekala na bantu: uwikala ne nama akaliwa*, which translates as, 'a person lives with people: he who lives with animals will be eaten.' In other words, "there are

---

69. In a provocative tone, Sigqibo Dwane, in talking about salvation as applying not only to souls but to all that people are, states categorically, "In Black society, the unit is not the individual, but the family which belongs to the nation. The idea of the salvation of souls is contrary to the biblical teaching that God manifests himself in and through the life of the *laos*, the people for the benefit of all his creatures. It is part of that individualistic pietism from the West which is repugnant to us, and with which our thinking cannot make common cause" ("Christology in the Third World," 8). This statement indicates an intense negative reaction against Western-style individualism.

70. Pobee, *Toward an African Theology*, 49; Kapolyo, *The Human Condition*, 23.

71. Kapolyo, *The Human Condition*, 22.

72. Ibid., 23, 35.

two alternatives for living: among people or away from people among the wild animals of the forest. To call a person *umuntu* [human] is immediately to associate that person with *abantu* [humanity] . . . in community."[73] Many African peoples, then, would have little place for the hermit, whether Christian or otherwise.[74] Likewise the virtues that define true humanity are in large part virtues oriented toward others, such as hospitality, generosity, care of others, consideration, and thoughtfulness.[75]

Another example of the importance of relationship and community may be seen in Diane B. Stinton's work, where she shares four common categories that define Christ in Africa—that of life-giver or healer, mediator, loved one, and leader.[76] Of these four categories for understanding Christ, only the first does not explicitly identify Christ as a part of the speaker's community: the mediator image envisages Jesus as an ancestor, the loved one names him a family member or close friend in the community, and the leader image casts him as king or chief, a leader from among the people. Clearly, these common metaphors for explaining the person and work of Christ rely upon an identity shaped by his familial relationship to the hearers: an identity defined by his communal, societal relationships.

This communal emphasis need not downplay or override the individual's place; William A. Dyrness argues that "the human person plays a central role in all African thinking, but always in the context of the community."[77] For instance, in traditional settings if a husband and wife fight, that disagreement "is an affair not only of that household but also of the whole village. For it destroys the coherence that holds things together."[78] Where people traditionally relied upon each other for their very survival, the concept of any matter being a purely private concern does not exist. The individual person certainly matters, but is a part of a much greater whole that must always be taken into account. What a modern, Euro-American

---

73. Ibid., 41.

74. In a discussion about holiness and wholeness not being 'solo' quests, Desmond Tutu points out that "even the solitaries of ancient memory and modern description do not account themselves as people who are alone. The Desert Fathers and Mothers relied on their spiritual strength and a firm recognition of the presence of God to sustain their solitude. Those who withdraw to the wilderness become keenly aware of the companionship of the plants, birds, and animals that make their homes in the places that other human beings have not yet populated" (Tutu and Tutu, *Made for Goodness*, 52). So these people experienced a connection with other creatures, something that bound them together, preventing the person from being detached or fully isolated.

75. Kapolyo, *The Human Condition*, 39.

76. Stinton, *Jesus of Africa*, 21.

77. Dyrness, *Learning about Theology*, 49.

78. Ibid., 50.

individualistic mind may mistake for something like communism—as in the case of Nyerere's Tanzania—is more properly interpreted as a strong value on communal identity.

Parratt says that not only identity but life itself is seen in terms of community. In his words, the African would say, "*Cognatus ergo sum*'—I am related by blood, therefore I exist."[79] An African orphan has no family, no name, no safety net, no shared bloodline, and no identity. It is almost as if they did not exist in any meaningful way because they have no one to whom they belong. African theology absolutely must address this question of a Christian's identity in Christ and relationship to the body of Christ. Pobee points out that "since belonging to a kinship group is a mark of a man, our attempt at constructing an African Christology would emphasize the kinship of Jesus."[80] The statement could be rephrased to say that until a person has learned something of Jesus's ethnic group and family lines, how could that person claim to know the Christ? No human person, the Christ included, can be a-contextual—so knowing a person involves having some grasp of the environment that has shaped them and the people to whom they belong.

Emmanuel Katongole's *The Sacrifice of Africa* provides examples of three people who are re-shaping Africa, in their own particular locations, by offering concrete examples of how the Christian story offers a new, more catholic identity and a new future. One example is that of Maggy Barankitse of Burundi, whose rediscovery of an intimate relationship with God transformed her life. She now leads a community of former orphans, offering them a home and a future where their ethnic identity is not a determinative factor in how they are treated. "Maggy's newly rediscovered relationship with God liberated her . . . [and] raised her beyond herself to a new place and a new story, into which she now wished to invite others. . . . This new story was not only bigger than her life, but bigger than the story of Burundi. It was as if a kind of new allegiance—a new claim on her life bigger than her Tutsi or Burundian identity—was revealed."[81]

Nationalistic and ethnic identities are a concern because of their exclusive nature and because of the treatment allotted to those considered 'outsiders.' Theologians reveal a concern that for Christians, loyalty to God would be the most important loyalty, and that this loyalty should generate a different type of ethos: one which welcomes outsiders and treats them

---

79. Parratt, *Reinventing Christianity*, 92–93.
80. Pobee, *Toward an African Theology*, 88.
81. Katongole, *The Sacrifice of Africa*, 172.

with care and respect. As we shall see, identity in Africa will need to address issues of life viewed relationally (in solidarity and interdependence) as well.

The other themes or pillars further help clarify the shape of communal identity, so I will return to the topic of identity at the end of this chapter. From the issue of identity we move to the concern with inculturation. Inculturation and the other themes examined here are concerns not limited to theologies in Africa, but the interwoven web of these five concerns plays out in particular ways in response to the African context.

Inculturation

Inculturation is in some ways a presupposition of African identity discussions. In other words, the debate assumes that a specifically African identity or identities can and should exist, that identity should be shaped by and intelligible in its particular context. Inculturation refers not only to a specific stream or method of theology in Africa, but more broadly to the notion that the Christian message and practices must be concerned with communicating in a manner that is understandable to the local culture.[82] The faith must become rooted in that particular context, providing a deep transformation of Christians. An emphasis on the need for inculturation and discussions of its method are prevalent in African theologies.

For example, John Pobee defines African theology as an "attempt to use African concepts and African ethos as vehicles for the communication of the gospel in an African context."[83] Here theologians are quite divided: some have a very positive view of African cultures and religions, while others are more cautious about the extent to which African cultures and religions can be employed in Christian theology, and there are many in-between positions. What is the best way forward? How far should inculturation go?

Kwame Bediako maintains that Jesus is the culmination and fulfillment of African religious beliefs.[84] E. Bolaji Idowu also believes that God has revealed himself primarily to all people through general revelation, and thus the biblical God was already real and known to Africans before

---

82. Bernard Onyebuchi Ukwuegbu suggests that inculturation "presupposes" enculturation (learning experiences by which a person becomes competent in their own culture) and acculturation (socialization outside one's family), but "transcends both in that it implies a semantic shift that includes in its scope a concern for a cultural group in relation to other groups and to the Christ-Event that may not be so central for cultural anthropology" (*The Emergence of Christian Identity*, 420 n. 72).

83. Pobee, *Toward an African Theology*, 39.

84. Bediako, *Jesus and the Gospel in Africa*, 28-30.

Christian missionaries arrived.[85] Bediako is not quite willing to go that far: he categorizes Idowu as one who would "radically indigenize" the church, while Bediako himself prefers the method of "translation."[86] However, both of these men posit a high level of continuity between African religions and Christianity, believing the two can be correlated with a few adjustments.

Stephen Ezeanya too clarifies that there will be qualifications to be made about inculturation, as African religious beliefs are not identical to Christianity: it is "not a question of trying to preserve everything in the traditional religion and cultures of African people simply because it is theirs, and trying to foster them side by side with Christianity."[87] Yet for the most part, those who have a high view of the past see only minor differences, and some will go so far as to say that their ancestors implicitly followed this God of Christianity and already were saved.

R. Buana Kibongi asks, "Would it be heresy or theological error if we were to admit, once for all, that Christ, by fulfilling what is positive in the Old Testament, also consummated all religions, social and cultural values which one finds outside the world of the Bible?"[88] His presumed answer is no. In other words, he proposes that non-Christian religions not only contain aspects of truth from general revelation, but actually have real salvific value. He sees a very high continuity in the conception of God, and some other theologians—Gehman suggests that John Mbiti is one of them, though Bediako believes Mbiti's approach is translation—liken African religions to Scripture, specifically the OT.[89]

Parratt expresses concern over the "high continuity" view, asking, if God was fully known before Christ, how is Christianity unique?[90] He believes that this issue is one which African theologians must still struggle with, suggesting the need for "a fuller argumentation both for the ground on which it is believed that African traditional religion has a real revelatory value and for the extent to which it constitutes such a revelation," because then how will the Christian be able to tell what is truly of God in them?[91] The danger in positing a high level of continuity is that eventually one must ask if there is a need for Christ at all, and if he has anything unique to contrib-

---

85. Idowu, "God," 20, 24.

86. Bediako, *Jesus and the Gospel in Africa*, 54–56.

87. Ezeanya, "God, Spirits and the Spirit World," 34.

88. Kibongi, "Priesthood," 54–55.

89. Gehman, *Doing African Christian Theology*, 55; Bediako, *Jesus and the Gospel in Africa*, 56.

90. Parratt, *Reinventing Christianity*, 64, 71–75.

91. Ibid., 208.

ute. Yet this struggle over continuity and discontinuity, regardless of where on the spectrum the particular theologian lies, points to a shared concern or belief that the Christian faith must speak to a person where she or he is, in their own location, becoming a faith they own rather than remaining a 'foreign' faith.

Accordingly John Pobee perceived three approaches to culture, one of which was adaptation (indigenization) of the faith; in his opinion, "Christianity is supra-cultural and not to be confined to one culture."[92] His theological argument for this approach is based on the fact of the Incarnation. This position seems to suggest the view that there can be some level of truth, possibly even revelation, in African religions, but not the high level of continuity proposed by Kibongi or Kibicho. However, Pobee is still very positive about the pre-Christian heritage, as can be seen in his comment on Hebrews 1, where he suggests that *paterea* refers to the Israelite patriarchs as well as to other men of old.[93] As mentioned earlier, Bediako places himself, John Mbiti, and Kwesi Dickson in this category of "translation" or "indigenization."[94]

At the other end of the spectrum stands Byang H. Kato, derisively labeled by Bediako as a "biblicist" who posits a "radical discontinuity" between Christianity and the pre-Christian heritage.[95] Kato's major work, *Theological Pitfalls in Africa*, firmly states that Christianity cannot in any way "incorporate any man-made religion" and disparages the attempt to find "so-called 'common ground' between Christianity and African traditional religions."[96] Other African theologians attacked Kato, suggesting he was merely a puppet for Western conservative voices.[97] Some wrote him off as irrelevant and ignored his works.

However, this picture unfairly and inaccurately charicatures Kato's actual stance. Kato stood firmly against the idea that African religions were on the same level as the OT, but he was not a-cultural. On the contrary, he specifically called for African theologians to indigenize the Christian faith, but without betraying Scripture.[98] Nor did he say that nothing could be learned from the pre-Christian past; rather, he wanted to be quite clear that "the call

---

92. Pobee, *Toward an African Theology*, 58–60.

93. Ibid., 73–74.

94. Bediako, *Jesus and the Gospel in Africa*, 54–56.

95. Ibid., 54–56.

96. Kato, *Theological Pitfalls in Africa*, 17.

97. Ferdinando, "The Legacy of Byang Kato," 169–71; Noll and Nystrom, *Clouds of Witnesses*, 93.

98. Kato, *Theological Pitfalls in Africa*, 16.

for recognition of 'clues' must be distinguished from the call for 'an integral Christianity.'"[99] Kato made a case study of the Jaba people in particular to demonstrate this point, and concluded that "to say the Jaba have some notion of the Supreme Being is not the same as saying that God has spoken to the priests of African traditional religions as He did to the Jewish prophets, which some African scholars maintain."[100]

In that respect, Kato disagrees with Pobee and Mbiti, referring to Heb 1:1–2 when he says firmly, "There is no evidence of a writer of a book of the Bible calling heathen ancestors 'our fathers.'"[101] Yet on the other hand, Kato protested against labeling African religions as "animistic," "witchcraft," or "primitive religion."[102] He felt that these were inadequate, poor descriptors, as well as derogatory, so he devoted a chapter of *Theological Pitfalls* to this terminology, which proves that Kato did not dismiss his cultural past, or desire to insult it, or view it as worthless. Rather, he explicitly affirmed, "I am fully in favor of the ever-abiding gospel being expressed within the context of Africa, for Africans to understand."[103] It would be most accurate, then, to conclude that Kato was not anti-cultural or anti-inculturation, though he opposed African religions being seen as vehicles of revelation. However, he is distinct from many of the theologians mentioned above in terms of his evaluation of African religions and what they have to offer.

Inculturation assumes there is some unique or specific message to convey, a message that impacts people and their culture even as the message itself—embodied in the ecclesial community—takes a culturally appropriate form. If this were not the case, why was the 1994 Rwandan genocide so jarring and unexpected? The situation confounded many specifically because Rwanda was a very 'Christianized' nation, and for a genocide to occur in such a place contradicted specific Christian values. Emmanuel Katongole expressed this bewilderment and sense of paradox when he wrote that

> the Rwandan genocide not only happed in one of the most Christianized nations in Africa; the churches themselves often became killing fields, with Christians killing fellow Christians in the same places they had worshipped together. This not only raised many questions about the famed African sense of community and sacredness of life, but also filled me with deep anger

99. Ibid., 38.
100. Ibid., 29.
101. Ibid., 44.
102. Ibid., 20–24.
103. Kato, *African Cultural Revolution and the Christian Faith* quoted in Ferdinando, "The Legacy of Byang Kato," 169.

and restlessness about the status of Christianity in Africa. I kept wondering whether Christianity in Africa had become so interwoven into the story of violence that it no longer had a vantage point from which to resist the violence.[104]

Katongole's words highlight the expectation that Christianity should alter cultures—it should uproot certain negative values—and at the same time become intertwined with the most basic self-understanding of people who claim that faith. Those who bear the label 'Christian' should not behave in such a way: it is inconsistent with a Christian identity.

Katongole's works explore the idea that Christianity is a story or script which requires Christians to enact and embody it in their particular settings; by following the Christian narrative, with its eschatological vision, people can bring about true and deep changes in their cultures, counteracting the false and destructive stories that produced genocide. Christianity failed in Rwanda, in this particular instance, because the Christian faith failed to disrupt a "political imagination" of violence and division. By submitting to the false, destructive story of "distinct races" competing with each other, the Christian faith lost its power to transform the situation, its ability to name this story as a falsehood and offer a different vision of the future.[105] Essentially, Katongole insists that Christianity 'failed' in Rwanda because it was not thoroughly, fully ingrained in the thoughts and acts of Rwandan Christians. So while the theologians above may disagree about means and degree of inculturation, all agree that inculturation itself is a vital issue.

In summary, inculturation raises questions about continuity and discontinuity, both in African theologies and in African Christian identities. Inculturation assumes that some connection or similarity, some continuity, exists between two items, but discontinuity also exists. To what extent will the past, with its negative, Euro-American-imposed view of Africa, affect the present and future of African identity? Further, for Christians, delineating the extent of continuity between non-Christian and Christian beliefs is vital, for if there is no discontinuity, then Christ would not be unique as orthodox Christian theology has historically proclaimed. The Christian identity must be both distinctive and culturally relatable. Christian identity must be inculturated in Africa, if it is to redeem African identities for Christ.

In terms of methodology, inculturation theology and liberation theology are often differentiated. Yet in one way, as other theologians have pointed out, these theologies should not be divided. Liberation theology is certainly concerned with speaking a message that is demonstrably relevant

---

104. Katongole, *The Sacrifice of Africa*, 8–9.
105. Ibid., 7–9, 17, 19, 21, 101.

to its context; the difference between liberation and inculturation theology is more one of method and emphasis, than that of opposites. To oversimplify, inculturation theology has tended to focus upon the past and traditional culture, while liberation theology works from the present context. Yet even inculturation theologies reveal a concern for liberation. Inculturation theology is based upon the premise that the gospel can and should be expressed in culturally appropriate forms, allowing Christians to grasp it in their own language and concepts. Successful inculturation gives Christians in Africa the freedom to be both Christian and African, to merge these two communal identities. It gives the ecclesial community an African face and voice, rather than assuming that some other culture's theology is dominating or final. In short, while liberation theology may focus upon social issues, inculturation theology (and inculturation as a general concern) is also interested in liberation to some extent, even if it may be defined somewhat differently.

Liberation

Liberation too, though, is a recurrent theme, whether dealing with sociopolitical realities, economic issues, the treatment of women, educational methods, necessities of using europhone languages, or the like. Broadly speaking, liberation is concerned with freedom from oppression and domination of various forms. For example, womanist theologians fight for the right of women to be treated as equals with men and study the Bible in light of their own experiences and with their own methods. Inculturation theology seeks liberation from the dominance and assumed universalism of Euro-American theologies and from Euro-American cultural identities being imposed upon the church. For example, in the field of literature, Kenyan Ngũgĩ wa Thiong'o wants to liberate his audience from the undue influence of 'Western' languages, culture, and financial manipulation. Theologians too emphasize that liberation flows from the gospel proclamation of redemption and freedom in Christ (cf. Luke 4:14ff.).

Even Tanzanian Charles Nyamiti, a proponent of inculturation theology, explicitly affirms the importance of liberation, stating firmly, "No theology can be adequately relevant to the needs of today's Africa if it neglects or ignores the demands of inculturation or liberation."[106] Elochukwu E. Uzukwu, another practitioner of inculturation theology, also addresses the importance of liberation in African contexts, expressing concern that Western powers still subjugate Africa. He desires to see the church in Africa become a free community, one that is neither dominated nor dominating

---

106. Nyamiti, *Contemporary Models of African Ecclesiology*, 114.

others but instead exists as an alternative society, a place from which people "participate in changing the continent."[107] The source of the Christian's liberation is none other than the Spirit.[108]

Agbonkhianmeghe E. Orobator likewise deals frequently with this theme of liberation. He contends that if the gospel is not being applied to all areas of life, something is wrong with our theology.[109] For him, liberation is inherently linked to the gospel. For those who dislike speaking of the church as serving society, Orobator objects that the gospel charges the church to seek justice.[110] He views his own theology as an approach that integrates this concern for liberation. Congolese Augustin Ramazani Bishwende too wants to integrate and synthesize the various theological streams in Africa.[111] Bishwende critiques both inculturation and liberation theologies, suggesting instead a full, dynamic inculturation approach that addresses the key concerns of other theological approaches, and hence integrates the struggle for liberation. So it is clear that even when different methodologies are involved, liberation remains a nearly pervasive concern for theologians in Africa.

Another way of saying this is that the church's message has present-day implications that cannot be ignored. If the church does not pursue liberation, it is essentially denying the gospel message's power. The church as a place of life must enhance freedom, seeking to renew and improve this world. If the church does not fight for such things, it denies the universal applicability of its message, and the power and hope that message proffers. Hence liberation is a prevalent, relevant theme for Africans and theologies in Africa, integrally tied to the gospel and the church's witness to God's Kingdom. The identity available to God's people ought to be a liberating identity, in other words.

How, specifically, is liberation linked with identity in Africa? Liberation involves freedom from distorted images of Africa, such as descriptions of the continent that only mention negative traits. Secondly, liberation for Christians means the freedom to have hope for the future and work for justice in the present. It is the independence to define Africa as Africans, not according to others' stereotypes. Theologians in Africa further envision that liberation from oppression of whatever type ought to result in a fuller, more freeing experience of life. Life, fullness of life, life force, a holistic view

---

107. Uzukwu, *Listening Church*, 7; cf. 152–53.
108. Ibid., 107–9.
109. Orobator, *Church as Family*, 13.
110. Ibid., 110.
111. Bishwende, *Église-Famille de Dieu*, 17–19.

of life—all of these are frequently used in African theologies and point to the next dimension, what liberation is for.

Life

Here too the necessity of contextualization is urgent, because 'life' in African writings is not limited to biological existence. It is a broader term encompassing more than mere survival. A certain absorption with the term appears repeatedly in texts from Africa: sometimes the focus is on the various threats to biological or social life on the continent, while other times the authors discuss traditional views of life, which are holistic and all-encompassing.[112] The holistic view of life is linked to a relational view of human beings, and this holistic perspective also explains the link with liberation in Christian writings. This holistic perspective prods the Christian communal identity to examine its own understanding of life, and to apply the Christian understanding of life to all facets of its identity.

Belgian Placide Tempels's *Bantu Philosophy* postulates the concept of "force" (a life force, or vital force) at the center of Bantu cultures, a force in which people participate.[113] This work, originally published in 1945, demonstrates the importance of 'life' among Bantu peoples. While aspects of Tempels's work have been much debated by theologians and sociologists, the importance of the theme itself is not the source of their disagreement. Similar to Tempels, V. Mulago gwa Cikala Musharhamina views vital participation as the "cohesive principle of the Bantu community": it is "the main if not the only basis of all their family, social, political and religious institutions and customs. This life is not static: it can increase or decrease; it is lived in the communion of its members."[114]

Mulago's chapter examines three aspects of vital participation, the first being "unity of life as the center of cohesion and solidarity among the Bantu."[115] This life is realized in closely bound blood relationships with the living and the dead, as well as relationships with the visible and the invisible (and animate and inanimate) realities in the world, certainly includ-

---

112. For a recent example, see Ilo, Ogbonnaya, and Ojacor *The Church as Salt and Light*.

113. Tempels, *Philosophie Bantu*.

114. Mulago, "Vital Participation," 137. This book (*Biblical Revelation and African Beliefs*, edited by Kwesi A. Dickson and Paul Ellingworth) is a collection of essays from African theologians presented at the 1966 All Africa Council of Churches conference in Ibadan, Nigeria.

115. Mulago, "Vital Participation," 137.

ing communion with God, the source of holistic life.[116] The goal of Bantu communities is to protect and increase their community's life. Mulago links this societal view with Christian theology in the following way: communion becomes the center of African ecclesiology. In his view, this life-relationship on which, among the Bantu, the unity of communities and individuals is founded; this communication which is a sharing in life and in the means of life; this effort towards ontic growth, self-transcendence and enrichment finds a sublime and transcendent realization in the Church of Christ, which is also a community of life whose vital principle is a sharing in the life of the Trinity, humanized in the Word of God made human.[117] He references 1 John 1:1–3 in support of his discussion about life and solidarity (in John's language, "fellowship"), finally describing the church as a "clan."[118]

Roughly three decades later, describing the needs of the African church in the future, Mercy Amba Oduyoye too turns to 'life' as a central theme in both African cultures and religions and Christianity. This similarity explains the many conversions resulting from the modern missionary enterprise in Africa: "Africans converted to Christianity because they saw an affinity between the gospel of Jesus Christ and the African worldview of the sacredness of life and the human attachment to life, fullness of life. They were drawn to the gospel's inclusiveness and wholeness, its care for the vulnerable and its affirmation of humanity's dependence on God."[119] The holistic view of life presented by the Bible and its affirmation of God's deep concern for all life imply that theology must have a "vigorous" theology of humanity's relationship to creation and maintain a sacralized view of the world in order to resist exploiting or oppressing others.[120] To have a future in Africa, the church must maintain unity amidst its diverse churches; by producing the fruit of the Spirit, the church visibly demonstrates that diversity-in-unity can become a blessing, an experience of "the riches of God's abundant life" and a contribution to the "fullness of life in Africa."[121] Thus, Oduyoye focuses on the theme of life, just as theologians did three decades earlier. Her own conception of life depends heavily on life being defined in a relational, holistic way; thus she ties together the concepts of dialogue, justice, and liberation.

116. Ibid., 138–45.
117. Ibid., 157.
118. Ibid.
119. Oduyoye, "The Church of the Future," 501.
120. Ibid., 501–2.
121. Ibid., 503.

Describing the model "church as family at the service of society," Orobator expounds on the view of life forming this 'family.' People in the community are viewed in a relational way: people are made for relationships, and thus life itself is relational.[122] Life in Christ is holistic: not just inner or spiritual, but including culture, politics, economics, and other social forces.[123] Life implies "sharing, hospitality, celebration and participation"[124]—concrete practices. To promote life, the community must fight against the forces of evil and death wherever they exist and walk with the suffering and needy as Christ did; in short, "*diakonia* presupposes *koinonia*."[125] Orobator emphasizes solidarity with the needy because of Jesus's ministry to them, and also because of the glaring reality that 'sub-Saharan Africa' is a place where "*not* to be poor is the exception."[126] Thus, a relational view of humans and life cannot neglect such a blatant wound in African lives.[127]

Titre Ande describes ecclesial identity in a similar manner. The community receives its life from Christ, and thus its life must be conformed to his. Those 'in' Christ affirm and seek life, as defined by and flowing from Christ. The life he gives is relational ("referred outside" one's self by the Spirit, shared with others, welcoming others) and liberative.[128] Ande directly states that 'life' in his theology is parallel to the usage of *zoe* in Johannine and Pauline writings: life includes vitality, natural existence, and health. And "if life is the cornerstone for African ecclesiology, the church must be Life-Community, living the life of Christ in its fullness and sharing Christ's life with others. Authority within the Church must be 'authority-for-life', not in the sense of dictation for life, but in the sense of 'authority for enhancing life.'"[129]

From the above examples, it is clear that the theme of life is a major, central one for African theologies. Specifically, life is seen as relational, holistic, and dependent upon God. Since human life is relational, then logically human identities too are relational in nature, meaning that relationships are key in defining personal identity. The communities to which a person belongs have great influence in shaping the person's self-perception, values, and so forth. Those who call themselves Christians are inescapably bound

---

122. Orobator, *Church as Family*, 150.
123. Ibid., 152–53.
124. Ibid., 150.
125. Ibid., 63; idem, *Crisis to Kairos*, 236.
126. Orobator, *Church as Family*, citing Donkor, "Structural Adjustment," 209.
127. Orobator, *Church as Family*, 150.
128. Ande, *Leadership and Authority*, 135, 144.
129. Ibid., 133.

up with the God's people, united by the Spirit to Christ, according to the NT. Christ, the community's center, gives life to the community and to the whole world. Christ orients the community's self-understanding, as well as that of the individuals within the community.

When life is viewed in highly relational, holistic ways, it is obvious why a fifth theme, solidarity in community, is an influential concept in African literature, whether the communities in question are ethnic, national, or ecclesial communities.

Community

When life is characterized in a relational, holistic manner, then one can see how the concept of life includes relationships with all aspects of human life, including other elements of creation. As people are made for relationships with God and fellow humans, it understandably follows that community and solidarity are common themes in African writings. The communal emphasis seen in Africa cultures often leads to a condemnation of modern Euro-American cultures, often characterized as possessing a dangerously strong individualist bent.

Despite numerous denunciations of individualism, African writers are agreed that it would be folly to suggest that the group-focus of their cultures is purely beneficial. Like all strengths, it also carries inherent weaknesses, at least in the context of fallen humanity. For example, the communal focus that pushes a person to be social and ever aware of their relationships with others also possesses the potential to manifest itself in ethnic conflict. Because a person is deeply tied to their own ethnic group, ethnocentrism is an ongoing difficulty for African churches. Thus, the struggle of contextualizing Christianity in such an atmosphere has led church and educational leaders in Africa to conclude that for theological training "new courses needed to increase ministry in the local context could include Justice and Peace, Conflict Resolution."[130] Ethnocentrism continues to tear at the church in Africa, highlighting that a relational emphasis contains the potential for blessing or curse; this danger is why examining the nature of ecclesial identity is vital.[131] Despite its dangers, theologians repeatedly affirm that community is central to God's existence and the existence of God's people: the Christian identity is inescapably communal, by God's design.

130. Chester, "'Reliable leaders,'" 373.

131. Hence Mbandi's *A Theology of the Unity of the Church in a Multi-Ethnic Context: Toward a Theological Understanding of the Unity of the Church in Relation to Ethnic Diversity*.

"The Church of the Future, Its Mission and Theology" discusses the value of religious communities, which sometimes replace deteriorating traditional family bonds and provide social support to the poor. "Africa's culture is communal," and "Africans of all three religions (African-Cosmic, Christianity, and Islam) are united by their extended-family obligations."[132] Indeed, "one clear function of the church in Africa is that of providing an active, supportive community for a people accustomed to living in caring communities"; further, the church as "a model of community . . . serves the function of sustaining the hope that human beings can love and care for one another."[133] Because these communities—and the continent—include a variety of people, cultures, and interests, Oduyoye desires for the church to live as "a community that demonstrates to Africa how variety and diversity may become a blessing. In other words, it should pick up the traditional African communal principles, enhance them with the good news of Jesus Christ, and enable caring communities to develop and thrive."[134] Hence some familiar themes rise to the surface: community as a necessary, central part of life, thus linking to relationality. Additionally, the community has powerful solidarity united with an equally necessary diversity. The community protects and enhances holistic life, encompassing issues of liberation from poverty with empowerment of women and other marginalized persons. One might sum it up by saying that within the church, no area of life is excluded in order that the church can "become once more the vehicle of good news to the world," the place where "fullness of life" can be attained.[135] This view of life links the gospel message, broader Christian theology, and a communal emphasis.

Orobator envisions ecclesial identity as one that strengthens and grounds a person while opening them to others. Christianity is a communal faith, one that is neither passive nor isolated from the rest of society.[136] The church is a community where life is protected and nurtured.[137] Within the

---

132. Oduyoye, "The Church of the Future," 497.

133. Ibid., 498. A sentence later, she admits that "on the other hand, the church can also be described as the worst example of divisiveness and intolerance of diversity and dissent." Later the article notes that "the only principle from African culture that will be honored [in new Christian movements] and appropriated is the sense of concentric communities that are open" while at the same time "community in Africa is being labeled tribalism and ethnocentricity and is being coopted [sic] by politicians for divisive and negative uses" (499, 500).

134. Oduyoye, "The Church of the Future," 498.

135. Ibid., 498–99.

136. Orobator, *Church as Family*, 46.

137. Ibid., 151.

church community, each person contributes and participates: leaders listen to laity, and laity fulfill their own important ministries.[138] This communal perspective reflects Paul's habit of referring to the church as an "organic unity."[139]

Here Orobator commends the palaver model, where the leader is essentially a listener, hearing the voices of his people; he does not force his will on them, but through dialogue the people find a solution they agree upon. An emphasis on the centrality of community and relationality coheres well with this model, because the palaver places a premium on interpersonal relationships and dialogue, restraining the church from overly individualistic or hierarchical views of the church.[140] An emphasis on participation and listening implies that there is diversity within the church, resulting in different types of ministry.[141] This diversity is from the Spirit and enriches the community.[142] Listening to its diverse voices grounds the church in reality, and incorporates the marginalized, such as women: the church should be identified as a community that unites diverse people.[143]

While Christ gives the church its distinct identity and mission, Orobator argues that the church also possesses a call to welcome all and to engage in the world in which it lives as a visible agent of transformation, extending the presence of Christ to all areas.[144] A church that fails to integrate the social groups and persons that constitute it does not reflect the 'universal assembly' that the Bible reveals as the eschatological goal.[145] Orobator envisions a community marked by participation, dialogue (indicating a desire to listen to diverse voices and arrive at consensus), and life. The Spirit provides the community with diversity and unity, and opens it to others, making welcome those who are different. This last is a necessity if the church is to remain true to the biblical vision and divine mission given to it.

Titre Ande also discusses God's design for God's people. His "Life-Community" model is based on a new, transformative identity in Christ and open to others by the Spirit, producing an "intra-ethnic consciousness," a "supra-ethnic community."[146] Without a supra-ethnic focus the church can

---

138. Ibid., 42.
139. Orobator, *Crisis to Kairos*, 209–10.
140. Orobator, *Church as Family*, 45.
141. Ibid., 142.
142. Orobator, *Crisis to Kairos*, 221.
143. Orobator, *Church as Family*, 31–32.
144. Orobator, *Crisis to Kairos*, 233, 243.
145. Ibid., 168–70.
146. Ande, *Leadership and Authority*, 144, 155, 157.

become contextual but isolated, or lost in the pressures of globalization.[147] The "Life-Community" can be

> a power base for unity as it is not simply a loose-knit collection of human beings in a geographical space or a direct biological relational community. Moreover, it is not anthropocentric, but built on the centrality of Christ in a Trinitarian basis. Therefore, Life-Community is not sociologically, politically and economically motivated, but it is a theological concept mostly Christ-centered on a Trinitarian basis, with sociological, economic and political implications.[148]

Instead of prioritizing African cultural and religious values, it highlights the primacy of Christ, source of life.[149] It is a community of unity, solidarity, and equality, engaging all spheres of life. Ande focuses on the Trinity because in his understanding "the ontological basis for the church is the communion of the 'Father-Son-Spirit' model."[150] Ecclesial identity reflects the social, communal nature of God.

In the Trinity each Person is fully divine (ontologically equal), and in the church community too there can be no ontological grading of persons; each community member has a vital role to play.[151] The relationality and communion described here point to a high degree of interdependence.[152] Ande envisions community structures that are not rigid and hierarchical, but more akin to those in the apostolic age, where leaders and community acted together.[153] Driven by the gospel, the church's communal identity shapes the personal identity of its members, people who seek to apply the Christian message to every area of life.[154]

Ande describes a community bearing similar traits to what Orobator and Oduyoye described. It is a community of life, dependent on God, marked by relationality and dialogue. Repeated emphasis on dialogue implies other values: humility and patience to hear another's voice and learn from them. The reminder of dependence on God for life also supports the importance of humility in Ande's model of community among God's people. He, like Orobator, invokes the doctrine of the Trinity as support for

---

147. Ibid., 156.
148. Ibid., 137.
149. Ibid.
150. Ibid., 143–44.
151. Ibid., 82, 145.
152. Ibid., 125, 145–46.
153. Ibid., 152.
154. Ibid., 121, 158, 169.

the communal emphasis: in short, if Christian identity is to be true to the Triune God, this identity must be highly communal.

While cultures in Africa have changed with time, many still strongly value community and desire to belong. This need for belonging is a universal human desire, perhaps, but it is especially deeply ingrained in African cultures. Several authors express the need for a community that accepts all persons as equals and encourages participation and interdependence. In order to integrate all persons and value each voice, multiple theologians recommend reclaiming dialogue as seen in the palaver model. For Christians, the church is in some ways analogous to the Trinity, reinforcing the notion that community and solidarity are not merely cultural values, but important aspects of God's plan for human thriving.

Summary

The previous sections show the extent to which themes of life and community are intertwined, almost inseparable. We also noted that inculturation and liberation are vital and interwoven concerns in Africa theologies. Finally we can now return briefly to the issue of identity, particularly how the concept is understood in African texts: identity can be viewed as the thread that unites the rest into the tapestry of theology in Africa.

Identity concerns arise the instant the terms 'Africa' and 'African' are employed. There is a struggle to redefine Africa in positive terms, to change the image and connotations that term frequently bears. There is also an ongoing debate about the nature of African identity, and a search for characteristics other than geography or common challenges that unite the people of this vast continent. Defining Africa primarily by race or geography is problematic. Kwame Appiah rejects the idea of a cultural unity across Africa or of European-imposed nationalism as adequate sources of unity or identity. A. E. Orobator proposes in response that one commonality is located in shared post-colonial socio-economic and political problems. However, this definition, though perhaps accurately describing challenges the church in Africa faces, paints an unduly and predominantly negative picture of Africa. Hence Orobator's definition is flawed and incomplete. Appiah also conceives of identity as a construct, a dynamic process that is ongoing, with persons and groups negotiating multiple identities. This approach is a more fruitful way to envision identity while giving Africans the agency to re-define the term 'Africa.'

Secondly, a concern with inculturation highlights the urgency of valuing and retaining aspects of African cultures. Ecclesial identities in Africa must be understandable in their contexts and have some continuity with the past, yet for Christians, continuity cannot threaten the uniqueness of Christ. In short, ecclesial identity must continually wrestle with the demands of inculturation and holiness, as Christians seek both connection with and distinction from broader cultures.

Thirdly, the ongoing relevance of liberation indicates that agency and freedom from neo-colonial control are major concerns for Africans. Freedom and agency take many forms: of particular interest here in relation to identity is the agency to redefine the term 'Africa' so that negative connotations are minimized, or at least are not allowed to be the sole defining traits. Theologians remark that Christ brings freedom in the gospel, which must be applied to all areas of life and produce visibly transformative results—including the identity of a new human community, Christ's body.

Fourthly, life is emphasized, perceived in holistic and relational ways, and the participation of every community member is encouraged. Hence identity discussions address how being in Christ is life-giving and communal, referring a person outside of their individual concerns. Due to relational and participatory emphases, concerns with solidarity and unity in diversity are natural. For Christians, life comes from Christ, is dependent on God, and brings the individual into interdependent relationships with others in Christ's Body.

Fifthly, then, community is a crucial component of the identity envisioned. In particular, the church's tightly knit communion should be marked by a high degree of solidarity, which has traditionally been a necessary, central part of life in African cultures. Within community, there is interdependence, and a need for equality of persons revealed in dialogue where all voices can be heard. Again, for Christians, the ultimate communal identity is found in the Trinity as revealed by Christ.

Given the past century or two of history on the African continent, it is not surprising that 'Africa' and African identities continue to be periodically problematic. A resilient, healthy African Christian identity must account for the major themes mentioned above as they provide points of contact with African cultures and religions: identity for Christians in Africa must be inculturated, liberating, life-giving, and communal. Another way of saying this is that while Orobator rightly perceives that Africa has a commonality rooted in a colonial history, he is wrong to leave Africa therefore mired in a negative definition based on contemporary problems. The themes identified in this chapter suggest how Africa might be redefined by a set of theological commitments that respond to a colonial history and contemporary problems with Christian initiative. Yet this identity must also transcend those moments when African (and other) cultures fall into a merely ethnic or clanlike form of solidarity. Thus theologians in Africa emphasize that Christian identity is founded in Christ, who gives his followers a new, transformative identity that 'supersedes' old loyalties and brings the person into a new community. Amidst the community of God's people, life, community, freedom, and context (including their continent, Africa, and particular cultural groups) are still central concerns, but reoriented around the Christ. These themes clarify in general terms—from a historical-theological perspective—what African identity must address and what it can be built on. But there is more to be said about developing a strong, positive African identity that can withstand the rapid changes and ongoing changes in African societies. To such confirmation and exploration of the ongoing African challenge of identity, and its ecclesiological significance, we will turn in the next chapter.

Chapter 3

Identities in Africa

The prior chapters established that identity has been crucial to speaking of "Africa," and more specifically that identity is primary among five key themes in African theology. As noted earlier, in this case 'identity' essentially functions synonymously with 'self-understanding' or 'self-concept.' The previous chapter highlighted African theology's concern with identity, specifically an identity that is inculturated, liberating, full of life, and shaped by community. Indeed, the latter provides a clue as how identity is being employed by theologians in Africa. This chapter argues that the focus of identity discussions in African theologies is a 'communal' or 'social' identity, and more precisely envisions a particular type of relationship between African and Christian communal identities. A particular concern with communal or social identity, related to group membership, would suggest that it is vital for African theology to explore ecclesial identity further, describing how that particular communal identity reflects the Lordship of Christ and the nature of God's kingdom. Hence the next chapter will explore the ways in which biblical texts are used as the basis of and further definition for the nature of this communal identity, before moving to ecclesiologies specifically in chapter 5.

On a broad level, this chapter demonstrates that identity concerns remain pervasive. More particularly, the chapter argues that (1) that these identity discussions are fundamentally centered on *communal* or *social* identities of Christians in Africa.

Furthermore, the chapter contends that (2) a certain relationship between African and Christian identities is desired by African theologians in order to achieve healthy Christian identities. The fact that concern with African social identity recurs in texts from multiple decades suggests that the issue is a persistent concern across various African cultures. Thus, the theological authors selected are purposely from different countries, with their works published in different decades and languages. These theologians focus on Christian identity in their various contexts, and highlighting both the consistency and diversity of this theme is the concern of this chapter.

The next two chapters, based on this one, will explore how this ongoing concern with communal identity shapes African ecclesiology. Pursuing the nature of communal identity, this chapter moves to theologians addressing the relationship between Christian and African communal identities: first V. Mulago gwa Cikala Musharhamina, from the genesis of modern African theology; then Kwame Bediako; and finally Mercy Amba Oduyoye. These theologians argue that the Christian identity encompasses other social identities, incorporating and not destroying African identities, and also that identity concerns are theological in nature since they arise from encountering the Gospel of the one Creator.

V. Mulago gwa Cikala Musharhamina[1]

Mulago (1924–2012) is one of the first modern African theologians. Chronological placement aside, Bénézet Bujo ranks Mulago as a "prerequisite" in African theology, "one of the precursors comparable to the Apostolic Fathers."[2] Kwame Bediako likewise considers Mulago a pioneer of African theology. One reason for Bediako's high assessment of the Congolese theologian is *Des Prêtres noirs s'interrogent*,[3] writings by Roman Catholic theologians that represent "the first concentrated effort by a group of African writers," where the opening chapter by Mulago is "clearly the keynote piece of the entire collection," addressing foundational issues about Christianity in and Christianization of Africa.[4]

---

1. Mulago was a Roman Catholic priest from Zaire (now the Democratic Republic of Congo [DRC]). Originally he published under the name of Vincent Mulago, but later used or was referred to as 'V. Mulago gwa Cikala', 'Mulago gwa Cikala', or 'Mulago gwa Cikala Musharhamina'. For example, see the bibliography in Mulago, "Traditional African Religion and Christianity," 119–34, which in itself shows various forms of his name. I have used "Mulago gwa Cikala M., Vincent" in the bibliography for all his works, and will use "Mulago" in the footnotes for simplicity.

2. Bujo, "Vincent Mulago," 13.

3. *Des Prêtres noirs s'interrogent: Cinquante ans après*. Mulago authored two chapters of this book: "Nécessité de l'adaptation missionaire chez les Bantu du Congo" (19–40) and "Le Pacte du sang et la communion alimentaire, pierres d'attente de la communion eucharistique" (171–87). We will focus more on the first, which describes his rationale and method.

4. Bediako, "A Variety of African Responses," 349. Bénézet Bujo called *Des Prêtres*

Born into the *Shi* ethnic group (hence a *Mushi*), his extensive education, and rare (at the time) doctorate from Rome earned him the nickname *Mushi Wasomire*, meaning 'the *Mushi* who has studied, the educated *Mushi*.'[5] He would go on to serve as a parish priest, teacher, director of a liturgical center, and founder of a center for study of African religions and of the journal *Cahiers des religions africaines*. Multiple *Festschriften* and works honor his legacy.[6] In short, he was a fervent advocate for African Christian identity.

His most representative work, *Un Visage africain du christianisme*, is based on his doctoral dissertation.[7] It contains themes that Mulago returned to repeatedly throughout his career: the need to deeply root Christianity in Africa, to validate African Christian identity, and to identify 'stepping stones' in Bantu culture that were fulfilled by Christian doctrine and sacraments. He also addressed ethical issues such as marriage.[8] Other frequent themes of his publications are the necessity of the adaptation method (and therefore also of African theology),[9] vital union as it relates to ecclesial unity,[10] sacraments,[11] and the place of the African religio-cultural heritage in the communal Christian identity.[12] Mulago's 'stepping stones' or 'adaptation' method has been heavily critiqued, even by friends and colleagues. However, this criticism does not negate Mulago's contribution to the discussion on African Christian identity.

---

noirs s'interrogent "the founding charter of African theology" ("Vincent Mulago," 15).

5. Bujo, "Vincent Mulago," 15.

6. Mushete, *Combats pour un christianisme africain*; Mulago, *Interpellations et croissance de la foi*; and Faculté de théologie catholique de Kinshasa, *Inculturation et libération en Afrique aujourd'hui*. Additionally, Mulago, *Théologie africaine et problèmes connexes* describes Mulago's intellectual and spiritual life.

7. Mulago, *Un Visage africain*.

8. Mulago, "Mariage africain et mariage chrétien," 547–64; Mulago, "Le Mariage traditionnel bantu," 5–61.

9. For example, Mulago, "Nécessité de l'adaptation missionaire chez les Bantu du Congo" and the preliminary chapter in *Un Visage africain* (15–34).

10. His dissertation, later revised and published as *Un Visage africain du christianisme*; "L'union vitale Bantu," 133–41; "Le Pacte du sang," 171–87; "Vital Participation," 137–58; "Traditional African Religion and Christianity"; "Symbolisme dans les religions traditionnelles africaines et sacramentalisme," 467–502; "Solidarité africaine" 86–134.

11. Mulago "Le Pacte du sang"; "Dialectique existentielle," 146–71; "Sauver la vérité des sacrements," 274–91; "Le nouveau ritual de la pénitence," 143–48.

12. For example, "La Théologie et ses responsabilités," 188–205; "Christianisme et culture africaine," 308–28; "Le problème d'une théologie africaine," 277–314.

Before examining specific aspects of *Un Visage africain du christianisme*, I will examine Mulago's 'stepping stones' or adaptation method and its presuppositions related to God's character, as well as his view of the relationship between universality and particularity. This method provides the rationale for the way in which Mulago construes the relationship between African and Christian identities. Adaptation is based on God's character: God is consistent, and does not contradict himself, so the ways in which he reveals himself in general revelation—among all peoples and places—are in agreement with Christ's revelation of God. Hence, there are genuine pointers to Christ in every culture, which must not be discounted.[13] The whole world, human nature included, is tainted by sin, but not so much that all hints of goodness and witness to God have disappeared without a trace. The theologian's task is to locate the good and the hints of divine illumination that remain in each culture, employing them for the benefit of the church and aiding people in understanding the Christian message. Adaptation, Mulago repeatedly insists, is not a reduction of Truth, but a means of illuminating an aspect of Truth to allow a person to grasp it more easily.[14] This approach treats all people lovingly and respectfully, seeking to enrich both individual persons and their society, and to integrate those riches into the church, moving it closer to its eschatological fullness.[15]

Furthermore, adaptation is not based on general revelation alone, but also on the Incarnation; Mulago's understanding of redemption propels him to the conclusion that cultural identities are purified to become part of Christian identity. In the Incarnation the Son of God enters into a context to purify it, using elements within that context to reveal himself. He does not utterly demolish the context, but works with the elements there and fills them with a new reality. In a similar way the church is called to embody the gospel and transform what she touches, not destroy or demolish the cultures she engages: in other words, this transformation is redemption, which is central to the church's beliefs. Hence African identities are redeemed, to be made part of the overarching Christian identity. Like Christ, the church must discerningly identify core values of African religio-cultures, then use those same values to present Christ as the fulfillment and goal toward which they were ultimately striving.[16] Mulago firmly, explicitly rejects the idea that Africa ever was or is, as some European thinkers supposed, a *tabula rasa*.[17]

---

13. Mulago, "Nécessité de l'adaptation missionaire," 22–23.
14. Mulago, *Un Visage africain*, 32–33, 37.
15. Mulago, "Nécessité de l'adaptation missionaire," 30–32, 38–39.
16. Ibid., 34.
17. Bediako notes that Mulago saw the theory of *tabula rasa* underlying not just

Once core values are identified, the point where the Christian message and cultural aspirations meet, then the theologian knows where to "graft" on the Christian message.[18] Mulago claims that 'grafting' was the Apostle Paul's method, as seen in his speech at the Areopagus.[19] What is clearly opposed to Christ must be rejected, but cultural aspects that retain some goodness can be redeemed. Such an approach allows the Gospel to be presented in a way that the people of that context can truly understand. For the Congolese priest, it is clear that "Rome wants us to penetrate the indigenous soul and wants us to adapt the presentation of Christian dogma."[20] Mulago insists that adaptation, like the Incarnation, is in no way a diminution or mutilation of the truth.[21] It requires adjusting the message's presentation, but not the core content or dogma itself.

As mentioned above, the first point this chapter argues is that identity discussions in African theology are concerned specifically with communal identity. Mulago advocates strongly and repeatedly for the Christian message and the Christian community taking a local or contextual 'face' (identity) in each culture: hence the book's title, *Un Visage africain du christianisme*. Secondly, Mulago envisions a particular relationship between African and Christian communal identities. He advocates that Christian (communal) identities in Africa must integrate African (communal) identities. His theological bases—God's character and the Incarnation—support his stance that Christian identity must be both universal and inculturated (shaped by local communities and their particular communal identities).

But with a strong emphasis on inculturation (the particularity of African identities), how does he negotiate the universality of the Christian message and the communal Christian identity? Rather than viewing these aspects as in tension, Mulago envisions universality and particularity having a necessary, reciprocal relationship. Specifically because the church claims to bear a universally applicable message, it must have a 'recognizable' face.[22]

---

colonial actions, but also the Western missionary enterprise, which logically led to an attempt to demolish African culture in its entirety, and a desire to 'rebuild' civilization on a Western cultural model (*Theology and Identity*, 350).

18. Mulago, "Nécessité de l'adaptation missionaire," 23, 29, 30 and "Le Pacte du sang," 183. Also *Un Visage africain*, 18.

19. Mulago, *Un Visage africain*, 30, and "Le Pacte du sang," 183. *Un Visage africain* also states that both Jesus and Paul used this method of moving from familiar, known imagery (the vine and branches, the body and its members) to unknown or mysterious Gospel truths (159).

20. Mulago, "Nécessité de l'adaptation missionaire," 24.

21. Mulago, *Un Visage africain*, 26–30.

22. Bediako, *Theology and Identity*, 353.

Bediako claims that it is this conviction of the church's universality "rather than simply a desire to vindicate an African cultural personality which really constitutes the *force motrice* of [Mulago's] argument."[23] The church claims to bear a message that is relevant for all people in all times and all places, so that relevance is manifested by the message becoming 'at home' in each setting. Note here that this 'face', this identity, is a communal one—it is the church's manner of manifesting itself in a particular society to which Mulago refers, not to an individualistic identity.

African identity is a necessary component of the Christian identity in Africa, because of the Christian identity's universal, global nature. At the same time as Mulago emphasizes the necessity of the church being inculturated in each context, Bediako points out that Mulago rejects the idea that only a so-called universal theology is valid, "since that kind of argument often hides the fact that what is meant by universal is also what is Western."[24] Universality does not mean that either theology or the Christian communal identity takes only one form. Instead, universality means that the Gospel story is applicable and relatable in all contexts, which is why the form it takes changes to some extent from one context to another. Mulago conceives of Christian unity and universality as rich and diverse in nature, in such a way that each Christian community bears a responsibility to bring their distinctiveness before God to enrich God's kingdom.[25]

Un Visage africain du christianisme explains Mulago's stance on African theology, his methodology, and then applies that method to his study of three ethnic groups: the Bashi, Banyarwanda, and Barundi peoples—Bantu groups that are linked geographically, physically, and culturally.[26] This work interweaves the concern with identity that is communal in nature, and with the desired relationship of the African and Christian communal identi-

23. Bediako, *Theology and Identity*, 354.

24. Ibid., 371.

25. Mulago, "Christianisme et culture africaine," 324; "Le Problème d'une théologie africaine . . . ," 119ff. (cited in Bediako, *Theology and Identity*, 371); and *Un Visage africain*, 227. Mulago's attitude toward 'universal' (or 'Western') theology may be partly a response to the debate between T. Tshibangu and A. Vanneste about African theology (Bediako, *Theology and Identity*, 371). Cf. Bujo and Ilunga, *African Theology in the 21st Century*, 1:183–99 for an introduction and English translation of the Tshibangu–Vanneste debate. Vanneste would later be Mulago's colleague. Despite disagreeing on the issue of whether or not all theological endeavors should attempt to be universal, Mulago later wrote that he appreciated Vanneste as a senior colleague who allowed Mulago the freedom to pursue his own project ("Projet de vie et itineraire," 30).

26. Mulago, *Un Visage africain*, 11. Mulago studied these three Bantu peoples, and he himself was a Bantu. However, there are many ethnolinguistic groups on the continent, such as the Nilotic, Hamitic, and Mande, among many others.

ties. His preliminary chapter discusses theology and its responsibilities. He contends that ecclesial unity-with-variety reveals her universality: variety around a united center (Christ) allows the church to adapt sufficiently that she can be at home in any place or time, due to her transcendent nature. The church incorporates and purifies peoples' aspirations, so that each people group can understand Christ's relevance in their own cultural terms. Again, note that Mulago refers to people groups, not to isolate persons: the identity he envisions is communal. The particularity of the message is necessary for Christianity to be deeply rooted, fully engaged, and vibrantly growing in a culture. The theologian's task is to carefully study a people's beliefs and practices, to find their foundational aspirations and then show how these values point to Christ.[27] Mulago asks, Is the numerical growth in the African church "simply an expression of the general Europeanization of the continent? Is our missionary method comprehensive? Is Christ incorporated, embodied in the African?"[28] He examines documents from the Holy See that support his argument, then proceeds to describe the principle of adaptation.

In the next two major sections of his book, he employs both a communal focus, and the relationship of cultural identities to Christian identities, as he studies the familial, socio-political and religious life of the three Bantu groups mentioned. He concludes that the concept of vital union is central to all aspects of Bantu life, from social structures, to ancestral worship, to blood pacts between persons or groups, and in religious rites such as the cult of Lyangombe. Vital union entails the idea that there is a dynamic common life involved between people; sometimes he speaks of this common life as vital participation, emphasizing the action involved.[29] Applying the concept of vital union to Christianity will help these Bantu groups grasp the Christian message in cultural terms with which they are familiar. In this way, the church, like her Lord, does not destroy but redeems, and hence African cultural identity or personality cannot be ignored or disregarded by the church. It is a gift from God, through which God works, and redeemed aspects of African cultural and religious identity are intended to enrich the church.[30] In fact, rather than prizing unity over particularity or vice versa, Mulago views contextual particularity as a manifestation of the church's universality. He designates Christ the founder of a new clan, race,

27. Ibid., 15–18.

28. Mulago, *Un Visage africain*, 18, my translation.

29. For Mulago, the phrasing of this concept as 'vital union' or 'vital participation' distinguishes him from Placide Tempels, who refers to 'vital force,' which Mulago rejects ("Vital Participation," 148 n. 23 and *Un Visage afraicain*, 157).

30. On this point, he cites Rev 21:24–26 (*Un Visage africain*, 29).

or people who will heal the divisions that currently exist among peoples, and sees no conflict in affirming unity alongside diversity because for him both God and the Christian message demand plurality-in-unity, a diverse, tightly-knit community. The church itself is not, in his mind, limited to or fully expressed by any one culture, be it Western, Asian, or African; at the same time, if the church is indeed "at home everywhere" and "if she is the mother as much of the Orientals as of Africans and Westerners, it is a sign that she is universal."[31] So the church's communal identity is universal, as well as necessarily adapting to its particular local context: if the Christian identity is universal, it must also be particular, including African identities. All people must be welcomed by and reflected in the church.[32]

What changes is doctrinal presentation, so that "then, but only then, gradually, Africans will understand that she [the church] is a community of life, where everyone, as in the Bantu community, has duties as a son or daughter and of father or mother. Eventually they will come to understand that the church is no more the church of priests than that of Europeans, but rather *their* church to them all and to each individually."[33] The Congolese theologian concludes his book with an allusion to Song of Solomon, suggesting that like the Bride in that book, the African church too has no reason to be ashamed of her "negritude," since God intends Africa—and every other culture and individual—to contribute to the wealth and fullness of God's kingdom. Like Solomon's Bride, the church in Africa replies to her critics, "I am black and yet beautiful."[34] Transcendence is not threatened by particularity; in God's design, particularity is a necessity. No person or group can claim to be the sole or full representation of Christ, and thus each culture must have its own theology, mine its own cultural resources and particularities, and offer them to God, thereby allowing all Christians to "better understand the transcendent wealth of the Master's life."[35] Again, we see Mulago's communal focus (on God's people in all places and times), and the reason that he believes African identities must be integrated into and under Christian identity.

A major hermeneutical key to Mulago's thought rests on the concept of vital union or vital participation, which he views as elementary to African worldviews; the cultural emphasis may be one reason he is predisposed to

---

31. Mulago, *Un Visage africain*, 223-24, my translation.

32. Ibid., 32. Here he refers to Pentecost, where the risen Christ is proclaimed to people in their own languages.

33. Ibid., 226, my translation.

34. Ibid., 227.

35. Ibid., 226, 227, my translation. Cf. pp. 15-18.

speak of communal identities.³⁶ Based on his extensive study of the Bashi, Banyarwanda, and Barundi peoples, he concludes that Bantu life centers on social unity, based on the solidarity of the family and extending from there to the clan, tribe, and nation.³⁷ This participation in the family's common life arises from sharing the same blood, and this union can be extended by participation; the church, too, is a community sharing Christ's blood and united by participation in his life.³⁸ In-depth examination of these groups led the Congolese priest to conclude that the concept of vital union affects family, social-political, and religious life: it is key to understanding Bantu thought, and the best place from which to explain the Christian message to Bantu peoples. Employing the concept of vital participation will help Bantu audiences to comprehend the story of Christ, who by his blood unites people to himself and to other people of God. Yet again, Mulago clearly is concerned with communities and communal identities, first of the Bantu and then of the church.

The theological foundation of communal identity is clear: Christian identity flows from and results in communal life. Ecclesial unity arises from sharing in Christ's life. Christians participate in his life, and also by extension participate in God's Trinitarian life.³⁹ Like the Bantu clan, people participate in the clan founder's life. Mulago examines biblical concepts of life, which in many aspects parallel Bantu views: life is holistic, includes the idea of fullness and intensity of life, has to do with one's relationship with God, and is a communal experience.⁴⁰ While there are parallels or indicators in Bantu culture of higher truths revealed in the Bible, Mulago does not deny that differences exist between Bantu views of life and vital union, and Christian views of life and union in Christ. However, his goal is to show that God leaves witnesses to himself and his truth in all cultures. The cultural indicators help a person grasp biblical revelation, which is why they are included within the all-encompassing Christian identity.

Ecclesial unity calls for the participation and efforts of Christians to bring others into this communion; Christian identity is intended to be communal. In other words, fullness of life requires involvement: life must be made manifest. Mulago's book draws heavily from Johannine writings in the NT; this third section cites Johannine literature over twenty times. He argues, from multiple passages, that John too saw the essence of divinity

36. Mulago, "Traditional African Religion and Christianity," 120, 131.
37. Mulago, *Un Visage africain*, 12.
38. Ibid.
39. Ibid., 161.
40. Ibid., 162–64.

as being life, and the manifestation and communication of the divine life was the goal of the Incarnation and the church's mission.[41] Because God is one and God's life indivisible, sharing in divine life unites the elect into a single body, bringing Christians into what Mulago terms "ontic union" with Christ.[42] Since the essence of Christianity, what makes it unique, is Christ, then Christian doctrine centers on the doctrine of the God-man, who has chosen people to act as his body in this world. The Holy Spirit creates life in and unity among Christians, and the sacraments of baptism and the Eucharist enact those truths. Ecclesial unity does not erase human individuality or confuse humans with God: God creates unity that maintains diversity.[43] Mulago suggests that the "Church is not a unity resulting from parts, no! In her, it is the unity which *makes* the parts."[44] Hence the need for all cultures—not just African ones—to redeem those aspects that point to Christ, and incorporate them into their Christian identities.

As life and communion are central in Bantu culture, so are these key biblical principles, and Mulago proposes that the definition of the church as *congregation fidelium* be replaced with a more life- and communion-centered definition of this identity: "The church is the community of partners-in-God's life."[45] This life in which individuals participate becomes their own life, while simultaneously being life that is shared among members. He later says that one can speak of "individual life lived socially or social life lived individually—it amounts to the same thing."[46] In other words, for the Muntu (the human), "to live is to exist within a community."[47] Social and individual aspects of life can be distinguished, but not separated, from each other.

In Bantu clans, there are means to maintain and increase the community's life, such as shared meals as a sign of fellowship and harmony, and the blood pact that unites people to the community. Clan unity stems from their common founder, and the founder's life must be passed along. What creates unity is not necessarily any outward similarity, but the fact that all participate in the same element.[48] Mulago hopes that realization of the unity of all humanity in Adam will break down sinful barriers between people; in Christ the original human unity is restored. The way in which Mulago

41. Ibid., 166.
42. Ibid., 165–69.
43. Ibid., 176.
44. Ibid., 175, emphasis added.
45. Ibid., 176.
46. Ibid., 193.
47. Ibid., 177.
48. Ibid., 179.

discusses clan unity versus vital unity in Christ makes it clear that the latter is far superior to, not a mere substitute for, the former.[49]

Why is African identity subsumed within Christian identity? These 'stepping stones' are not ones that Mulago believes he has created in order to make his point; he sees these cultural values not as coincidences, but as results of divine providence, allowing the Bantu to grasp church doctrine.[50] At the same time, these indicators in Bantu culture are incomplete, awaiting fulfillment in Christ.[51] This is why the Christian identity is the primary identity, as well as why the 'stepping stones' must be integrated into the Christian identity. Mulago values these Bantu 'stepping stones', particularly the central concept of vital union (highlighting life and communion), because they offer protection against and freedom from dangerous Western individualist, materialist thinking.[52] He also believes that the notion of solidarity and unity is "a distinctive note of African civilization and culture" more broadly, not just among the three Bantu groups previously mentioned.[53] If Mulago is correct, then the principles he identifies ought to apply to ecclesial identity in Africa as a whole, not just among the Bantu.

---

49. Ibid., 186, 193.

50. Ibid., 160. He clarifies that this method of going from a known thing to a new thing is the same method Jesus and Paul used, and that it does not imply that Christian union with Christ is merely a substitute for Bantu vital union (159-60). The former is perfect and transcendent, while the latter concept is not, but it can serve as a bridge or door for the African to enter into the Christian worldview and deeply root it in his or her own culture.

51. Ibid., 221, 222.

52. Ibid., 222. Englebert Mveng's essay in response to Mulago's book emphasizes the same concern: since 'Western' theologies have little concern for communion and participation, what place does the church truly hold in such cultures? Will Western cultures end up 'crushing' the church, or denying its essence? At the same time, Mveng realizes the danger of one hegemonic model (Western) simply being replaced with another, and warns against reducing the church to a singular, narrow, and outdated model. The church must be universally relevant and also always have a local face wherever it is found (Mveng, "Un Visage africain du christianisme," 134-35). For a critique of Mulago's method by a colleague who disagreed strongly, see fellow Congolese Ngindu Mushete's "L'histoire de la théologie en Afrique," 30-48 (particularly pp. 35ff).

53. Mulago, *Un Visage africain*, 221, 222. "Vital Participation" states that "as we have extended the area of our research to other Bantu groups in the Congo, we have so far found no difficulty in applying to them the conclusions of our study. . . . For example, participation or vital union is also the key to the customs of the Bakongo, the Baluba, the Babira, etc" (137 n. 2). He further notes that Placide Tempels has reached a similar conclusion, though Mulago disagrees with aspects of Tempels' work, including his term 'vital force' (as opposed to Mulago's use of terms like vital union, communion, or vital participation). Mulago's terms emphasize relationship and action, not just a power or force.

This pioneer in African theology broadly, and in ecclesiology specifically, made lasting contributions. Mulago offers a rationale for African theology, as well as for the necessity of plurality within the church's unity and universality. He proposes a method for African theology, based on his view of God's general revelation. Rooting his ecclesiology in thorough ethnography, he provides a vivid example of an inculturated Christian communal identity and an implicit argument for the importance of ecclesiology in Africa. He identifies themes that are still central in African theology today: solidarity, life, and communion, incorporating these into the Christian communal identity he envisions. He demonstrates that life and communion are core concepts not just in Bantu thought, but in church documents and the Bible itself.

Regarding identity, throughout his career Mulago affirmed the value and necessity of drawing on cultural identity to communicate and shape Christian identity and theology. His strong arguments for the necessity of inculturation imply that the African Christian identity should be liberated from imposed, Western identities. Mulago believed in one church, and equally in the universal church's contextual necessity. So when he discusses the importance of preserving an African cultural identity—'personality' as he occasionally terms it—this does not mean prioritizing African identity over Christian identity. Mulago makes it clear that the cultural analogies he identifies are just that: limited analogies, inadequate and incomplete but nevertheless pointers to the sublime truth. He mentions analogies when comparing the church to the Bantu clan, with which the church shares some similarities but greatly transcends. Not surprisingly, then, one passage Mulago draws upon in his ecclesiological work is Gal 3:26-29, which affirms that all other identities are relativized in light of the 'in Christ' identity.[54] On the other hand, relativized is not remotely the same thing as destroyed. African heritage and cultures ought to be affirmed and valued, yet relativized in light of Christ.

From all we have seen in Mulago, it is clear that he discusses communal identities, and argues why African identities must be included yet relativized in Christian identities in Africa. Here some may perceive a lacuna in Mulago's work: he addresses only two identities at work in African Christian contexts—an African identity (Bantu), and a Christian one—with the Bantu identity appearing to be rather monolithic. Mulago has identified the stepping stones in Bantu culture, and thus contextualized the church's teaching for Africa as a whole. Now the relationship between African identity and Christian identity appears clear. But are there not other identities at work?

---

54. For example, Mulago, *Un Visage africain*, 193, 208.

And what if the identities themselves are not fully static but have some dynamic elements, or African culture is more pluralistic? Mulago presents a strong case for the necessity of adaptation, as well as universality and transcendence, meaning that the church will become 'local' in each context, but he nevertheless could be accused of oversimplifying or overlooking some important facets of communal identities along the way. However, we must remember that Mulago was a pioneer in the field, presenting an apologetic for African theology and African identities. He had to first defend the value of African culture and identity and their use in theology. An exploration of the plurality and dynamism in African identities would await later theologians; Mulago laid the foundations for such work. Undeniably, identity concerns—specifically communal identity of African Christians—pervade Mulago's work, and the Christian communal identity is given priority while incorporating African identities in itself. In Mulago's mind, the Christian identity must be marked by solidarity and a universality that results from the particularity of inculturation.

Mulago gwa Cikala Musharhamina laid the groundwork for later theologians of the continent. One of those later theologians is Ghanaian Kwame Bediako, who published articles and books from the early 1980s into the 2000s. Bediako represents a Protestant counterpoint to Mulago, a later temporal period, and a greater emphasis on Christianity as a non-Western religion. Despite the difference in era and ecclesiastical affiliation, Bediako too was greatly concerned with Christian identity in Africa and the question of culture's relationship to theology.

Kwame Bediako

Kwame Bediako (1945–2008) is described by some as a "colossus" among African theologians, and with good reason.[55] His most substantial work, *Theology and Identity: The Impact of Culture upon Christian Thought in the Second Century and in Modern Africa*, is recommended as compulsory

---

55. Asamoah-Gyadu, "Bediako of Africa," 9. Another Protestant theologian is Nigerian Byang H. Kato. There are several reasons I have chosen to focus upon Bediako rather than Kato, though Kato merits engagement. First, Kato's career was very brief (he died before his fourth decade), and thus while he wrote many essays and articles, he only published one major work, *Theological Pitfalls in Africa*. Secondly, Kato is a polarizing figure, and there are other Protestant theologians more engaged in subsequent dialogue. Moreover, it is important to represent theologians from various eras. Kato could be categorized as one of the earlier writers (he died December 17, 1975), while Bediako continued to write in the 1990s and beyond, serving as a transitional figure chronologically. For these reasons, Bediako is more appropriate for the purposes here.

reading for those interested in African theology.⁵⁶ The scope and length of this book, as well as its topic, make it a natural focus for those seeking to understand Bediako. *Theology and Identity*, based on his doctoral dissertation, is a work of historical theology that has implications for theological method and foci. Bediako compares four second-century theologians with four theologians in modern African theology, arguing that there are intriguing similarities between these two groups. For example, the second-century theologians lived amid religious pluralism, and wrestled with the nature of Christian identity in their cultural contexts. Bediako contends that for these theologians, and modern theologians in Africa, identity is a theological issue that touches on fundamental aspects of Christianity.⁵⁷ *Theology and Identity* argues that discussions of Christian identity are essential because they are a natural consequence of the Gospel, in that the Gospel is universally relevant and offered to all, but always meant to be inculturated, answering cultural questions.⁵⁸ Those who claim Jesus as Lord are claiming that Jesus is Lord over every area of life and relevant to each of those areas.

Identity concerns are prominent in this work, quite explicitly, and again communal in nature. When Bediako discusses Christian identity, he clearly states that its basis is essentially religious.⁵⁹ Yet there must be integrity in conversion: a person brings all of who they are to Christ, and Christ is at work in the person as a whole, united being.⁶⁰ So for Bediako Christian identity, in Africa and all other contexts, includes both cultural and religious aspects, because God transforms people in their contexts, in their communities.⁶¹

Bediako begins by examining Greco-Roman culture of the second century, then focusing on Tatian, Tertullian, Justin Martyr, and Clement of Alexandria; the focus on cultural identities as they related to Christian identity indicates communal identity is being explored here. Tatian highlighted the radical nature of Christian identity in relation to Greek or Roman identities.⁶² Tertullian too emphasized that Christians were not born but made,

---

56. Bediako, *Theology and Identity*; recommended by John Parratt, "Review of *Theology and Identity*," 172.

57. Bediako, *Theology and Identity*, 6, 31–33.

58. Ibid., 48. Bediako's emphasis on the necessity for theology to engage with contextual issues was made clear to his students, as Asamoah-Gyadu testifies ("Bediako of Africa," 8).

59. Bediako, *Theology and Identity*, 36.

60. Ibid., 4.

61. Ibid., 10.

62. Ibid., 67, 71, 76.

and thus a distinct group whose identity was essentially religious.[63] For Justin, truth finds its unity in Christ, and thus Christ is the interpretive key for understanding one's past as well as one's present.[64] Bediako suggests that Christianity gave Justin a "heightened Gentile self-consciousness," perhaps indicating that faith gave him a greater awareness of the grace of God that transcended ethnic and social barriers.[65] Bediako closes this section with Clement, who realized the significance of conversion for a proper appraisal of one's past and culture.[66] Clement also suggested that Christianity 'supersedes' other traditions by absorbing or integrating them, implying that Christianity is the apogee of all religious traditions and therefore the Gospel is relevant in every context.[67]

The second part of *Theology and Identity* assesses modern African theology, continuing to address the nature of a healthy relationship of cultural identities to the Christian identity. It explores how four theologians— Bolaji Idowu, John Mbiti, Mulago gwa Cikala Musharhamina, and Byang Kato— understood the relationship of African cultures and identities to Christian theology.[68] The modern African predicament, as Bediako terms it, resulted in a modern identity dilemma. As others have argued, modern African cultures have been greatly shaped—largely in deleterious ways—by contact with European cultures; this contact produces a clash of communal identities, though Bediako does not phrase it in those terms. The modern African context is one of Western ethnocentrism, denigration of African culture, and therefore a denial of the African memories of the past; hence issues of communal identity come to the forefront again.[69] Missionaries believed that Africa needed Christianity along with European civilization, and hence aimed to produce "Black Europeans" as opposed to African Christians.[70] The major problem with the advent of Christianity, then, was mission-

---

63. Ibid., 104–5, 112, 115.

64. Ibid., 142, 148, 149, 155, 160.

65. Ibid., 137.

66. Ibid., 175, 183.

67. Ibid., 180, 197, 207.

68. Mulago's works are also published under other names, as mentioned previously.

69. Bediako, *Theology and Identity*, 234–37. Tinyiko Sam Maluleke is but one example of a theologian who agrees with Bediako that the African Christian must address the issue of identity, motivated by the search for self-respect, integrity, and a coherent identity ("Identity and Integrity," 28–29). He also situates the quest for identity in African theology against the backdrop of the larger quest for identity in Africa, illustrated in pan-Africanism, Négritude, philosophies of African personality, etc. "The question therefore is not merely what it means to be an African Christian convert, but what it means to be an African, period" (ibid., 31).

70. Bediako, *Theology and Identity*, 226, 228, 234.

ary ethnocentrism, which misunderstood the role of culture in Christian identity.[71]

To repeat, Bediako is advocating a specific type of relationship between cultural identities and Christian identity. In any context, denying Christians their past is problematic because "theological memory is integral to identity; without memory we have no past, and having no past, our identity itself is lost."[72] What NT Gentiles received from Paul was a gospel that grappled seriously with Gentile thought and transposed its message into that context. But Africa had no Paul, and thus experiences alienation.[73] Could this lack result in Judaizing of Africans? At the least, efforts to make African Christians culturally European indicate that missionaries misunderstood the nature of the Gospel, Bediako concludes.[74] The Gospel applies to all people in their contexts, bringing them freedom. African theologians therefore understandably wrestle with the significance of the Gospel in their cultures and the ways in which Christ's Lordship shapes African identities and applies to African realities.

Bediako begins with Bolaji Idowu, who emphasized the need for a radically indigenized church in which old cultural ways were fulfilled in this new gospel reality.[75] Idowu insisted that Christianity was not and should not be tied to Western culture, and that Christianity should create persons who find unity and integrity in their conversion.[76] John Mbiti echoed similar sentiments, suggesting that the Gospel is unchanging, but Christianity is always indigenous.[77] Because Christ offers both freedom and a new identity to his followers, the church must always seek to understand what it means to follow Christ in a particular context. Hence a church that is aware of its own identity will speak in its own theological voice.[78] A church that does not understand and embody the Gospel cannot fulfill its mission of proclaiming the message to others.[79] Again, we see that communal identity concerns are central, and that Christian identity is understood as a theological matter. Further, Bediako conceives Christian identity as incorporating cultural traits, but not tied to any single culture.

71. Ibid., 235, 237.
72. Ibid., 237.
73. Ibid., 240.
74. Ibid., 251–52.
75. Ibid., 272, 274, 278, 285.
76. Ibid., 273, 280.
77. Ibid., 304, 306.
78. Ibid., 307, 319.
79. Ibid., 309.

The third theologian Bediako examines is Mulago gwa Cikala Musharhamina. Mulago proposes that Christianity meets and exceeds the religious aspirations of African cultures.[80] Christ does not ask the African to become non-African, and the church worldwide should respect the African sense of self-worth and make room for African contributions in that global communion.[81] The church in all locations is called to show how Christ fulfills the peoples' needs; the church always adapts, discerning what is and is not in line with the Gospel, assuming a local face, as it should in Africa.[82] Finally Bediako examines Byang Kato, whose stance Bediako labels 'bibliology.' Kato strongly rejected many aspects of emerging African theology, and suggested instead that while Christ answers the needs of the human heart, he does not fulfill non-Christian religions.[83] For Bediako, this means that Kato fell into the error of affirming Africa as a *tabula rasa*, which implied that African experience could not be brought to bear on Scripture, and assumed that the Gospel was a-cultural.[84] Regardless of the different positions of Mulago and Kato, they both address communal identities, specifically the relationship of African identities to Christian identities and theology.

Again, as so many times before, Bediako's argument returns to the relationship between African and Christian communal identities. He concludes by reaffirming that the desire of African theology—and presumably, by extension, African Christian identity—to draw upon its past and its religio-cultural context is neither aberrant nor indicative of syncretism. Christianity should allow a person to remain in their culture and draw upon it, producing not syncretism but synthesis and indigenization.[85] All thor-

---

80. Ibid., 350, 351, 359.

81. Ibid., 348, 371.

82. Ibid., 354.

83. Ibid., 390.

84. Ibid., 391, 407, 413. As noted earlier, this interpretation of Kato is erroneous. Denying that Christ fulfills non-Christian religions is not the same as saying that Africa is a *tabula rasa*. Kato does not deny general revelation's existence, or the idea that African cultures and religions have any value; he simply refused to equate those things with Christian Scripture and religion, and held that salvation is through Christ alone.

85. Bediako, *Theology and Identity*, 427, 428, 431, 432, 434–36. Tinyiko Sam Maluleke accuses Bediako of failing to take the modern African context on its own terms, and instead describing it mainly with reference to European actions on the continent ("In Search of 'The True Character,'" 212). This accusation may be a misreading of Bediako, who, along with several others, agrees that the European relationship with and image of Africa in the last centuries has been massively influential in how Africans view themselves. Bediako explores the reasons why Africans may have a negative image of the continent and their cultures, or have a difficult relationship with their past. Maluleke also objects to Bediako's treatment of African religions, asking if the view that they are preparation for the gospel is all that can be said about them (216).

ough theology produces indigenization. In addition, the Gospel message is offered to all, and God rules over all creation; thus his actions are universal and he provides coherent integration of past, present, and future.[86] The Gospel transcends old divisions and barriers, rooting identity in Christ.[87]

In other words, Bediako advocates a particular relationship between Gospel, culture, theology, and hence Christian communal identity. The theological rationale for his argument means that this understanding of the relationship between cultural and Christian communal identities is one that ought to apply in all cultures, not just in Africa, though the situation in Africa has particularly highlighted this issue. Bediako continually reiterates that the Gospel is simultaneously universal; namely, applicable to all persons, and particular; namely, indigenized in each context it engages: it is translatable.[88] Receiving the Gospel inherently entails evaluating one's

---

Hinne Wagenaar concurs with Maluleke on this point ("Theology, Identity and the Pre-Christian Past," 372). Yet, in light of Bediako's goal of clarifying African Christian identity, Maluleke's and Wagenaar's critiques are unjust or at least off point: if this is what Bediako intended to do—view the African past and culture from a Christian perspective—why should he be faulted for doing exactly that? Bediako's goal was not to provide a non-Christian perspective on African religions, and given his commitment to the uniqueness of Christ, his attitude toward those religions is understandable. Benno Van den Toren affirms that Bediako studies them from a self-consciously Christian perspective, but suggests that since no truly neutral stance is possible, using a Christian perspective is not problematic ("Kwame Bediako's Christology," 226). Van den Toren is concerned with what he sees as Bediako's over-emphasis on theology's contextuality. Bediako says little about the general human condition and God's consistent nature, which (van den Toren charges) Bediako "dangerously leaves aside in his study of the contextuality of theology" (230).

86. Bediako, *Theology and Identity*, 435. This truth was particularly personal for Bediako. Hans Visser and Gillian Bediako, Kwame's wife, relate that in his youth, Kwame was a committed atheist. During his university studies in France this situation changed: "One day, the fact that Christ is the Truth, the integrating principle of life as well as the key to true intellectual coherence, for himself and for the world, was impressed upon him with irresistible force" (xi–xii). So his emphasis on Christ as integrating force was not an abstract, intellectual stance Bediako chose, but one based on a deeply vital experience that changed the direction of his life (Visser and Bediako, "Introduction," xi–xvii).

87. Bediako, *Theology and Identity*, 441. Earlier in the book, he stated that Paul does not see the church as a people but as a "new creation," a "third race" of sorts (35, 41). From his conclusion, it appears that what Bediako meant by Paul not viewing the church as a people is that it is not a people unified by any of the old categories (ethnicity, language, etc.) but a distinct, new category due to the life-giving, transformative work of Christ, a group of people whose foundation lies beyond this fallen world.

88. Hinne Wagenaar uses Bediako's approach to analyze his own (minority) Frisian identity and culture in relation to Christianity. Rarely do North American and European theologians apply African insights and methodology to re-analyze their own culture's reception of Christianity, which makes this article particularly noteworthy ("Theology,

context, as the convert seeks to understand how Christ's lordship will be displayed in that context.[89] The Gospel always relates and adapts to the local culture in order to become fully rooted and a transformative force in that context. Thus, Bediako's view of the Gospel coheres with his case that culture and identity questions are inherently related to the Gospel's reception, so the relationship between Christianity and culture is not anthropological or sociological in nature, but rather theological.[90] Andrews Walls identifies the relationship between Gospel and culture as a key motivating factor for Bediako, who "labored so that generations of scholars, confident equally of their Christian and their African identity, might be formed in Africa."[91] African religio-cultures are part of the African Christian's heritage, redeemed and purified by Christ.[92]

Studying second-century theologians, Bediako proves that modern African intellectuals are not alone in their argument that African religio-cultures deserve more attention and appreciation. He also demonstrates that efforts to relate Christianity to culture in no way means rejecting Christ's uniqueness. Culture is the context for Gospel reception, which clarifies why European denigration of African cultures was so devastating for Africans and African identities, Christians or otherwise. Bediako repeatedly affirms that the Gospel values and redeems culture.[93]

If culture provides the soil in which the Gospel takes root, then theology—and hence, ecclesiology, Christian communal identity—is one of the first fruits of the Gospel's growth in a context. Theology deals with the implications of Christ's lordship in a particular context, addressing questions arising from that context, and inculturation goes awry if it completely alienates Christians from their past.[94] Christians who cannot understand what Christ means for their context cannot be effective in life and witness.[95]

Identity and the Pre-Christian Past"). While van den Toren is concerned that Bediako pays too much attention to context, Wagenaar accuses Bediako of moving too hastily from the particular Akan perspective to "the universal biblical perspective" (370) in his book *Jesus in African Culture: A Ghanaian Perspective*. Wagenaar concludes that as a result, Bediako's approach emphasizes "universality at the cost of particularity" (371).

89. Bediako, *Theology and Identity*, xvii, xviii.

90. Ibid., 32.

91. Walls, "Kwame Bediako," 188. Bediako viewed Western theologies as inadequate, particularly since they overlooked or misunderstood some aspects of African cultures (189).

92. Bediako, *Theology and Identity*, 4.

93. Ibid., 273.

94. Ibid., xv, 240.

95. Ibid., 274, 276, 278.

Thus African theology's concern with culture and Christian identity reflect "fundamental questions" of Christianity.[96] An indigenized church develops its own theology, demonstrating intentional reflection on its relationship to both Christ and culture: in other words, it develops its communal identity by integrating biblical, theological, and cultural insights. Indeed, culture must bring its questions to Scripture and expect that culture also contributes to theology.[97] The Gospel brings freedom in Christ, while conversion brings people to assess their culture, forming in them a new identity; as mentioned many times previously, these musings are largely concerned with communal identities.[98]

How then does Bediako envision Christian identity's relationship to cultural identities? Theologically it incorporates both gospel and culture, yet "the basis for Christian self-definition [is] to be essentially a religious one, not national, nor cultural, nor social."[99] Since the primary self-identifier is religious, cultural aspects play an important, but secondary, role. Conversion should place all aspects of a person's past and identity under Christ.[100] There will arise situations where Christians' identity and obligations intersect "with their identity and obligations as members of a family or a community or a state" (again, all communal identities).[101] However, people entirely severed from their past lose an important part of their theological memory and identity.[102] Asamoah-Gyadu, a student of Bediako's, terms such persons "schizophrenic Christians."[103] Walls notes as well that "a period of Western dominance too often led either to blanket rejection of all things evidently African or to a division of life into parallel streams of 'Christian' and 'African' activities that never met. The end product could be a sort of religious schizophrenia, a fractured identity."[104] Because Christ and the Gospel about him are unique, there will always be differences between Christians and their culture, which they assess according to Christ, their standard.

---

96. Ibid., 6–7.
97. Ibid., 407.
98. Ibid., 252, 273.
99. Ibid., xvii, 36.
100. Ibid., 4, 280.
101. Walls, "Kwame Bediako," 190.
102. Bediako, *Theology and Identity*, 237.

103. Asamoah-Gyadu, "Bediako of Africa," 14. Keith Ferdinando testifies that "the question of identity has indeed emerged as a leading issue in many of the theologies coming out of churches in the Two-Thirds World," indicating that African theology is not atypical for focusing on this topic ("Christian Identity," 121).

104. Walls, "Kwame Bediako," 190.

On this point, Ferdinando is concerned that Bediako does not sufficiently stress the Christian identity's discontinuity with culture. Ferdinando refers to Andrew Walls's "pilgrim principle," which points out that there is "an inevitable degree of cultural alienation for all believers. By its very nature the Gospel is counter-cultural . . . If this is not the case then Christian faith simply degenerates into 'cultural Christianity.'"[105] On the other hand, God redeems people, and therefore African Christians are not required to become non-African when coming to Christ; instead, Christ gives them a proper perspective on their culture and how to integrate aspects of it into their new identity in Christ.[106]

Bediako briefly mentions Paul's contribution to the issue of Christian identity and its relationship to other identities. Twice Bediako states that the apostle viewed Christians—and hence the church—not as a people, but as a new creation, citing 2 Cor 5:17 and Eph 2:14ff.[107] What does Bediako mean by describing Christians as a new creation as opposed to "a people"? It seems that here he agrees with Harnack, whom he quotes just after these statements. Harnack identifies Christians as a group that supersedes old divisions, because they belong to an altogether different plane.[108] Like Mulago, Bediako is quite concerned to explore the communal Christian identity and its relationship to African identities, viewing the Christian identity as foundational, and other identities are integrated within it. He repeatedly emphasizes that the Gospel introduces a new, overarching category that transcends the importance of communal identities based on gender, ethnicity, and so forth—clarifying that a person's identity is rooted in Christ.[109] The old identities are not destroyed, but incorporated in and subservient to that final, ultimate identity.[110]

In the work of Mulago and Bediako, there was a great deal of concern with African and Christian communal identities and the type of relationship between these two identities that is necessary for a healthy Christian

105. Ferdinando, "Christian Identity," 135.

106. Ibid., 136–37.

107. Bediako, *Theology and Identity*, 35.

108. Ibid., 35–36, citing Adolf Harnack, *Mission and Expansion of Christianity in the First Three Centuries*.

109. Bediako, *Theology and Identity*, 441.

110. Ferdinando references Gal 3:28 when stating, "The believer's fundamental identity derives from being 'in Christ,' which relativizes while not obliterating all other cultural distinctives" ("Christian Identity," 139). He further criticizes Mbiti, Idowu, and Bediako for their "somewhat backward-looking orientation," suggesting that "[Christians] finding their identity in Christ in fact moves the orientation of their identity away from the past and toward the future; the center of gravity has shifted in a decisive way," as seen in the New Testament (ibid.).

identity. These foci are interwoven throughout their works. There are differences between the two, but there are many points of overlap. With the next author, the picture becomes more convoluted: African and Christian identity are further fleshed out, positives and negatives of both located, and the intricate and sometimes contradictory relationship of these two to African women's identities is considered. For the sake of argument, I have distinguished multiple threads woven into her argument, though in reality it has a tightly knit, organic unity.

Mercy Amba Oduyoye

Mercy Amba Oduyoye (b. 1934)[111] is a Ghanaian scholar who organized what is believed to be the first pan-African women's theology conference in Ibadan, Nigeria in 1980, initiated the Circle of Concerned African Women Theologians,[112] taught in seminaries on three continents, has been a leader in the ecumenical movement,[113] and established the Institute of African Women in Religion and Culture at Trinity Theological Seminary, Accra, Ghana.[114] Throughout all of this, with a publishing career beginning in the late 1960s and including multiple books and over 80 articles, she has consistently advocated on behalf of African women.[115] As a feminist, she is concerned with all who are marginalized, without a voice or an agency, dehumanized and without dignity. For her entire career she has sought to liberate African women who are "doubly and triply burdened" by religion and culture.[116]

Though she does not always explicitly employ the term 'identity,' her emphases on the nature of the personhood of African women is indeed a concern with identity. Her frequent references to the agency, self-hood, naming, and humanity of African women all have to do with identity. Pui-lan Kwok highlights Oduyoye's questions about the legitimacy of constructing

---

111. She published initially as Mercy Yamoah; 'Oduyoye' is her married name. She also published as Amba Oduyoye.

112. Oduyoye, "The Story of a Circle," 97–98.

113. Nottingham, "Review of *Daughters of Anowa*," 164.

114. Njoroge, "A New Way of Facilitating Leadership," 29–32.

115. Kwok, "Mercy Amba Oduyoye," 7, 19.

116. Oduyoye, *Introducing African Women's Theology*, 24. See also Oduyoye, *Who Will Roll the Stone Away?*, 63. By religion she is referring to African religions, Christianity, and Islam; she sees all three as guilty of dehumanizing women at various points (for example, see Oduyoye, "The Search for a Two-Winged Theology," 42). She also finds within Christianity and African religio-cultural aspects that affirm and empower women, and highlights these in her writings.

"a generalized and universalized cultural identity for the whole African continent. Such a construction collapses differences into sameness because it does not consider the diversity of African cultures and development over time."[117] It also overlooks the fact that most male theologians in Africa have constructed an African identity that represents only the male perspective; the African identity so described does not account for women's experience, and thus does not accurately describe the identity of African women.[118]

Whereas Mulago and Bediako are concerned with African identity, and specifically the way in which Christian identity relates to African identities, Oduyoye discerns more complexity within this situation. Her examinations of theology from Africa, such as the South African Kairos Document and Jean-Marc Ela's *African Cry*, have brought about the realization that "typically none of these see the women's experience of Africa as any different from men's," yet women have a "right to be treated as human beings bearing separate identities."[119] From her perspective, feminism, is "an instrument for the re-examination of 'identity' and 'relationships' in the human community," which has the goal of improving the community's functioning and better meeting the needs of both individuals within the community and the community as a whole.[120]

Feminism is an important part of Oduyoye's theology, both methodologically and in terms of content. It also underscores that her concern with identity is about communal identities: women's identities, African identities, and Christian identities in Africa. Oduyoye frequently expresses concern with women's identities in Africa. For example, she avers that "women describe themselves as being in the image of God even if sexism denies their dignity."[121] Women are seeking to reclaim their God-given identity, one of dignity and worthy of respect. The image of God is key in this regard; we will return to this later. Unfortunately, women's identity has been "bound up with their sexuality," their biological ability to bear children, and their identity and worth are suggested to spring solely from child-bearing.[122] A woman's ability to participate in religious rituals—African or Christian—is limited because of her gender, and often further limited by further 'female' factors.

---

117. Kwok, "Mercy Amba Oduyoye," 13.

118. Ibid, 14.

119. Oduyoye, "The Search for a Two-Winged Theology," 41, 43.

120. Oduyoye, "A New Community," 26.

121. Oduyoye, "The African Experience of God," 500.

122. Oduyoye, "A Critique of Mbiti's View," 344; see also Oduyoye, *Hearing and Knowing*, 122.

Oduyoye insists that women have been degraded, oppressed, and silenced by both religious and cultural factors. "The impoverishment of women that has resulted from the joint effects of western Christianity and Islam, Arabic and African cultures, is still being overlooked."[123] While both Christianity and African cultures have aspects that honor women, they also have negative elements, and women theologians seek to identify and remove these elements from their identities.

Yet some women "have no independent identities and do not wish to name themselves."[124] Oduyoye calls attention to Chikwenye Ogunyemi's point that "naming is a political matter. We Africans are always being named, our 'bi-racial personal names,' the names of our cities and rivers, our lakes and waterfalls; so now we are expected to name ourselves after one or other of the self-named groups."[125] With regard to African women, Oduyoye argues that what matters

> for women of Africa is not whether we are feminists, womanist or 'benign women,' communist, socialist or capitalists. What is important is creating an atmosphere, a culture in which our human dignity will become a non-negotiable fact. In this, as in other aspects of Africa's development, the way forward is to name ourselves, to make a contribution to world culture. The way forward that women advocate, is to find our contribution from our African culture, cleared of all that demeans our humanity, especially that of women.[126]

In contrasting self-naming with being named by those who are 'Other,' Oduyoye does not advocate an isolated individual naming herself outside of community. Identity is shaped by community and relationships, and having a voice within that community. As Oduyoye says, "I cannot be alive in a community that ignores my existence;" existence and identity-formation are communal in nature.[127] In fact, people "are human because we are jointly responsible with others for what happens in our community. In a community a person's word must be heard and evaluated alongside that of others."[128]

---

123. Oduyoye, *Beads and Strands*, 60–61, 69–72, 75. For more on how women are imaged in Akan culture and the Bible, see Oduyoye, "Naming the Woman," 81–97.

124. Oduyoye, "The Search for a Two-Winged Theology," 47.

125. Oduyoye, *Introducing African Women's Theology*, 124. She is here referring to whether or not African women theologians should call themselves feminists or womanists.

126. Ibid., 126.

127. Oduyoye, "Be a Woman," 49.

128. Ibid., 49.

The individual, then, is part of a community, yet "not entirely subsumed" into it.[129] She is concerned that the church recognize and live out the reality that all persons, female and male, are made in God's image, learning to prioritize that common human trait "over the biological sex category" and other differences.[130] Excluding any part of humanity from this respectful treatment will damage humanity as a whole; it damages the divine intention for a united human identity that includes diversity.[131]

In other words, she is not advocating an anti-communal form of self-identification. Rather, her concern is that the "power to define—to enable a group to name itself the representation of true humanity—is truly an awesome power. The person or group defined is then in a position of non-being that is only active to the extent that it is allowed to be."[132] So if men are perceived as the 'standard' by which humanity is defined, women are seen as lesser human beings. On the other hand, if women are recognized as equally bearers of the *imago Dei*, they will be listened to and the African identity constructed by male theologians will be enlarged to include African women.[133]

There are at least two reasons, then, why Oduyoye fights for women's identity to be respected in the church: first, it would end the dehumanizing of women, if they were treated as image bearers as God intended, and secondly, Christian identity in Africa would be more accurately reflected in African theologies. The African identity described by male theologians is flawed because it is incomplete and partial, as it were. Thus women's communal identity is not just a concern for women; their identity impacts the church's communal identity and its ability to fulfill its mission and reflect God. Along similar lines, much of male-authored African theology has envisioned a "generalized and universalized cultural identity for the whole African continent. Such a construction collapses differences into sameness because it does not consider the diversity of African cultures and development over time"; it presents a very limited perspective of Africa.[134]

Oduyoye acknowledges her communal perspective arises in part from her culture. For example, "The African Family as a Symbol of Ecumenism" employs a traditional African understanding of family, specifically that of the Abusua clan of the Asante people of Ghana, to illustrate how branches

129. Oduyoye, "'In the Image of God,'" 44.
130. Oduyoye, "Naming the Woman," 82.
131. Oduyoye, "'In the Image of God,'" 44.
132. Oduyoye, *Beads and Strands*, 96.
133. See Oduyoye, "A Critique of Mbiti's View," particularly 360–61.
134. Kwok, "Mercy Amba Oduyoye," 13.

of the church should relate to each other.¹³⁵ Within an Abusua, "one surrenders individualism in order to promote full individuality. It is a group within which the 'self' is as important as the 'other' for one defines the other."¹³⁶ This kin-group is marked by cohesion, participation of all, and unity but not uniformity; it is not isolated or exclusivist, but outward-looking and welcoming new members.¹³⁷ The article concludes that the communal focus of the Abusua, as well as specifically its structure and ethos, "may have something to offer to our search for models of manifesting the unity of the church of Christ."¹³⁸ While not stated it in these exact words, this article suggests that the Abusua view of identity-in-community should be adopted by Christians: it should shape their own understanding of their Christian identity and that identity's solidarity. This article highlights some of the same concerns that ecclesiologies in chapter 5 address, such as the church's response to diversity within and without, and its high degree of solidarity. "The African Family as a Symbol of Ecumenism" also demonstrates that African cultural elements can, indeed must be redeemed by and integrated into Christian identity in Africa. On this score, Oduyoye's argument syncs with those of Mulago and Bediako.

Another instance where Oduyoye employs an aspect of her culture to understand and further shape Christian self-understanding is in "'In the Image of God . . .': A Theological Reflection from an African Perspective."¹³⁹ Here the Akan understanding of humanity and Christian sources are employed to correct misunderstandings about the *imago Dei*. Again, where the male theologians emphasize positive elements in African cultures, Oduyoye offers a more nuanced viewpoint: she acknowledges strengths, but also critiques the blatant injustices in both African and Christian worldviews, showing where they are inconsistent and wrong-headed.¹⁴⁰

So, when describing a communally shaped identity, she critiques African worldviews in which a woman's identity and "social status depends on these relationships [of wife and mother] and not on any qualities or achievements of her own"¹⁴¹ or on the more basic, foundational identity of being made in God's image.¹⁴² On the other hand, later in the same work

135. Oduyoye, "The African Family," 465–78.
136. Ibid., 470.
137. Ibid., 466–67.
138. Ibid., 477.
139. Oduyoye, "'In the Image of God,'" 41–53.
140. For example, see Oduyoye, "Naming the Woman."
141. Oduyoye, *Hearing and Knowing*, 122.
142. For instance, see Oduyoye, *Beads and Strands*, 54.

she affirms that the Akan worldview has positively contributed to her understanding of communal identity.[143] She says, "In the Akan worldview that operates in the dark mysterious center of my being there sits a sense of my being mystically incorporated into an ever expanding principle of human be-ing. Hence my attraction to the dialectics of the themes of community and self-hood."[144]

Since the previous chapters acknowledged that African theologians are frequently concerned with community, and draw upon the Bible and their cultures to understand and shape their view of it, we shall now move to exploring Oduyoye's theological bases for prioritizing community and its influence on an individual's 'self-hood.' For one, God's Triune nature demonstrates that relationality and community are central to God's identity, thus this doctrine could provide a model for healthy human community.[145] The Trinity calls Christians to reject individualistic, isolated ways of living, hierarchies, and attempts to enforce uniformity.[146] The Trinity is also "the ground and goal of the church," providing a rationale for and insight into the nature of the Christian communal identity.[147] She repeatedly emphasizes a relational view of God, and a non-hierarchical view of the Trinity as she describes what healthy, integrated community and communal identities look like.[148]

Besides the Trinity, her focus on communal identity is also supported by the biblical creation narratives. In these narratives, God creates Eve "to correct the state of alone-ness and to create a community" of equality and mutuality.[149] Genesis 1–3 exposes the failure of human communities, which are so often marked by dualism, domination, or acquiescence—these traits undermine God's design for healthy community.[150] Because humans, female and male, are created in the image of the Triune God, they are intended for relationship and communal living. Feminist theologians emphasize relational language about God because it shows that partnership and equality describe God's own being and are God's intention for humanity as well.[151]

---

143. In *Beads and Strands* she specifically employs the phrase "African communal identity" (50), one of the few places where she directly uses that expression.

144. Oduyoye, *Hearing and Knowing*, 148.

145. Ibid., 136–37.

146. Ibid., 140.

147. Ibid., 144. Another trinitarian analogy is found in Oduyoye, "A Critique of Mbiti's View," 363.

148. For instance, Oduyoye, *Hearing and Knowing*, 143.

149. Ibid., 92.

150. Ibid., 94, 95.

151. Ibid., 136; she also shares a Bemba creation myth that expresses the same

African beliefs affirm that all humans are made by God, which expresses "the unity of humanity" and its integral relationship with God.[152] An emphasis on humanity's unity in the God-given identity, and healthy community being marked by equality and appreciation for difference, may also be why African women theologians are committed to "a collaborative model of doing theology in what has been called 'communal theology'" for a theology that claimed to be communal but did not include the multiple voices in the community would be a contradiction in terms.[153]

A third biblical support for this communal perspective comes from God's plan as seen in the Exodus event: God is creating a people, transforming diverse persons and groups into an organic whole.[154] Similarly, the NT concept of union with Christ again communicates that God's plan is the creation of a community of redeemed, restored persons. Baptism is a rite that indicates joining God's family, which is described as one body with many members, the beginning of a new humanity.[155]

This new community is described as a community marked by reconciliation, a transformation of human relationships.[156] If sin is alienation from God and others, then salvation includes restoration of relationships and a responsibility toward the community of reconciliation that one has joined.[157] Salvation is not about individuals isolated from community; rather, it is liberation 'in a familial context' and into a liberated community, but not a freedom that is "experienced at the expense of 'the other.'"[158] It is freedom for and empowerment on others' behalf. To sum up, some theological themes that Oduyoye names in support of a communal view of life and identity include the Trinity, the creation narratives, God's plan to create diverse persons and groups into a new humanity, baptism and salvation, and union with and in Christ. The communal perspective, and hence the importance of communal identity, is supported on both cultural and theological grounds. The question then remains, How do the African and

---

message that the Creator's goal in creating the two sexes was to have partnership between the two: "To learn to appreciate, respect and value one another as primarily human," but at the first test of humanity, "they failed the test of mutuality and began taking unilaterial actions" (*Introducing African Women's Theology*, 66).

152. Oduyoye, "'In the Image of God,'" 43–44.

153. Njoroge, "A New Way of Facilitating Leadership," 35.

154. Oduyoye, *Hearing and Knowing*, 79, 91.

155. Ibid., 116, 137; see also Oduyoye, *Introducing African Women's Theology*, 61, 116, 119.

156. Oduyoye, *Introducing African Women's Theology*, 63, 66.

157. Oduyoye, *Hearing and Knowing*, 96, 101, 103, 106.

158. Ibid., 148–49.

Christian communal identities relate to each other, and what is the nature of the Christian communal identity?

First of all, like Mulago and Bediako, Oduyoye agrees that African communal identities must be redeemed and integrated into Christian identity; not wholesale, but integrated nonetheless. "Christianity and African Culture" directly addresses the relationship of the two, advocating further study of their interaction.[159] Here the phrase 'crossroads factor' and 'crossroads Christianity' describe the encounter and interaction between African religio-cultures and Christianity, particularly western forms of Christianity.[160] In the mission era, leaders of African institutions "became Christian only when they were ready to give up the traditional roles. Both sides of the contest [African religio-culture and western Christianity] demanded this [sacrifice of traditional roles for Christians]. Becoming Christian was presented as ceasing to be fully African."[161] Oduyoye rejects this position; just as Christianity adapted to and became at home in Bavarian culture, it can and must do the same in African cultures.[162]

She affirms that all "human cultures have elements that are incompatible with religion of Jesus and the way of life he exemplified; the challenge of the good news he brought and lived is to all human cultures."[163] While there are elements in every culture that must be eliminated, there are also aspects in all cultures that are worth redeeming, elements that can be "lifted up to reinforce the Jesus culture."[164] For theology to be authentic in a particular context, it must reflect its context in some degree, and simultaneously "if the theology is Christian it cannot help but throw light upon some universal issue."[165] In short, she finds no legitimate reason why African religio-culture should not affect Christianity and the form it takes in Africa, as has happened in every other context where Christianity took root. To view Africans as a *tabula rasa*, cutting them entirely off from their religio-cultural background, is what has produced an "identity crisis in Africa," for "a people 'without a history'" cannot "respond as responsible human beings."[166] This position echoes that of Mulago and Bediako, who affirm that Christanity

---

159. Oduyoye, "Christianity and African Culture," 78.

160. Ibid., 80, 82. One logical extension of this concept is the necessity of a hybridized, somewhat dynamic and flexible, identity.

161. Ibid., 83.

162. See Kwok, "Mercy Amba Oduyoye," 12; Oduyoye, "Christianity and African Culture," 85.

163. Oduyoye, "Christianity and African Culture," 87–88.

164. Ibid., 85.

165. Oduyoye, *Hearing and Knowing*, 52.

166. Ibid., 54.

theology is always both particular and universal, and that the Christian communal identity should provides integrity and integration in conversion.

One example of incorporating African religio-culture into Christianity is her use of the African view of family, specifically much of her experience of the Abusua, which she suggests should affect the Christian communal identity in Africa. She singles out traits such as "the unity, integrity and solidarity of the Abusua," proposing that "its structure and ethos may have something to offer" to models of ecclesial unity, as well as its emphasis on the parts and their responsibility to the community as a whole.[167] What she does, in other words, is apply an African communal identity—that of the Abusua—to the Christian communal identity. In the Abusua, and hopefully in the church, the self is defined relationally without a loss of individuality.[168] Clearly, Africans do have something "to offer to transform Christianity in Africa, not to speak of world Christianity."[169]

Oduyoye wishes that African religio-cultural aspects would be engaged with and transform Christianity, and vice versa. She affirms certain aspects of African cultures, such as communality, solidarity, relationality, and more. She also isolates stories and proverbs that offer positive, affirming images of women. However, in "Christianity and African Culture," she asks, "Why do I cringe every time I read African self-identity or African authenticity? Then I realized that it is the male writers who make me cringe," because it is unclear whether or not they are condemning aspects of culture that degrade and dehumanize women.[170] Often these male theologians "do not include in their critique and appropriation of culture a sensitivity to the fact that societies do not culture women and men in the same way."[171] This oversight produces a short-sighted picture of 'African identity' showing only a portion of the reality. In Oduyoye's analysis of 'crossroads Christianity' and rejection of a generalized cultural identity for all of Africa, Pui-lan Kwok sees parallels with the postcolonial theory and critics such as Homi K. Bhabha who

> has pointed out that myths of homogeneous national or cultural identity have been created to benefit those who are in the majority or who are in power. The postcolonial perspective, he insists, forces us to rethink the limitations of a consensual

---

167. Oduyoye, "The African Family," 477.

168. Ibid., 470.

169. Oduyoye, "Christianity and African Culture," 78; cf. Oduyoye, *Hearing and Knowing*, 11, 36.

170. Oduyoye, "Christianity and African Culture," 86.

171. Ibid., 87.

sense of cultural community, because it tends to exclude minorities and women, as well as migrant, diasporic, and refugee populations.[172]

The implication for African self-identity as described by most male theologians is straightforward: constructed by men, it fails to account for minority perspectives, painting an inaccurate picture where the discordant, minor voices are silenced. Hence the African identity so described is partial at best, as well as defective and unsound.

In the 'crossroads' between African cultures and Christianity, Oduyoye criticizes aspects of African cultures without fear; however, she is equally willing to identify and criticize biblical passages that dehumanize or mistreat women, as well as areas where western Christianity has misread or misused the Bible and thus contradicted its own message. All elements that she criticizes, regardless of their source, she calls contrary to the way of Jesus, "the One who came to promote a domination-free culture."[173] For example, some biblical passages seem to attribute the origin of evil to women, or are popularly used to do so. Proverbs 31, too, is problematic for Oduyoye, because it "illustrates the 'raison-d'être' of womanhood in Israel—her desire is her husband. She labors that he might have worthy sons and be well-spoken of and respected in the gate."[174] There is certainly nothing wrong with having sons, or caring for her husband, but for these attributes to be her sole source of worth or self-identity is not healthy. Must a woman be subordinate, dominated, and solely other-focused? This viewpoint falls into the trap of viewing women mainly from their biological function, not the more foundational *imago Dei* identity. They have a right to be treated as human beings with 'separate', independent identities.[175]

On the contrary, the Yahwist account of creation, properly read, describes woman as a counterpart of man, not lesser or negative in any sense.[176] The priestly account in Genesis 2 shows both sexes being created simultaneously in God's image, suggesting that "both sexes are equal factors in creation."[177] She concludes that subordination and domination is a human institution, a result of the Fall. She reads Paul's earlier works as being more egalitarian in tone and content, which seemingly changed later in his

---

172. Kwok, "Mercy Amba Oduyoye," 13, quoting from Bhabha's *The Location of Culture*.

173. Oduyoye, "Christianity and African Culture," 85.

174. Oduyoye, "Naming the Woman," 92.

175. Oduyoye, "The Search for a Two-Winged Theology," 43, 47.

176. Oduyoye, "Women from the Perspective of the Bible," 163–65.

177. Ibid., 165.

life. For example, in Gal 3:28, "according to Paul, for those in the household of faith all divisive tendencies in human organization, including sexism, disappear." Unfortunately, later in life, when writing 1 Corinthians 14, Paul 'reverts' to applying 'traditional norms' to women, according to Oduyoye.[178]

While it may sound from the above that the Bible is teaching contradictory messages, Oduyoye seems to suggest that the problem is that Jesus's message has always conflicted with human communities, demanding more than they wanted to give.[179] When the Bible shows negative or subordinate images of women, we are seeing biblical cultures in resistance to God's plan for humanity; culture is never identical with God's will, and a gendered approach to theology can expose injustices in culture and in the Bible.[180] Christianity is intended to be a counter-cultural force, to some extent; the danger of Christianity in Africa is that it could become "established, respectable, coopted," instead of revolutionary and liberating as Jesus intended it to be.[181]

Oduyoye determines which elements of African religio-culture and Christianity are redeemable, and which aspects must be discarded by asking if they create a liberating community where identities and relationships are being transformed.[182] "In the Akan, Bavarian and biblical traditions, the religions and cultures have both liberation and domination elements. Even biblical Christianity has aspects that are not domination-free, especially viewed from the experience of women"; such aspects are to be rejected.[183] Again, "no Christianity that ignores the oppression of women should be made at home in Africa as Christ cannot be at home in a domination-riddled Christianity."[184] The freedom and dignity Christ brings should cause a Christ-follower to resist dehumanization and oppression. Oduyoye notes that "in Africa, the very idea of a 'free woman' conjures up negative images. We have been brought up to believe that a woman should always have a suzerain," when in fact Jesus sets women free, empowers them to reject de-

---

178. Ibid., 168, 169.
179. Oduyoye, "Christianity and African Culture," 89.
180. Phiri, "Major Challenges," 9.
181. Oduyoye, *Hearing and Knowing*, 9.
182. Oduyoye, "Be a Woman," 49; "Christianity and African Culture," 80; *Hearing and Knowing*, 121, 146–49; *Introducing African Women's Theology*, 17, 57, 58, 63; and *Beads and Strands*, 96. *Hearing and Knowing* indicates that God's concern with "redemption/liberation/salvation" manifests as early as Genesis 2–3, where God seeks to "correct" Adam's "state of alone-ness and to create a community" (92). Note too that liberation, redemption, and salvation are roughly equivalent here (92, 148).
183. Oduyoye, "Christianity and African Culture," 85.
184. Ibid., 87.

humanization, and invites them to be God's agents of salvation.[185] Another way of saying this would be that Jesus frees oppressed people from false imposed identities, and renews the *imago Dei*, restoring their dignity and divine calling.

How is the divinely granted identity characterized, aside from liberated? Oduyoye envisions freedom in Christ being used for particular ends: it is freedom on behalf of others, freedom in a communal sense instead of freedom "at the expense of the 'other'" or in isolation from others.[186] In this community there is no place for those who link their identity to domination of others, as Pharaoh did.[187] Domination and hierarchy undermine community, and ignore "individuals' ability to contribute."[188] Neither patriarchy, matriarchy, nor any other type of domination is Oduyoye's goal, or her understanding of God's goal for the Kingdom: the focus is on learning to live as "beings-in-partnership," on developing mutuality and participation by all.[189] In such a community, there will be a focus on the 'other' as one made in God's image, and thus one to respect and value. If women were more valued in the church, they would have integrity in their humanity, in their identity as God' children. The Christian identity brings freedom and mutuality, as well as recognizing a person as a subject, not an object: a responsible agent with a voice and a role to play in God's plan.[190]

Like Mulago and Bediako, Oduyoye advocates that African identity be integrated into Christian identity, and that Christian identity redeem and transform African culture. Unlike her male counterparts, Oduyoye provides much more pointed criticisms of African religio-cultural elements, western Christianity, and some biblical cultural elements, while affirming that oppressive elements in any of these are contrary to the life and teaching of Jesus. Her perspective reveals a situation that is much more complex, one in which the biblical texts and western Christianity bear responsibility (at times) for failing women and other marginalized persons. Though she specifies many ways in which women's God-given identity, their very

---

185. Oduyoye, *Beads and Strands*, 69; Oduyoye, *Introducing African Women's Theology*, 57–58.

186. Oduyoye, *Hearing and Knowing*, 102, 106, 148–49.

187. Ibid., 84–85, 94.

188. Ibid., 95.

189. Oduyoye, "A New Community," 25; *Hearing and Knowing*, 94, 134, 136, 140; "A New Community," 26; "The African Family," 467, 472; "Calling the Church to Account" in *Beads and Strands*, 97.

190. Njoroge, "A New Way," 29, 34; Oduyoye, "Be a Woman," 49; Oduyoye, *Introducing African Women's Theology*, 10 n. 3; Oduyoye, *Beads and Strands*, 59, 90, 98.

humanity, is damaged, she does not give up but clings to the hope that God is at work, bringing liberation and transformation.

Summary

To sum up, the previous chapter highlighted key common themes in theology in Africa, suggesting that the first, identity, is often implicitly the crucial factor underlying and integrating the others. Thus the present chapter examined the prevalent theme of identity: (1) honing in further on the type of identity being discussed (communal), and (2) detailing the nature of a healthy relationship between African and Christian communal identities.

Mulago's works sought to reclaim an African past, a heritage with dignity and value. He paints a rich picture of Bantu life, negating the notion that Africans lacked culture and history before Europeans arrived, and reminding the reader that African cultures have dignity and value that must be treasured. Mulago rejects the notion that Africa was a *tabula rasa* before Europeans arrived, and also advocates that African religio-cultures should not be destroyed or ignored, as this attitude would deny God's self-revelation in all times, places, and peoples through general revelation. The signs of God in each culture should be redeemed, with the result that the church enriches and transforms them. While Mulago did not explicitly address diversity and plurality, as well as the continuing development, within African cultures, this omission is most likely due to his apologetic focus. He insists that the very universality and transcendence of the Christian message require particularity and inculturation, hence his proposal of the adaptation method, which is open to the possibility of development in cultures and identities. If Mulago's main points are true, then authentically African theology is imperative, rightly drawing on African cultures. Mulago insists that theology must engage the core beliefs of a culture if Christians in that culture are not to be 'uprooted' persons. Thus Mulago emerges as a defender of African cultures and identities, for the sake of the Gospel and God's Kingdom. Identifying solidarity and community as distinctive emphases of African cultures resonating with the biblical message, Mulago demonstrates the importance of African ecclesiology, an ecclesiology that relativizes but does not destroy other identities. Instead, the Christian identity refines and draws upon those secondary identities, manifesting the richness and diversity within God's kingdom. For Mulago, a choice between a Christian identity and an African identity is a false dichotomy.

For Kwame Bediako, the relationship of Christian identity to African identity touches core issues of the gospel. In the modern African context, there has been a denial and loss of the past, which leads to identity struggles, because identity always draws on the past. Like Mulago, Bediako emphasizes that the Gospel is both universal and particular, and that God does not destroy but transform culture. Therefore, Bediako affirms that both cultural and specifically theological sources contribute to a unified Christian identity. Yet cultural identities, gender, ethnicity, and the like are secondary and transcended in Christ, so that when other identities conflict with Christian identity, the Christian identity has priority.

Mercy Amba Oduyoye's perspective is less apologetic in tone and intent, and more of a critique of existing African and Christian communal identities in Africa as they affect women's identities. Thus she argues for further, closer examination of African religio-cultures, Christian tradition, and the influenced of culture on biblical texts. She is also explicit about the fact that culture is constantly changing, and thus that African communal identities are changing to respond to various pressures, including the homogenizing force of globalization. In this context, African women and other marginalized persons must be intentional about developing their own voices and agency, in order that they will have a hand in naming themselves and thus describing their identities in ways that more accurately reflect God's plan for human beings: to be responsible agents, identified first and foremost by the *imago Dei*.

Thus these theologians are all addressing communal identities, which is an often overlooked or simply unstated aspect of identity discussions in African theology. Clarifying the concept by use of more specific terminology would aid theologians in conveying their point, and in engaging with other disciplines as well as theologians from more individualist contexts. Theologians in Africa are exploring African and Christian communal identities, and the relationship of the two. They specifically seek appreciation of African identities and their incorporation into Christian identities; in theological terms, they insist on the redemption of African identities, their purifying baptism into Christ's body. This concern arises repeatedly, despite differences in cultural, temporal, and ecclesial locations. The authors claim that solidarity and difference are necessary for healthy communal identities, which remain distinctively essential in shaping African personal identities. Hence, African identities ought to be treated with dignity. Indirectly, the concern for fully inculturated Christian identities also indicates the necessity of a more fluid identity, one that is not static, fixed, and rigid, but can adjust to cultural changes. Because the continent has gone through rapid change in the last century, the ability to adapt while still appreciating the value and dignity of one's past is crucial. Fixation on the past can be just as dangerous as Euro-American attempts to repress, destroy, or deny the African heritage.

Theologically, Mulago examines how to best appropriate Bantu beliefs within a Christian identity, while Bediako continues to wrestle with how Christians in Africa historically have and theoretically can and should interact with their cultures and contextualize their Christian identities. Both believe that God redeems African cultural identities into Christian identity. When Mulago and Bediako focus on Christianity's relationship to culture (in the singular), they sometimes tend to depict 'culture' as a relatively static, stable entity rather than a dynamic one, focusing on past traditions and not necessarily those that are currently developing; Oduyoye's work brings a corrective to this tendency, providing a more complex and critical view of culture and indeed of Christianity. Mulago's arguments for the adaptation method, along with Bediako's case for integrating culture with Christian identity, highlight divine consistency and trustworthiness, providing reassurance of a stable foundation for Christian communal identity in a rapidly changing world and amidst negotiation of evolving identities and cultures. Oduyoye argues for the importance of the divine image in all persons being foundational for identity. The points of stability are the *imago Dei* in humans and the Christ, the universal Savior, the perfect and exact representation of God. All these theologians direct attention to the enduring, supra-ethnic and supra-racial nature of the Christian social identity, an identity that should subsume and unify other identities within itself.

Yet a crucial emphasis on a stable Christian identity need not deny the range of forces influencing African identities: relationships with African religio-cultures, Euro-American neo-colonial forces, globalization, the individual's roles and memberships in other communities, religious beliefs, and more. Mushete recognized and addressed a multiplicity of influences at work in modern African identities: this situation indicates that African identities must be able to negotiate complex, dynamic cultures, and that dynamism and multiplicity can be strengths in constructing a healthy communal identity. Africa's present and future challenge African theologians to address the Gospel-culture relation dynamically and not just statically.

Perpetually focusing upon the past, or viewing culture as a static entity, will limit, damage, and potentially threaten both the present and the future of persons and cultures. Just as African identity in general should not focus solely on the past, so Christian identity should not remain confined to exploring the relationship between African religio-cultures and the Christian gospel. Multiple forces shape African identities, and a healthy Christian communal identity requires in-depth dialogue with these forces, examining the role it now plays amidst them. Focusing mainly or only upon culture in a broad sense as it interacts with the gospel neglects other important nuances influencing African and Christian identities, such as gender.

From a specifically Christian perspective, African identities must contribute to Christian social identity. Identity in Christ is of prime importance but it embraces who we are called to be as particular people and cultures. The Christian enters a new community, God's people who are in Christ by the Spirit; this communal theological identity provides a perspective on and transformation of other identities. Thus we can begin to explore African ecclesiologies more specifically in succeeding chapters, now that we have sketched the broader cultural framework within which identity, particularly the nature of the communal identity of God's people, becomes a particularly prominent concern. The next chapter examines biblical appeals in African theologies before the succeeding chapter details their major concerns, various ecclesial proposals, and what these theologians desire for the Christian communal identity in Africa.

Chapter 4

≈

Communal Identity in Scripture

This work argues that it is crucial to specify the type of identity with which theologians in Africa are concerned, in order to advance identity discussion and also show its link with ecclesiology. Chapter 3 argued that identity discussions in Africa are concerned with communal identity, specifically the complicated relationship between African and Christian communal identities, and described the relationship theologians envision between these identities. The proposed Christian communal identity in Africa takes up the concerns with inculturation, liberation, life, and community (chapter 2), drawing on past traditions, but also responding to the present and considering the future, and displaying some flexibility as cultures are ever-changing. Mulago and Bediako were prone to emphasize the stability and preeminence of the overarching Christian identity; Oduyoye too stressed the foundational nature of the Christian identity, as well as the *imago Dei*, which unites all humanity. All three of these theologians emphasized the large role of community in shaping personal identity, and find cultural, theological, and biblical rationales supporting this emphasis on community. So for multiple reasons, relationality and communal identities remain central in African cultures, even if their forms may be changing.

This chapter explores biblical texts concerning Christian communal identity that are explicitly referenced by African theologians. This chapter is a contribution to existing scholarship, in that most discussions on communal solidarity and ecclesiology do not provide much exploration of their biblical bases. By examining how some African theologians ground their concepts of communal identity and its nature in Scripture, we build a further bridge to the explicit ecclesiologies studied in the next chapter. These theologians unanimously reject the idea that differences within God's people should be abolished, while at the same time they recognize that solidarity should characterize the communal identity of God's people. Since they find such solidarity characterizing African cultures and creating contextual resonance with the original biblical cultures, they can appeal to the OT in concert with directly ecclesiological passages in the NT. Thus, passages to examine include Joshua 2 and 6 (and less directly Joshua 7), Ezekiel 18, John 17, 1 Corinthians 12, and Galatians 3. The goal is to examine what these texts contribute to African arguments about the nature of Christian communal identity, and in particular its relationship with diversity and the individual's place within the whole.

Communal Identity among 'God's People'

Unfortunately, the concept of communal identity is sometimes disparaged by more individualistic cultures, relegated to peoples who are pre-modern or less 'advanced'. The phrase can carry certain negative connotations and misunderstandings, such as the notion that this mindset is the result of a simpler view of the universe, or is unable to properly distinguish the individual from the group, or is purely a cultural rather than theological trait (and accordingly limited to the OT period).[1] However, communal or social identity most simply refers to the part(s) of a person's identity formed by group membership: this shared identity bonds the individual to others in the group, and the group as a whole. Communal identity is not merely present in ANE cultures, but is central to God's plan for humanity: YHWH's intent is to form a people for himself. It is therefore a factor everywhere, and perennially, to some degree, with all cultures fitting on a continuum of social factors in their approaches to identity. When it comes to the Bible, then, James A. Sanders discerns the importance of corporate identity, concluding that "the principle issue of patriarchalism in the Bible was that of survival of the corporate identity of the chosen family or tribe, just as eventually the central issue of the Exile in the sixth century BCE was whether the people

---

1. The possibility of development in the concept from the OT to the NT is not ruled out. OT and NT are used rather than 'Hebrew Bible' and 'Christian New Testament', respectively, because the former are the terms typically used by the African scholars cited here. A canonical approach studies the texts as they currently are, and in relationship with other texts within the Bible, as opposed to devoting time mainly to source or form criticism. From a canonical and creedal perspective, one should indeed put the study of one passage or book within the wider context of the canon (Jenson, *Canon and Creed*, 87).

whom God has chosen would survive with identity intact, and not assimilate to the culture of the conqueror, thereby losing identity."[2]

The communal identity examined in this chapter is 'God's people', with other social identities then relating to it and how it shapes the place of the individual with respect to the community. The biblical texts examined here are all texts alluded to by Africans exploring the communal identity of God's people and the way in which that communal identity responds to difference and individuality. For the NT passages, the selected texts are important to or frequently mentioned in specifically ecclesiological works in Africa. Even though African Christians are sometimes said to be partial to the OT, ecclesiologies rely heavily on the NT in describing the character of this communal identity.

Knut Holter refers to Kwesi A. Dickson's 1973 article, which noted this "so-called African predilection for the Old Testament"; Holter agrees that this "special interest" in the OT "was reflected already in the publications of the *Gründer*-generation of African theology" in the 1960s–70s.[3] D. T. Adamo refers to the comparisons between African religio-cultures and ancient Israel, listing John S. Mbiti, Emmanuel B. Idowu, Kwesi Dickson, and others as pioneers of these comparative studies in the 1930s–60s.[4] Adamo highlights the hermeneutical role of African religio-cultures: they were "stressed as a means by which the Old Testament Scripture could be appropriately understood."[5] Grant LeMarquand draws attention to Knut Holter's work, which concluded that particularly in regard to the OT, Bible translation resulted in a recognition that many aspects in African traditional culture paralleled those of the OT world.[6]

Laurenti Magesa also underscores the prominence of the OT in Africa "on account of the similarity in symbols, metaphors and rituals described in the Old Testament and those found in African religiosity, to which African Christians seem to be attracted and drawn." Furthermore, he observes that "many—perhaps the majority—of the AICs exemplify this intuitive preference, which in these churches goes to the extent of not only including the

---

2. Sanders, "The Family in the Bible," 118.

3. Holter, "Old Testament Scholarship," 56, referring to Dickson's "The Old Testament and African Theology." Dickson observes this "predilection for the Old Testament," then proceeds to explore the nature of the OT, the reason African Independent Churches have this attitude toward it, and the ways in which the OT can contribute to an African theology (32ff).

4. Adamo, "The Historical Development," 14.

5. Ibid., 15; cf. also 17–18, 20ff.

6. LeMarquand, *An Issue of Relevance*, 17 n. 37. Cf. Mugambi, "Africa and the Old Testament," 7–25.

word 'Israel' in their nomenclature but also replicating many Old Testament rituals (such as mandatory circumcision) and symbols (such as dress) in their religious vision and practice."[7] Given this widely affirmed importance of the OT in African theology, it is unclear why the OT seems to be generally neglected in ecclesiologies from Africa. Perhaps it is simply a matter of citing texts that are obvious and easy to use; it remains surprising, however, because the OT aids in underscoring the nature of the corporate identity 'God's people'.

Hermeneutical Differences

Contextual differences result in hermeneutical differences between African and non-African theologians. For example, Justin Ukpong charges that Western hermeneutics falls prey to individualism and intellectualism.[8] In contrast, African frameworks emphasize community, pragmatism, and a "unitive view of reality."[9] This is not to say that community issues should displace all references to the individual, but that being attentive to communal aspects of the text will bring out more holistic, balanced readings that are more in line with God's communal purposes.

In a similar vein, Teresa Okure emphasizes the need for a holistic approach to biblical studies that does not separate the various disciplines but draws upon them all, studying "a given text from the perspective of the whole of life, theological and otherwise, keeping always in view its faith dimension as its fundamental key to meaning."[10] She shares,

> A Nigerian Ibibio proverb holds that the legs of the bird that flies in the air always point to the ground ('*Inuen afruroke ke enyong ukot asiwot isong*'). Biblical criticism took off from the ground and remained poised in flight for a greater part of the twentieth century. In the process it all but lost touch with life on the ground as it explored various imaginative ways of reconstructing the biblical texts and their contexts. Scholarship now needs to land on the ground, reconnect with life and critically assess its aerial view findings for the benefit of life on the ground."[11]

---

7. Magesa, *Anatomy of Inculturation*, 113.

8. Ukpong, "Inculturation Hermeneutics," 24.

9. Ibid., 24-25. In this hermeneutic, context is highly critical (23-29). Cf. LeMarquand, *An Issue of Relevance*, 85.

10. Okure, "'I will open my mouth in parables,'" 454, 461.

11. Ibid., 463.

This approach values the role of context in the hermeneutical process. Okure also stresses that "God's gospel should help to expose [one's contextual prejudices] as we become socialized into Christ and learn to cultivate his mind (Gal 3:28; 1 Cor 2:16). A reading that loses its counter-cultural edge, or fails to transform lives and promote the good in the culture, may be an inauthentic reading."[12] Ukachukwu Chris Manus affirms Okure's observation, noting a tendency of Western exegetes to be interested in 'stylistics' rather than 'theological signification,' with the result that "themes are not brought down to earth to touch on life but are only considered valuable at the level of historical and literary criticism." Manus urges that such tendencies require "Africans to launch out for a paradigm shift."[13]

Grant LeMarquand's *An Issue of Relevance* was written specifically to test Okure's contention "that biblical scholarship as it is normally practiced in the North Atlantic world is substantially different from the way biblical scholarship is normally conducted in modern Africa."[14] LeMarquand concludes that the goals of these two traditions differ: the North Atlantic primarily seeks to understand the text in its original context, "with little regard for its relevance to contemporary circumstances" while in "modern African biblical scholarship, a major purpose of exegesis is to meet current needs."[15] In essence, Western scholarship focuses on the past, and African scholarship on the present.[16] African hermeneutics might be termed hermeneutics with a pragmatic or praxis-oriented bent, as revealed in the way scholars in Africa employ the following texts.

Old Testament Texts

Joshua 2, 6, and 7

In his ecclesiology, Kenyan Paul Mbandi underscores the importance of Rahab's story to elaborate on the communal identity of God's people, particularly its relationship to ethnic identities.[17] Rahab's story also aids in understanding the place and role of the individual in this corporate uni-

---

12. Ibid., 448.

13. Manus, *Intercultural Hermeneutics*, 59. For examples of this tendency, see pp. 16, 23, 29, 46–47, 48, 65, and chapters 9 and 10.

14. LeMarquand, *An Issue of Relevance*, 3.

15. Ibid., 3. For examples, see 80–81, 84, 164. For his conclusion that overall Okure is correct, see 219–20.

16. Ibid., 4–5.

17. Mbandi, *A Theology of the Unity of the Church*.

ty.[18] The contrast with Achan (Joshua 7), the ethnic Israelite who is cast out from God's people, further supports Mbandi's argument.[19] On the one hand, the solidarity of the communal identity is theologically, not just ethnically, defined; Achan is judged. Yet, on the other hand, he and his household are judged precisely because his actions affect the unified faithfulness of the community. So too Rahab, in the reverse as it were: she rescues her family by responding in faith to the God of Israel. As a result, she comes to enjoy a crucial place in the history of Israel. Yet Rahab is a controversial figure. Some female and postcolonial theologians denigrate Rahab for 'betraying' the citizens of Jericho, viewing Rahab's actions as 'selling out' to the enemy and perpetuating a colonialist, patriarchal mindset. Others doubt the veracity and/or motivation of Rahab's confession.

A prostitute in Jericho, Rahab hides two Israelite spies, and asks that in return, when Israel attacks Jericho, the Israelites spare her and her family. The spies agree, before escaping the city and reporting back to Joshua. In Joshua 6, Joshua honors the agreement, and thus Rahab's family lived in Israel. Indeed, "she was not only spared, but she was fully incorporated into the people of God. She married into the tribe of Judah," becoming an ancestress of David and Jesus.[20]

Mbandi highlights the Rahab narrative to support his argument about the nature of ecclesial unity. He emphasizes that God "wanted other nations and ethnic groups to observe his grace and blessing to Israel and glorify him (cf. Deut 4:5–6, 26:19). The incorporation of Rahab, the prostitute, into the covenant community" testifies to God's inclusive plan.[21] Mbandi employs Rahab's story for practical purposes: to argue that God's people are intended to include ethnic diversity; another way of saying this is that for the communal identity 'God's people', ethnicity is not a core identity marker, on the basis of which a person would be included or excluded from the community. By contrast, while some preliminary groundwork aids in understanding the text, the failure of many non-African scholars to move from preliminaries to such substantive engagement with its theological implications is unfortunate. Scholars debate what type of prostitute Rahab might have been, if the spies were right or wrong in making a treaty with her, whether or not she was a hero or a traitor for leaving her people to join Israel, in addition to

---

18. For insight into Mesopotamian and Israelite social life that aids in more fully understanding and situating corporate unity in the ANE context, see Toorn, *Family Religion*.

19. Bernice Letlhare mentions Achan when comparing corporate personality in ancient Israel and among the Botswana people ("Corporate Personality," 474–80.

20. Mbandi, *Theology of the Unity*, 61 n. 259.

21. Ibid., 61.

the standard source, form, and redactional issues.[22] However, non-African scholars rarely focus on the corporate identity of God's people and the nature of their unity here to the extent that Mbandi does.[23]

Must emphasis on a unified corporate identity repress individuality and personal responsibility? Though Mbandi does not examine corporate unity in the Rahab narratives, I suggest it is worth noting that Rahab's story negates the notion that corporate identity requires suppression of individuality. Despite a context that tended to subjugate women, Rahab spoke on behalf of her family, saving their lives. In her aggressive bargaining with the spies, Rahab made it clear that the spies owed her, and that obligation extended to her family. The text indicates that Rahab had male relatives (Josh 2:13, 18), yet surprisingly she acted as if she had the right to speak for the whole family.[24] Despite Rahab's socially unacceptable role as a prostitute, her family maintained a relationship with her, and was saved from death by complying with her directions.[25] In light of Oduyoye's concerns with women's agency and responsibility, it is important to highlight Rahab in this regard too, not just for the fact that she was integrated into Israel in spite of her ethnicity.

Rahab is certainly a liminal character.[26] Perhaps her story "has been placed at the beginning of the book of Joshua, which makes us ask about foreigners 'in the midst of Israel,' a theme that echoes throughout the book of Joshua. . . . [The story] focuses on the question of what it means to be a member of the people of promise (ethnicity, geography, or confession and

---

22. For example, see Begg, "The Ai-Achan Story," 1–20; Bird, "The Harlot as Heroine," 119–39; Mehlman, "Rahab as a Model," 193–207; Robinson, "Rahab of Canaan," 257–73; Rowlett, *Joshua*; Sherwood, "A Leader's Misleading," 43–61.

23. Scholars who directly mention corporate unity in Joshua 2 or 7 are Butler, *Joshua*; Howard, *Joshua*; Kaiser, *Toward Old Testament Ethics*; Matties, "Reading Rahab's Story," 57–70; Woudstra, *The Book of Joshua*; Stek, "Rahab of Canaan and Israel," 28–48. Nevertheless, these discussions are relatively brief. Even Stek does not deal specifically with corporate unity, though he moves into the text's meaning and implications. The notion is touched upon, but not directly addressed, by McConville and Williams, *Joshua*.

24. Rahab's taking responsibility for her family and acting on their behalf is atypical for her cultural background (Robinson, "Rahab of Canaan," 267).

25. Bird explains that the *zônâ*, or prostitute's, "social status is that of an outcast, though not an outlaw, a tolerated, but dishonored member of society" ("The Harlot as Heroine," 120).

26. Cf. Kuan and Tran, "Reading Race," 27–44. Corinne Lanoir identifies Rahab as a marginal or "frontier" figure in several senses: geographically due to her house's location in the city wall, socially because of her profession, politically in her relationship to Jericho and the Israelites, existentially in terms of being the dividing line between life and death for the spies and her family, as well as literarily and mythically ("Rahab?," 36–37).

covenant loyalty)."[27] Some scholars believe that Joshua and his spies failed in their duties by sparing Rahab and her family, interpreting the sparing of Rahab's family's lives as a violation of the ban (Deut 7:2) upon Canaanites. But in Deuteronomy 7 an Israelite is defined by worship of YHWH alone. Israelites were forbidden to intermarry with other ethnicities and nationalities because those marriages would likely lead to worship of other gods (Deut 7:16, 25).[28] In other words, God's ultimate concern is not with ethnicity, but with faithfulness.

Bernard Robinson's interpretation supports Mbandi's reading. Robinson argues that because Rahab converted, "the harsh law of חרם does not apply. After a temporary exclusion from the Hebrew camp . . . she wins for herself and for her enduring clan a place in the heart of Israel."[29] Mehlman's analysis of Rabbinic tradition concurs: the final picture of Rahab is that of a woman whose faith is greatly rewarded.[30] In the NT, Rahab merits a place in Jesus's genealogy (Matt 1:5), as well as among heroes of the faith (Heb 11:31) and a commendation for saving the spies (Jas 2:25). Kenyan David Oginde succinctly highlights the change in Rahab's communal identity: "A Canaanite turned Israelite!"[31] Rahab's religious identity changes, and her ethnic identity is not immutable, nor the defining aspect of her identity; instead, her relationship to YHWH and his people ultimately defines her.

Further warrant for this reading comes from the Book of Joshua. Typically actions of which God disapproves receive swift punishment, such as failure to conquer a city (Josh 7:1–5). Yet there is no mention of punishment that comes upon the Israelites for sparing Rahab's family. Instead, Joshua 7 tells of an ethnic Israelite—Achan—who is cast out of Israel for his disobedience to YHWH. Ghanaian J. Kwabena Asamoah-Gyadu references the Achan narrative to argue that while the OT concept "that the consequences of individual actions affect the whole community is present in traditional Ibo thought," the Western "missionary Christian practices tended to favor individual rather than the communal implications of salvation."[32] Essentially, Asamoah-Gyadu charges that missionaries erred in minimizing the Bible's communal perspective; presumably the communal aspect of Christian

27. Matties, "Reading Rahab's Story," 67.

28. This reason is mentioned in Deut 7:1–5 and Exod 23:31–33, where the command is given; Judg 3:5–6 and 1 Kgs 9:20–21 record that intermarriage and close relationships with previous inhabitants of the land did lead the Israelites to abandon YHWH.

29. Robinson, "Rahab of Canaan," 257.

30. Mehlman, "Rahab as a Model," 197.

31. Oginde, "Joshua," 273.

32. Asamoah-Gyadu, "'The Evil You Have Done,'" 49, 51.

identity too is minimized.³³ Yet Asamoah-Gyadu associates Achan's story with the Ezekiel 18 proverb, seeming likewise uneasy with the notion of corporate unity, at least as it is linked to corporate judgment: "As expressed in the book of Ezekiel . . . collective justice is not justice. One of the most poignant examples here is" Achan.³⁴

Achan's story is the mirror opposite of Rahab's; here the ethnic Israelite disobeys, and he and his family fall under YHWH's judgment.³⁵ Juxtaposing these characters reveals that YHWH's foremost concern and the primary marker of the God-follower identity is neither gender (as Oduyoye highlighted, and as Rahab's story demonstrates) nor ethnicity (per Mbandi's exploration of Rahab's story), nor even one's sinful past; what is most central is a covenant relationship with YHWH. The relationship to YHWH and YHWH's people is prioritized over other identities (as Mulago and Bediako advocated), which makes ethnically Canaanite Rahab an 'insider' whereas ethnically Israelite Achan becomes an 'outsider.'

In conclusion, Rahab's story clarifies the nature of the communal identity 'YHWH's people': it is based on exclusive loyalty to YHWH. Thus there is solidarity between people of different ethnicities who together worship YHWH and thus share that communal identity in common, whereas an ethnic Israelite who disobeys and forsakes YHWH is no longer a 'true' Israelite.³⁶ I proposed that Rahab's story also illustrates that this communal

---

33. Andrew M. Mbuvi also highlights the intriguing similarity between the possibility that Okonkwo's actions could bring judgment on his community in *Things Fall Apart* and the Achan narrative ("Missionary Acts," 149).

34. Asamoah-Gyadu, "Mission," 402. Later he affirms that the "integrated and interdependent nature of human life and existence means that, for the world in general, human actions have consequences far beyond the control of those who initiate them" (405).

35. Oginde emphasizes the communal consequences of an individual's sin, commenting that "although only one man sinned, all Israel was held liable." Sin "often affects not only the sinner, but it spreads its consequences to their family, fellowship, or the whole church. Achan's sin led to the defeat of Israel and the death of his family!" He suggests that in order to experience God's blessings, "we must deal with sin in our lives as individuals and as a fellowship" ("Joshua," 274, 276). Oginde gives no indication that he finds this communal judgment unjust, or that it in any way negates or is in tension with the idea of individual responsibility before God (274-76).

36. John H. Stek asserts that "Israel's most distinct characteristic was its monotheistic Yahwism—their sense that they were Yahweh's special creation, and that they and Yahweh were bonded by a covenant that dated from the wilderness wanderings" ("Rahab of Canaan and Israel," 34). Stek later concludes, "Only those—*but all those*, even a Canaanite prostitute—who take Yahweh seriously as the one and only Lord of creation and of history and who accordingly make the choice that Rahab made, laying her life on the line in abandoning her Canaanite identity, community, and religious heritage and seeking inclusion in Israel, will have place among the people of Yahweh and thus

identity in no way removes an individual's agency and responsibility. At the same time, the individual's actions affect the community, as both Rahab and Achan demonstrate. It is also noteworthy that this communal identity marked by unity with God's people applies not just to Rahab but extends also to her family. Letlhare differentiates between 'interdependence'— described as a strong bond between a person and the social groups to which they belong—and collectivism, which attaches greater importance to the community.[37] In Rahab's situation, YHWH accepts the person who shows faith, regardless of her gender and ethnicity, and extends mercy to her family, an example of interdependent unity, not collectivism.

Rahab's life reveals YHWH's concern with creating a communal identity marked by an interdependence and solidarity that includes and respects diverse ethnic identities while prioritizing their shared foundational identity as YHWH's people. This is of particular, practical concern to African scholars observing churches split by ethnic differences. Yet how does the communal identity emphasis here reconcile with a text that some suggest focuses on the individual in opposition to corporate unity and identity?

Ezekiel 18

Is Ezekiel 18 an argument against the prominence of communal solidarity and social identity, a sign of evolution beyond this idea? In this chapter the prophet berates his fellow Israelites for a proverb they use. Their trust in God shaken, the people have succumbed either to cynicism or despair. The proverb blames their forefathers for the suffering the current generation is undergoing. The exiles exploit communal identity to vindicate themselves. The proverb reaches Ezekiel's ears, and he responds with a disputation oracle.[38]

Through his mouthpiece Ezekiel, YHWH indignantly asks, "What do you people mean by quoting this proverb about the land of Israel: 'The parents eat sour grapes, and the children's teeth are set on edge'? As surely as I live, declares the Sovereign LORD, you will no longer quote this proverb in Israel. For everyone belongs to me, the parent as well as the child—both

---

have a part in the future triumph of Yahweh's kingdom" (48, emphasis in original). Stek's phrasing reiterates that Rahab's commitment to YHWH involves a communal identity shift.

37. Letlhare, "Corporate Personality," 474, 479. Letlhare acknowledges that interdependent relationships can have "negative connotations," as in Achan's case (476–77).

38. According to D. F. Murray, disputation involves a thesis, counter-thesis, and dispute ("The Rhetoric of Disputation," 99).

alike belong to me. The one who sins is the one who will die" (vv. 2–4).³⁹ Some suggest that this passage contains a highly developed understanding of the autonomous individual, which is said to represent a more advanced stage of development in Israel's theology from earlier notions of corporate solidarity and the importance of communal identity.⁴⁰ This autonomous, independent view of the person is said to replace the older, more archaic or primitive notion of communal identity.⁴¹ Nigerian Chinua Achebe concludes that "western culture" may have used Ezekiel 18 to justify the idea that "the West's emphasis on the supremacy of the individual is somehow the right one," as opposed to viewpoints that emphasize the person-in-community and communal identity as African cultures do.⁴²

How does Ezekiel counter the exiles, and what does this say about the place of the individual and individual responsibility with regard to communal identity?⁴³ The proverb provoking the oracle occurs in verse 2. The phrase "the parents eat sour grapes" conveys the idea that the forefathers have sinned, while "the children's teeth are set on edge" states that the children—the present generation in exile in Babylon—are innocents suffering

---

39. The same proverb occurs in Jer 31:29, though the verb tense differs. Ezekiel uses the imperfect form of the verb לבא—the fathers 'eat'—while Jeremiah uses the perfect form—the fathers 'ate.' According to Rodney R. Hutton, Ezekiel's audience claimed that the proverb was eternally valid, while Jeremiah expresses the point that the people will come to a new understanding: God does not work this way ("Are the Parents," 278, 282–83). Hutton is not alone in arguing that Jeremiah and Ezekiel are making different points in their respective uses of the proverb. For example, Joyce, "Ezekiel and Moral Transformation," 143.

40. Paul M. Joyce provides two examples of this 'developmental' view: F. Baumgartel, and W. Eichrodt (*Divine Initiative*, 79). Joyce later concedes that "it may well be that the engagement with the problem of undeserved suffering in the book of Job and also the emergence of a belief in personal resurrection (reflected, it seems, in Dan. 12:2) are related to an increased concern for the life of the individual and to the wish to vindicate the justice of God in relation to a particular life. The likelihood that certain developments of this kind took place may readily be acknowledged. What must be resisted, however, is any tendency to generalize from such specific developments and to postulate a simple, one-way development towards increased individualism" (85). Among those who believe that Ezekiel 18's unique contribution is individual responsibility for sin instead of collective guilt, Joyce lists Zimmerli and Eichrodt ("Individual Responsibility?," 185). Joel S. Kaminsky lists Halpern, Lindblom, and Von Rad as scholars holding this view (*Corporate Responsibility*, 139).

41. Paul Joyce's definition of individual responsibility emphasizes personal autonomy: "The moral independence of contemporary individuals; in other words, that particular men and women are judged in isolation from their contemporaries" (in *Divine Initiative*, 36).

42. Achebe, "The Nature of the Individual," 205–6.

43. For application of this passage to contemporary Ghana, see Asamoah-Gyadu, "Of 'Sour Grapes,'" and "Mission."

for their forefathers' sins, which in turn means that YHWH unjustly punishes innocents (v. 25).[44] Ezekiel vehemently disagrees, firmly stating that "the one who sins is the one who will die" (v. 4, 20) and offering three cases in which the person is judged by his own life.[45]

Does this passage contradict African theological claims regarding the necessity of corporate unity and communal identity? Can these two poles—the responsibility of the community as a whole and the responsibility of the individual within it—both be retained, or must one be jettisoned? Eritrean Tewoldemedhin Habtu introduces Ezekiel 18 by stating,

> Biblical scholars have long debated the relationship of corporate and individual responsibility in the life of God's covenant people. This chapter, which is often invoked in that debate, does not present individual responsibility as being in contradiction to the corporate responsibility of the nation before God. Rather, it shows that Israelites are both corporately and individually responsible to the covenant Lord.[46]

Letlhare understands Ezekiel 18 as quoting a proverb "which called attention to the individual" in such a way as to question their relationship to the society as a whole, and Ezekiel's response implies "that individual responsibility is inherent" in society, regardless of whether the society is marked by a 'corporate personality' mindset or not.[47]

---

44. Rodney R. Hutton disagrees, saying that the Israelites are not accusing YHWH of being unjust when he punishes children for the sins of the fathers (cf. "Are the Parents?," 277–78). Daniel I. Block argues that the exiles are not questioning God's justice, but expressing "belief in an inevitable and uncontrollable determinism": they believe that God is either disinterested or impotent (*The Book of Ezekiel*, 560, 561). Barnabas Lindars concludes that whether the proverb is a protest against YHWH's injustice, or the exiles truly believed it (and thus absolved themselves of responsibility for their current predicament), Ezekiel's response closes the door on both of those beliefs ("Ezekiel and Individual Responsibility," 462). Asamoah-Gyadu suggests that Achan's story in Joshua 7 is an example of just such an occurrence, in which a father's sin sets the teeth of his descendants on edge ("Mission," 402).

45. Here Ezekiel draws upon Deut 24:16, which teaches that fathers are not to be put to death for their children's sins, or vice versa; instead, each dies for his own sins. Gordon H. Matties notes that elsewhere Deuteronomy acknowledges that the community could suffer the consequences of one person's actions, in part depending on the person's status and the nature of their offense ("Individual Responsibility," 128, 130). Block resolves the tension by arguing that "on the surface the Decalogue formation appears to be contradicted by this law. However, Exod 20:5 deals explicitly with the *divine* administration of justice, while Deut 24:16 is designed to rein in abuses in *human* judgments" (*The Book of Ezekiel*, 563, italics original).

46. Habtu, "Ezekiel," 952.

47. Letlhare, "Corporate Personality," 479.

J. Kwabena Asamoah-Gyadu pairs Ezekiel 18 with John 9:1-3, concluding that these passages are "repudiations of the worldview that people will always inherit the punishment for the sins of their ancestors."[48] Ezekiel 18 is, further, a "new dispensation," "in which each person was the only one who would be responsible for his or her wrong-doing," an emphasis that will not allow the Israelites to deny personal responsibility.[49] He views Ezekiel 18 as an evolution in Israel's thinking, yet still affirms that the "integrated and interdependent nature of human life and existence means that, for the world in general, human actions have consequences far beyond the control of those who initiate them."[50] Asamoah-Gyadu's statements here parallel Letlhare's reminder that personal responsibility is always relevant.

How do these two perspectives—the individual's place and responsibility and a united corporate identity—relate in Ezekiel 18? First, "it is essential to take account of the fact that the exile was a national crisis, which inevitably affected everyone. It is the 'House of Israel' which Ezekiel addresses (18:25, 29, 31) and his answer to the 'sour grapes' proverb must offer an explanation of the suffering of the nation as a whole."[51] YHWH asks the exiles (second person plural) why they quote this proverb.[52] The chapter describes three individuals (vv. 5-20)—righteous grandfather, wicked son, and righteous grandson—being judged each by his own actions, while seeking to explain why an entire generation (Ezekiel's audience) is exiled in Babylonia.[53] Ezekiel presents these test cases where an individual lives

48. Asamoah-Gyadu, "Mission," 402-3.
49. Ibid., 405, 406.
50. Ibid., 405.
51. Joyce, *Divine Initiative*, 37.
52. In Ezekiel 18, v. 2 is the thesis, and the counter-thesis is in v. 4b: "The soul who sins is the one who will die" (which recurs in v. 20). Leslie C. Allen notes that the passage presents "a second, related counterthesis" in v. 21 and 24 (*Ezekiel 1-19*, 268).
53. Ezekiel's listing of a grandfather, son, and grandson may not be purely hypothetical. It could signal (1) a reference to the Davidic line, particularly Josiah (righteous), Jehoiakim (wicked), and Jehoiachin (potentially righteous) (see Laato, *Josiah and David Redivivus*, cited in Block, *The Book of Ezekiel*, 555), or (2) Ezekiel's reliance upon earlier writings, such as Exod 20:5, 34:7 or Num 14:18, which state that God's wrath will extend to the third and fourth generation (Lindars, "Ezekiel and Individual Responsibility," 462). However, Block suggests, "Although the statement is generally interpreted vertically, i.e., the punishment is carried out in successive generations, even after the guilty person has died, it may also be understood horizontally, according to which the 'third and fourth generations' represent the maximum number of generations that live together in an extended family. The punishment is applied in the case of Achan" (*The Book of Ezekiel*, 559 n. 26). Jurrien Mol also follows this line of thought, noting that both Ezekiel 18 and 20 are "making use explicitly of the line of the generations.... Three generations are necessary for the formation of a 'house of the father,' a 'family'"

in a manner opposite of his predecessor; each time, YHWH's verdict rests not upon what the immediate ancestor did, but what the individual himself does. This is the first reason for Ezekiel's use of the individual language: he draws on the priestly, legal tradition "for both the style and the substance of his argumentation," as seen in (1) the test cases, (2) the argument's structure, and (3) the lists of virtues and vices.[54] Ezekiel re-applies the language of criminal law to the context of divine retribution.[55]

Again, in the initial examples, each man represents a generation.[56] "Although a single man is considered in each of the three test-cases, it is the cause of the nation's predicament which is being explored; the proverb blames the sins of previous generations for the sufferings of the present, and accordingly the individuals of the test-cases each represent a generation,"[57] just as in the proverb 'fathers' and 'children' refer to whole generations. Joyce agrees that Ezekiel

> takes for granted the general principle of 'individual responsibility' in the realm of legal practice (and employs it in considering his three hypothetical cases), but the possibility of Yahweh judging individuals in isolation from their contemporaries is not considered. This is because the question at issue is a different one, namely, 'Why is this inevitably communal, national crisis happening?'[58]

Individual judgment before YHWH is on the basis of each person's deeds, but here YHWH addresses exiled Israel as a whole (vv. 25, 29, 30, 31), urging her to get a "new heart and a new spirit" (v. 31, singular). In closing,

---

(*Collective and Individual Responsibility*, 239). Mol emphasizes that in Ezekiel family is the "unit of responsibility," the "moral community" and unit of "internal judgment" (243–44). He claims that the family is the basis for responsibility: "Individual responsibility is constituted within the community, namely in the family. . . . The constituting family structure is the ground of existence of collective responsibility and solidarity" (245).

54. Block, *The Book of Ezekiel*, 557.

55. Paul Joyce suggests that "recognition of this reapplication of language is the key to the understanding of the chapter" (*Divine Initiative*, 41).

56. It was mentioned previously that the individuals in these test cases may represent not Israelites in general, but the final kings of Judah. If so, the point is still valid: the present generation seeks to blame previous persons, or a single representative person, for present-day suffering.

57. Joyce, *Divine Initiative*, 46.

58. Ibid. From an African perspective, it could be argued that the possibility of judging an isolated individual does not arise not only because of the question at hand, but also because the "autonomous individual" concept is not God's perspective on human beings.

Ezekiel exhorts his audience to accept responsibility for their actions, resist despair, and repent.[59]

Secondly, Ezekiel 18 uses individualistic language because it "indicates that God addresses the nation through the individuals who make up this nation."[60] Tewoldemedhin Habtu similarly says, "God's final impassioned appeal to the Israelites to repent is addressed to the *house of Israel* corporately, but also stresses individual responsibility in that he promises to judge *each one according to his ways*."[61] Using examples of individuals suits Ezekiel's hortatory purpose. In Darr's words, the goal of this "proverb performance" is not foremost to change beliefs about transgenerational retribution; the intent, once the exiles correctly assess their situation, is "to provide the people with a means to survive their *present* circumstances."[62] Ezekiel urges his audience to take responsibility for their lives and live rightly before God. To make the exiles feel the weight of that responsibility and to encourage them to hope in YHWH's mercy, the prophet couches his argument in terms of individuals. Each person must realize her agency and responsibility in Israel's communal identity to effect a corporate renewal. It is not God who is inequitable, but rather their own ways are unjust and must change. Asamoah-Gyadu believes that Ezekiel rejects the proverb because he "saw in [the proverb] an escape route for a people who wanted to deny their personal responsibility in the troubled times that the exile had brought upon them."[63]

As Habtu notes, Ezekiel's emphasis on individual responsibility does not negate unified corporate identity; instead, it is a matter of which perspective is emphasized in a particular context. Based on the insights from theologians of the previous chapter, I suggest that communal identity and individuality are not concerns confined to the Bible or African cultures, but are always part of human societies. Indeed, Jurrien Mol believes that while there can be change in the relationship of the two, the evolutionary or developmental approach fails because "collectivism and individualism are entities in the Old Testament era which neither succeed or relieve one another,

---

59. Ezekiel thinks corporately regarding renewal too. "The overwhelmingly corporate nature of the chapters dealing with judgment is echoed in the hopeful material in the book, where we find that renewal is consistently presented as a corporate experience." As proof, Paul M. Joyce points to the promise of a new heart and spirit for the house of Israel (ch. 36), the 'dry bones' which are Israel (37:11), and the new life promised to 'my people' (37:12, 13) ("Ezekiel and Moral Transformation," 146).

60. Kaminsky, *Corporate Responsibility*, 171.

61. Habtu, "Ezekiel," 953, italics original.

62. Darr, "Proverb Performance," 222, italics original.

63. Asamoah-Gyadu, "Mission," 406.

nor are they mutually connected in an evolutionary manner."[64] This point is important to Mol, and he reiterates, "Each model which attempts to remove or bridge tension between the individual and the collective, in fact denies the existence of both the individual and the collective."[65] If Mol is correct, then many scholars are guilty of trying to flatten emphases that play an important role in biblical accounts of identity. I would add these are aspects of identity relevant in all cultures and ages, not confined to biblical accounts.

Another point deserves mention: in each case in Ezekiel 18, the individual is judged based on his actions. The majority of the actions cited are communal, related to how the person treats his or her neighbors, either oppressing or assisting them. When speaking of an individual's righteousness, Ezekiel does not describe the person as an autonomous being, who will only be judged on his heart's attitude toward YHWH or on so-called personal, private beliefs.[66] On the contrary, for people whose identity is shaped by covenant with a holy God, called to live in a holy community, it is natural that righteousness has both vertical and horizontal dimensions.[67] Holiness for YHWH's people has a major communal element.[68]

In conclusion, Ezekiel 18 uses personal language with the aim of urging the house of Israel to repent and mend their ways. The personal language may or may not indicate a change or growth in the way individuals were understood, but both Habtu and Letlhare affirm that the tie between individual and society is unbroken, and the responsibility of both the individual

---

64. Mol, *Collective and Individual Responsibility*, 211. A page later, he commends Kaminsky's work on the topic, and points out Kaminsky's contention that the developmental model remains popular with some scholars due to their "individualistic bias."

65. Ibid., 249. For corporate personality as it appears in and/or is relevant to African theology, see Azuh, "Corporate Personality"; Boganjalo, "Personnalite collective," 177–88; Letlhare, "Corporate Personality." Letlhare cites Josh 7 and Ezek 18, among other texts (475, 476–77, 479).

66. In 1 Sam 16:7, God tells Samuel that humans judge by outward appearances, while God looks at the heart. Other biblical passages teach that what is in the heart leads to outward actions. Jesus sums up the law with the commands to love God and neighbor. Indeed, it is impossible to be in right relationship with God, and at the same time hate one of God's people (1 John 2:9–11).

67. Daniel I. Block comments that the robbery is against a brother, "another member of the covenant community . . . [which term] reflects the perception of the entire nation as a consanguineous extended family." Moreover, the phrase about one who misbehaves 'in the midst of your people' (v. 18) "reiterates the communal concern of the oracle. This man's own wicked and anticommunal behavior has resulted in his death sentence" (*The Book of Ezekiel*, 578–79). The point is that even when the individual is highlighted in an OT text, the communal element has not disappeared or lost its importance.

68. See Adewuya, *Holiness and Community*.

and the corporate whole remain.⁶⁹ Ezekiel 18 champions a person taking responsibility for their actions, while simultaneously not forsaking corporate unity and identity.⁷⁰ In Block's words, "Children may not hide behind a theology of corporate solidarity and moral extension that absolves them of personal responsibility for their own destiny."⁷¹ To rephrase and apply this concept to an African context, Asamoah-Gyadu quotes Emmanuel Asante: Africa's situation makes it clear that African Christians need "a savior who has the power not only to deliver the believer from individual powers but also transform the lives of the bewitched and the dehumanized, enabling them to live actively in community."⁷² Both the individual and the community that shapes their identity and in which they participate matter in such a formulation: they are complementary.

Hence, from Joshua 2, 6, and 7, and Ezekiel 18 as Africans interpret them, we may conclude that YHWH looks at persons on the level of the individual as well as on the level of the corporate whole. Corporate solidarity arising from a communal identity does not downplay the importance of the individual; it simply situates a person within communities that have shaped them. A person is judged by their life (especially their relationships with others), while remaining subject to the consequences—whether good or ill—that fall upon Israel as a whole. So YHWH justly punishes Israel after Achan's offense precisely because corporate solidarity in the communal identity exist in deep, meaningful ways.⁷³ If not, how could another man,

69. It may be that corporate solidarity is most relevant when Israel is in the land with a king ruling over them. If there is no king, or the people are exiled, the focus of address out of necessity shifts toward the more individualistic end of the spectrum. However, if kingship in the united land is the paradigm, then corporate identity remains normative, though not necessarily monolithic. If this were the case, then it would not be problematic to identify diachronic development in the concept of individuality and individual responsibility, yet argue that corporate unity must not be dismissed.

70. Mol's *Collective and Individual Responsibility* offers in-depth examination of these chapters.

71. Block, *The Book of Ezekiel*, 589.

72. Asamoah-Gyadu, "Mission," 392, quoting Asante, "The Gospel in Context: An African Perspective." The article concludes that the Christian mission is to remove barriers to abundant life in Christ, who "shows compassion towards all people irrespective of race, nationality, color or circumstance," as seen in Gal 3:28 (405–6).

73. Kaminsky, *Corporate Responsibility*, argues that "the persistent tendency to denigrate various corporate ideas found in the Hebrew Bible stems from a larger Enlightenment bias that places greater value upon moral systems that emphasize the individual over against those that value the community. This proclivity to stress the atomistic autonomy of the individual has resulted in the disparagement of other societies—be they earlier or contemporary—that focus less on the rights of the individual and more on the individual's responsibilities to society. Additionally, it has led to a failure to recognize the importance that collective ideas continue to exert even today"

centuries later, claim to be the representative of Abraham's descendants, through whom those with Abrahamic faith might gain the promise of forgiveness, resurrection, and eternal life? Since African ecclesiologies rely heavily on the NT, though, we now move to some sample texts they reference with regard to specifically Christian communal identity (ecclesiology).

New Testament Texts

John 17:11, 20–23

Non-African Johannine scholarship in the first part of the twentieth century was often preoccupied with the Johannine community: its existence, nature, and so forth. By contrast, the approach here is what Stephen C. Barton calls *"readerly,"* meaning that instead of focusing on re-constructing the world in or behind the text, this approach engages deeply with the historical text

---

(179–80). Further, "the greatest flaw in the thinking of those who highlight passages like Ezekiel 18 and denigrate the importance of older corporate ideas falls under the rubric of logical coherence. It is presumed that the individualistic theology of Ezekiel 18 is theologically more perceptive than the older corporate theology because it is closer to our own [Western] modern notions of justice" (185). The author concludes that "inasmuch as the biblical view of the relationship between the individual and the community takes account of both poles, but places more emphasis upon the community and the individual's responsibility in that community, it can provide a much needed corrective to current ethical thinking. . . . A more nuanced theology that takes greater account of one's personal responsibilities toward the larger community will be necessary in the attempt to solve many modern issues, inasmuch as they are global issues (economics, environmental protection, the drug problem, energy planning, disease control and eradication, arms control etc.)[.] Acknowledging our responsibility to the larger communities in which we live will not only facilitate solving global issues, but it will create a greater sense of meaning, inasmuch as it will allow individuals to realize that we all share a common narrative. Indeed, it is time that we accepted the fact that we are our 'brothers' keepers'" (188). I cite Kaminsky at length to show that some Euro-American scholars are beginning to recognize their Enlightenment biases regarding individualistic readings of Ezekiel 18 and the Bible in general.

Though the examples here are from narrative and prophetic books, this theme applies to other genres in the OT, such as wisdom literature. One might say that wisdom literature particularizes Torah for the individual, but always portrays the flourishing individual as living in community. For example, Psalm 1 refers to the ways of the righteous person, and then contrasts the future of the righteous person with that of the wicked person. The wicked will not be welcomed into "the assembly of the righteous" (v. 5). The righteous person, by contrast, will enjoy fellowship with God and God's people. Another example is Prov 3:3–4, where the sage recommends wisdom, including holding tightly to "love and faithfulness," which will bring "favor and a good name in the sight of God and man." Hence, the sage assumes that wisdom is not a private, individualistic, inward pursuit alone, but one that affects relationship with both God and neighbors.

itself "*as Spirit-inspired*," with the goal of producing individual and communal transformation.[74] Barton describes this approach as "a form of critical reason which is *theological and ecclesial*." This accords with the tendency of theologians in Africa to employ pragmatic hermeneutics with a communal focus. This does not mean that questions of historicity and re-construction of the world in and behind the text are irrelevant, but the priority is examination of the text itself, seeking to read it as it was intended to be read: as a message for the God-following community.[75]

John's Gospel has been popular with scholars across Africa, from Nigerians Justin S. Ukpong and Teresa Okure to Kenyan Samuel Ngewa, to South Africans Dirk G. van der Merwe and Gert J. Malan. Perhaps this is because of its focus on life, or its teachings on unity among God's people. This section focuses on John 17, often referred to as 'the high priestly prayer.' Okure describes John 13–17 "as a resumé of the meaning of Jesus' mission, the aim of which is to explain more fully to the disciples the full meaning of this mission and its significance for them personally."[76]

Before focusing on vv. 11, 20–23, it is helpful to sketch the major themes of John 17. Ukpong finds four: (1) glorification of the Son, (2) glorification of the Father, (3) the world-versus-disciples contrast, and (4) the unity of all God-followers.[77] Verses 11, 20–23 echo these themes. Jesus prayed for the unity of his disciples (v. 11), not that they would become one, but that they would maintain their God-given unity.[78] Okure's dissertation examines mission in John's Gospel,[79] concluding that

74. Barton, "Christian Community," 284–85.

75. On the other hand, Gert J. Malan regards the view that the apostle John authored the Gospel as an un-academic, naïve approach, and he presupposes the Johannine community was an 'antisociety,' against other communities, even other Christian communities. In his reading, the book is not an eyewitness account, or historiography, and the Johannine community's Jesus is a figure who legitimates their group. At the time he wrote the article, Malan was a research associate at the University of Pretoria, South Africa ("Does John?," 1, 2, 4, 7–9). Teresa Okure critiques a secessionist, sectarian view of the Johannine community; she contrasts a "sessesionist [*sic*] or 'heretical'" group with the Johannine or 'orthodox' group, rather than seeing the Johannine group itself as sectarian, and argues that John's Gospel focuses on mission (xvi, xix). She lists John 17:20–21 as one of the "overtly missionary passages" in the Gospel (*The Johannine Approach to Mission*, 19). Andreas J. Köstenberger agrees, noting that those who accuse John and the Johannine community of being sectarian, in contrast to the Gospels of Luke and Matthew which command love of neighbors, disregard the strong emphasis on mission in John's Gospel (*A Theology of John's Gospel*, 515).

76. Okure, *Johannine Approach to Mission*, 54.

77. Ukpong, "Jesus' Prayer," 53.

78. Köstenberger, *John*, 493–94.

79. Musa W. Dube describes Okure's method as a "biblical hermeneutics of life," and

> given the importance attached to the community as the visible locus of the reality of Jesus' mission and to mutual love and service as the authenticating marks of this community, the worst that could happen would be for the disciples to love the world or assimilate its evil ways. . . . Worse even than this would be the presence of disunity and lack of love within the community itself; for then this community would betray itself and, if it were possible, make nonsense of Jesus' mission.[80]

Thus Jesus requests the Father to protect the disciples by the divine 'name' so that the disciples will be one. The Father's name links the disciples' unity to the Son's revelation of the Father, and Jesus further compares the disciples' unity to the unity between the Father and the Son. Okure's remarks highlight that a high degree of solidarity in the new identity is vital for the church's mission: it is central to who God's people must be, and what they are called to do.

In this text, unity is centered on Jesus's person. Here the larger context comes into play: Jesus has spoken in John 15 about the vine and branches metaphor, indicating that receiving life and love require 'abiding' or 'remaining' in him. Jesus will abide 'in' them through the Spirit (John 14), and thus all three members of the Godhead, united while distinguished, are involved in modeling and creating unity amongst God's people: the basis of their communal identity is the divine communal identity. Kenyan Samuel M. Ngewa underscores that Jesus's unity with the Father and Spirit is not a total identity of person, but a unity marked by common purpose and goals. Likewise, Ngewa urges God's people to maintain unity of purpose and message, without losing the diversity among the persons constituting the community.[81] Congolese Kuzuli Kossé too emphasizes that unity means different elements are formed into an organic whole "characterized by agreement and internal coherence."[82] He affirms that for God's people,

> unity that God brings extends to all believers of all nations, denominations and times. Tribalism, ethnicity and

---

a "life-centered hermeneutic," a method Okure supports with passages like John 10:10 (Dube, "*Talitha Cum* Hermeneutics," 144).

80. Okure, *Johannine Approach to Mission*, 209. She earlier discussed the importance of Christian fellowship for (and in) mission. Fellowship "defines the reality of [the disciples'] Christian existence here and now," and John conceives of fellowship "as something that has to be socially and concretely expressed" (204, 205). Okure also emphasizes that this Johannine perspective closely parallels Pauline theology, specifically 1 Cor 12:12–31.

81. Ngewa, *The Gospel of John*, 321.

82. Kossé, "Unity of Believers," 1288.

denominationalism are hindrances to the unity of God's people and must be resisted. Of course, each ethnic group or tribe has its place in the church, but only as links in a long chain. There is no place for ideologies that consider one ethnic group or tribe superior to another.[83]

Again, Kossé's concern is pragmatic in the rich sense of that word: the Christian identity must be marked by visible unity, and differences must not divide God's people, as distinctions in the three Persons do not divide the Trinity. Like Mulago and Bediako, Kossé urges that the Christian identity must be greater than ethnic and denominational identities: it is primary, while they are secondary.

When the Farewell Discourse as a whole is the context for interpreting John 17, it is evident that the themes of Trinity and community are interdependent, though the term 'Trinity' is anachronistic.[84] Francis Watson argues that the underlying logic of John's Gospel is Trinitarian, in that it continually addresses the divinity and unity of Father, Son and Spirit, propelling its hearers toward later councils' conclusions about the Trinity.[85] The triadic God-language in John's Gospel prevents reducing this divine tri-unity to a stark monolith. Thus this language must "be taken with full ontological seriousness: God really and eternally is as this language asserts God to be," so that reading John's Gospel in a Trinitarian light is "to read it retrospectively, in the light of an understanding of God that it does not explicitly assert but that later imposed itself as the appropriate and indeed normative rendering of its theological logic."[86]

Verses 20-23 address the unity of future people of God. The disciples' unity flows from and attests to divine unity; the human unity testifies to God's presence and work, thus supporting the community's identity and message. Given that the community is charged with carrying on Jesus's mission, its credibility and testimony are vital for completing this mission, as

83. Ibid. Kossé specifically contrasts church unity with familial and ethnic unity, which he views as limited and vulnerable, possibly viewing outsiders as enemies.

84. Watson, "Trinity and Community," 171. Indeed, John 17 is clear that Father and Son are not identical though perfectly united. If one fails to distinguish between Father and Son (and Spirit), emphasizing supposed unity without any distinction, the Gospel no longer makes sense (to whom is the Son speaking here?) and one falls into the trap of modalism or some other deficient, heretical view of God. Thus, the text must be read in a trinitarian manner.

85. The prayer in John 17 focuses upon the Father, Son, and the disciples (present and future), without mentioning the Spirit. However, in the preceding chapters (14 and 16) Jesus teaches about the Spirit, so the Spirit has not been overlooked; he is simply not the focus in John 17.

86. Watson, "Trinity and Community," 169, 183.

Okure emphasized. For God's people to display God's love, they must be in community; how else can they witness to the divine unity and love which signifies the new life in their midst?[87]

These verses reveal a complex relationship: the Father is in the Son Jesus, and vice versa. Jesus is also in the Christ-follower (v. 23a), and the Christ-follower is to be in the Father and Son (v. 21b). Certainly, then, one must conclude that Christian unity is grounded in and a result of the divine unity. In fact, Jesus prays that his disciples will participate in the Father and Son's unity (v. 21b), not merely imitate it.[88]

God's people participate in the divine communion because of Christ's work; therefore their unity results from union with Christ.[89] As in the OT, the oneness of God's people "is bound up integrally with the oneness of God."[90] Furthermore, union with Christ and each other is not the *telos*; rather the church's unity is part of its witness to the unbelieving world. The community identified by life and love draws people to Christ:[91] D. G. Van der Merwe describes this aspect of ecclesial unity as its "revelatory-salvific function" because it attests to Christ.[92]

Ukpong highlights the vital role unity plays here: since the Father and Son are one, "belonging to them means being one in them" and with others who belong to them.[93] In other words, the unity—and communal identity—of the disciples does not rely upon "any sociological or anthropological considerations. It arises from the unity of the Godhead to whom the disciples belong."[94] To repeat, Ukpong claims that solidarity in the Christian communal identity arises from the divine, not any cultural preference. Hence the communal identity of God's people should be prioritized everywhere that the church exists. Ukpong draws several implications about the nature of unity from this chapter: believing in Christ means unity with him, unity in faith and in proclaiming the gospel message.[95] Thus the unity Jesus prays about is "essentially invisible," but expressed "in a visible form."[96] Drawing

---

87. Lincoln, *Truth on Trial*, 245.
88. Bruce, *The Gospel of John*, 335.
89. Cadier, "The Unity of the Church," 175.
90. Barton, "Christian Community," 290.
91. Ngewa, *The Gospel of John*, 325. Ngewa comments further that the unity of Christians is, above all, unity "around a person" (326).
92. Van der Merwe, "The Character of Unity," 226.
93. Ukpong, "Jesus' Prayer," 57.
94. Ibid., 58.
95. Ibid.
96. Ibid.

on John's terminology, Ukpong stresses that unity flourishes only where there is love, and hence Christians' verbal witness will be useless "if we do not treat our fellow human beings with love."[97] So one mark of the Christian identity is loving others, whether or not they share that identity. Before concluding, Ukpong emphasizes that

> the type of unity that Jesus talks about transcends racial and national boundaries. It would be a false type of unity if Christians were to feel united to only those of their own national or racial group. The mission of Christians implies also the unity of Christians.[98]

Ukpong, then, understands unity in John 17 as flowing from divine unity and visibly uniting those with faith in Jesus—in other words, giving them a new communal identity marked by love for others and diversity-in-unity. As the quotation above shows, this identity is understood to be primary, to transcend other communal identities.

However, Gert Malan states that this prayer is often misread, arguing that it does not endorse unity but instead encourages tolerance of diversity within the church while simultaneously legitimizing the Johannine community.[99] Yet the article's conclusion views John 17 as a prayer for the Johannine community's unity and solidarity, as well as a probable means to "to legitimize non-confirmation [sic] of the Johannine community with opposing groups, even within the Christian fold. Understood in this way, it should be read as a plea for ecumenical diversity rather than structural, or even theological or confessional, unity."[100]

Malan opposes traditional readings of this passage, but how well does his interpretation represent the text? Despite the prevalence of the terms ἓν and ἐν in the pericope, Malan argues that the passage promotes 'ecumenical diversity'. Ignoring the passage's own language and emphases, however, undermines Malan's argument, and places him in disagreement with the other African scholars here. Even so, Malan touches on a central point ecclesiologies will raise: unity is not uniformity, and the unity between Father and Son, and among God's people, is a unity that includes difference or distinction within itself. Those distinctions cannot be glossed over or suppressed, for they are vital for the type of unity described. Suppression of distinctions is a major concern of every African ecclesiology in the next chapter: true

---

97. Ibid., 59.
98. Ibid.
99. Malan, "Does John?," 1, 4.
100. Ibid., 9.

unity always implies diversity, whether that is diversity of gender, socioeconomic group, ethnicity, language, or other social barriers. A communal identity with a high degree of solidarity does not erase the individual's voice or responsibility, either. Every theologian studied agrees on this point: unity in the church includes diversity, by God's design. Christ unites diverse individuals from all these groups into one new community, giving them a new identity in Christ.

Analyzing the grammar of vv. 20–23, D. G. Van der Merwe applies the tools of discourse analysis. The author charts verses 11, 21, and 22, highlighting their shared terminology and structure. "In all three texts the ἵνα particle is used to indicate that 'unity' is the main objective. The particle of comparison, καθώς, also occurs in all three texts to indicate that the unity to which the disciples are called relates to the unity between the Father and the Son" and has the goal of revealing Jesus to the world.[101] Furthermore, both structurally and theologically vv. 20–21 and 22–23 are equivalent.[102] Where verses 20 and 21 relate the Father-Son relationship, verses 22 and 23 describe Father and Son being 'in' Christ-followers, and Christ-followers are one only when they are 'in' Jesus and the Father. Divine unity and ecclesial unity are not identical, but a significant parallel exists, as is clear from the use of the καθώς particle.

One obvious difference between divine and human unity is that the Father and the Son are 'in' each other, while the disciples cannot be 'in' one another directly, or in the same sense. They "can only become ἕν through their mutual being ἐν Jesus and Jesus being ἐν them."[103] So Christian unity is a result of remaining 'in' Jesus (personally and in union with others 'in' Jesus), and is unity characterized by love. Jesus's love is a self-sacrificing love, as John's Gospel indicates. Thus, for "the disciples, love is a group expression—a disciple's identity is determined by and becomes clear from his relationship with the other disciples."[104] This quotation certainly describes a communal identity: an identity shown by relationships with others of a particular community. This identity requires love for and unity with fellow disciples.

If Van der Merwe's analysis is correct, the unity described in John 17 is not primarily structural, although that type of unity has the potential to be

---

101. Van der Merwe, "The Character of Unity," 226. The crucial nature of ecclesial unity highlighted by Van der Merwe parallels Okure's point that solidarity in this new community—or communal identity—is necessary for the church to fulfill its commission.

102. Ibid., 227.

103. Ibid., 242.

104. Ibid., 243.

one aid or means for God's people to visibly display their accord. The communal identity described in John 17 is founded in unity in Christ; structural unity is not the goal of this text. Per Ngewa, unity in John's Gospel is also not confessional or creedal per se, but unity 'in' Jesus, who is "identified as having been sent from the Father."[105] Strictly speaking, then, this is a personal *and* corporate unity grounded in the Triune God, marked by obedience and self-sacrificial love on the part of a person of God. John 17:24 offers a glimpse of God's eschatological plans: the Sent One, Jesus, returns to the Father, bringing many others with him. Christ's mission is restoration of communion in broken relationships: this is a divine priority, not just a cultural emphasis of Africans. The Christian communal identity assumes a place of preeminence with regard to other communal identities, restoring relationships among those whose prior communal identities had divided them.

Several ecclesiologies in the next chapter link Christian communal identity to the Trinity. By contrast, some scholars may be uncomfortable with what may seem like a move toward strongly social trinitarianism. Yet this move is actually better understood as involving a relational view of the Triune God, whose eternal communion is the source of human communion in Christ. The doctrine of the Trinity is applicable to other *loci* of systematic theology, particularly ecclesiology, without necessarily entailing a mere projection of human ideals onto God. Indeed, the "question of who God is" will always be "*the* theological question," and therefore "contemporary trinitarian theology is right to understand the doctrine of the Trinity as the comprehensive context for all theological reflection."[106] To speak of an 'analogy' between Triune unity and ecclesial unity is, at its most basic, to insist there is some relationship involving similarity as well as dissimilarity—not univocal identity. The doctrine of the Trinity does not answer all questions about ecclesiology. But it is crucial to insist that who God is, however mysterious that Triune existence may be, has some bearing on the identity of God's people, calling them to a unified communal identity characterized by love. This is simply an acknowledgement of God's relational nature and the identity of God's people as image-bearers.

1 Corinthians 12:12–27

Where John 17 focuses on the unity of God's people, 1 Corinthians 12 examines the relationship of diversity to that united communal identity—hence the reason it has been a much-used text in African ecclesiologies. This

---

105. Ngewa, *The Gospel of John*, 325.
106. Watson, "Trinity and Community," 170.

text presupposes that diversity is necessary for a healthy, functional body. First Corinthians addresses a congregation Paul had mentored, which in his absence was experiencing conflict and dissension. Thus Paul wrote to them, emphasizing the true nature of the gospel, the Christian identity, and the lifestyle that reflected them.

In chapter 12 Paul discusses diversity and unity—specifically, the diversity of gifts and roles from the Spirit, and the unity brought about by the Spirit in whom it is both possible and essential for diverse people to function as a single organism. The pericope repeats 'one' five times in the first two verses.[107] Some scholars focus on the latter verses, particularly vv. 28–30, employing them in discussions about the spiritual gifts (their number and importance), and debates about whether particular ones have ceased. Yet the majority of the chapter focuses on unity and the interdependence of the various parts. Paul urges the Corinthians to put an end to their divisive ways (1 Cor 1:10–12) and be of one mind.

This is not the first or only time Paul uses the body analogy.[108] Here he emphasizes unity, but not at all a stultifying, homogenous uniformity; rather, the body functions properly only if its various members each perform their distinct roles. Paul makes a point of saying that all members are to be treated honorably, regardless of whether they are areas of the body considered unseemly, feeble, or even shameful. The diverse roles assigned to the multiple parts are clearly intentional, and seen as a necessity by God who created the body (v. 18). The three-in-one God values both similarities and differences in relationships with others, and finite humans all the more so need other persons to broaden their perspectives and do what they cannot.

African readings of 1 Cor 12:12–27 often focus on the communal aspect of Paul's imagery; this text provides yet more biblical support in favor of a relational perspective and the nature of the communal identity of God's people. For example, the *Africa Bible Commentary* only specifically mentions two gifts (apostle, administrator), focusing instead on Christian unity, both in suffering and in joy. Two African proverbs express the point in a less propositional way: "The left hand washes the right and the right hand

---

107. Verses 12–13, ESV; in Greek ἕν [2x], ἑνὶ, and σῶμα and πνεῦμα (both in the singular; hence the English gloss 'one').

108. This Pauline imagery of God's people as a single 'body [in Christ]' appears in other passages, such as Eph 3:6, 4:12, 5:23; Col 1:24, 3:11–15; Gal 3:26–28. All these passages describe God's people as a single body, in Christ, due to the work of Christ and the Spirit: 'A strange family in the world/one source, one final goal/one body, though not yet whole' (Furler, "Unified"). Being in this body entails participation and certain actions toward others in it, in order to maintain unity.

washes the left" and "One hand cannot lift a [heavy] load."[109] It is impossible and inconceivable that a person lives and succeeds totally independent of others. Datiri focuses on the interdependence and communal nature of humanity; implicitly, these two proverbs also suggest a need for diversity, for the 'other.'

Paul highlights the body's unity; in other words, the corporate angle—communal identity—is his first concern. The weight of the verses themselves supports this argument: the majority of the chapter details common bonds unifying God's people (their shared identity markers). The specific, varying gifts allow the body to function in a healthy manner, enabling it to fulfill its purpose. If diversity were lost, the body would be irreparably impaired; in fact, it would no longer be a body at all. The gifts are given for the good of the whole community: they are vital components in its identity.

The congregation's purpose is to be God's dwelling place, a community that above all loves in a sacrificial, selfless way (1 Cor 13), as modeled by their Lord. This purpose involves relationships, for (biblical) love is not solitary. Love is a verb—involving motion and deed—that requires a recipient. Love entails relationship. As the triune God is always in relation, God likewise intends that beings made in the divine image should also be integrated into relationships among fellow people of God.

If the community and its nature rather than the individual is the frame of reference, then the closing verses about gifts may be read differently. Since the thrust of the passage is about being unified and working in harmony, the final verses (noting differences) should not receive greater attention. An individualistic reading goes against the grain of the text, repeating in a new context the old Corinthian error of divisiveness. Such readings, then, do not offer an alternative viewpoint, but in fact misinterpret the text. It is insufficient to only seek to discover what God says about individual people and gifts; the next step is to seek to understand the purpose of these gifts, which are community-oriented. There is a crippling danger on the solitary road; all parts of the body working in interdependent unity is the way to health, to an identity reflecting the wholeness of the Triune God.

Nigerian Pandang Yamsat identifies the letter's theme as "the need for partnership or solidarity with fellow believers in the blessing (1:2–5) of Christ who has invited us into his partnership (1:9). This thesis that believers are partners in the work or things of Christ and not rivals, cuts across every issue that is dealt with in this letter, except may be [sic] chapter 15, but even this exception is debatable."[110] An extended argument buttressing Yamsat's

---

109. Datiri, "1 Corinthians," 1392.

110. Yamsat, *An Exposition of First Corinthians*, 16, 19. Again we see the link between

position comes from Margaret Mitchell, who makes an impressive case built upon extensive comparison with other ancient rhetorical texts, that each of the "theological motifs [in the letter] is knitted into Paul's deliberative argument for the elimination of factionalism. The result is a coherent and systematic ecclesiology."[111] Mitchell further notes that this interpretation of the letter agrees with early Christian interpretations of it, lending further credence to Yamsat's position.[112]

Indeed, Mitchell identifies still another parallel: common *topoi* of rhetorical arguments occur in 1 Corinthians. With regard to 1 Corinthians 12, two of these elements are particularly pertinent: first, the appeal to end factionalism and seek concord, and second, an appeal to τὸ συμφέρον (*utilitas*, advantage). For example, in 6:12 Paul repeats a Corinthian slogan about freedom to do what one wants. This slogan "assumes that the answer [of whose advantage to consider when making a decision] . . . is 'the individual.' Paul counters by defining the basic sphere of advantage for the Christian not as the individual, but as the entire ἐκκλησία."[113] Mitchell's point supports the arguments of Mulago, Bediako, Oduyoye, and the scholars of this chapter who argue that the Christian communal identity is foundational.

This ecclesial focus is reflected in Paul's discussion of the church as a body, with the joy or honor of one part affecting all the others (12:26). The concern with schisms and the urging of unity are reflected in Paul's language of 'building up' into a single unit. Paul repeatedly urges the Corinthian Christians to cease fighting for their own advantage and honor, replacing those attitudes with selfless love for fellow Christians. Their true interests "are only served when those of the entire community are served. . . . This whole appeal is substantiated by Paul throughout the epistle by his insistence upon the communal identity of the Corinthians," one example being the 'body of Christ' imagery in chapter 12.[114] Yamsat offers an analogy from his own culture, where

> unity and beauty is not in one color or several colors mixed together into one color, but in a combination of several colors in the same dress. Each of them retain their identity while they all relate to each other to form a beautiful material. In unity, we do

---

solidarity in the Christian identity and the community's mission.

111. Mitchell, *Paul and the Rhetoric of Reconciliation*, 5 n. 12.
112. Ibid.,, 17–18.
113. Ibid., 36.
114. Ibid., 37.

not lose our identity but share our identity with others to form a common and more beautiful identity.[115]

From Yamsat's perspective unity is drastically different than uniformity, which is undesirable and even the opposite of Paul's point in this passage.[116] In fact, God's people should value their different gifts, and "*see each other as indispensable within the community of faith. No one can claim to have nothing to give for the nourishment of God's people and none can claim to have everything that God's people need.*"[117] The communal identity Paul advocates is marked by interdependence, despite the trend toward individualism in many cultures today.[118] Also, Yamsat's analogy raises the point that other communal identities are not lost in this type of unity—instead, they contribute to a new shared identity, which encompasses the previous identities.

Yamsat argues that Paul's desire is to combat factionalism. The book's opening verses highlight this goal: what is significant in the address is that all share a common call, thanks to God's grace, and this common call makes them partners in the saving work of God.[119] Paul addresses the Corinthians as 'the called ones,' attempting "to replace old terms of ethnic identification with a single, unified identification for the members of the church community."[120] Yamsat later concludes that because all receive the Spirit at conversion and are united with Christ and each other, "racial and social distinctions that used to separate us" lose their force as the common identity in Christ becomes more important.[121] These differences can and should exist, per the body metaphor, but they should not separate people. Paul does not urge uniformity. Rather, "in 1 Cor 12:24 . . . he depicts the creation of the community at God's hands using . . . [a] technical term for the 'mixed constitution' in Greek political thought. . . . Like Numa and Alexander the Great, Paul in 1 Corinthians is attempting to create solidarity within a new political group; that group, too, is a 'mix' of what were previously different social communities," a new communal identity.[122]

---

115. Yamsat, *An Exposition of First Corinthians*, 154–55.

116. Yamsat returns to the topic of the nature of unity later, insisting that "we do not all have to agree on something to show that we are united, because unity is not the same thing as uniformity" (ibid., 165).

117. Ibid., 167, italics original.

118. Ibid., 161.

119. Ibid., 17, 18.

120. Mitchell, *Paul and the Rhetoric of Reconciliation*, 88.

121. Yamsat, *An Exposition of First Corinthians*, 165.

122. Mitchell, *Paul and the Rhetoric of Reconciliation*, 115.

The 'body' metaphor assumes and relies upon the understanding that a body has different parts, each with its own function. Diversity is a presupposition; urging unity and concord is the goal. Indeed, the specific organs Paul mentions (hands and feet, eyes and ears, the necessity of weaker or shameful parts) are those used in other ancient rhetorical speeches. Thus, Mitchell determines that Paul applies "a common political metaphor to the Corinthian situation, Christianizing it" by applying it to the Spirit-unified body of Christ.[123] Love and 'building up' combat factionalism—hence the placement of 1 Corinthians 13.[124] Yamsat concludes that the various gifts and roles within the body mean that no person is independent of others; instead, all of God's people are indispensable for the proper functioning of Christ's body.[125] What is crucial in gifting is whether one's gifts are used with love to edify the community: otherwise, the gifts fail to meet their intended purpose.[126] This communal identity, then, is designed by God to have a high degree of solidarity and interdependence.

Literary analysis aside, "we can expect on sociological grounds that the Corinthian divisions would naturally exert great influence on whole church gatherings."[127] Differences between Jew and Greek, slave and free, male and female, higher and lower social status, one spiritual gift and another—all these would influence times of common worship, as reflected in the issues raised in 11:2–14:40. Paul does not suggest erasing differences but erasing barriers to fellowship. The reality of being 'in Christ' and having the one Spirit matters more than gaining power or honor over others in the congregation. In fact, the differences are God-ordained, aspects to value rather than denigrate, as Yamsat's analogy of the colorful clothes emphasized.[128] Thus, Paul urges them to excel in love, valuing all persons and their differences. Since the love of Christ is other-centered love, when the Corinthians act with this type of love they will reflect Christ and their new shared identity in him. This is, in a nutshell, Yamsat's reading, focused on the aspects most relevant to 1 Corinthians 12 and confirmed by rhetorical and other trends in non-African scholarship.

Elsewhere in the book Paul encourages people to stay in the state in which they were found (7:17–24, 26), and endorses, to some degree, different practices in worship for men and women (11:4–15). Paul's body metaphor

---

123. Ibid., 159–60.
124. Ibid., 165–68.
125. Yamsat, *An Exposition of First Corinthians*, 167.
126. Ibid., 171.
127. Mitchell, *Paul and the Rhetoric of Reconciliation*, 259.
128. Cf. ibid., 268.

requires different roles among the members of the body. Further, the apostle does not suggest that the 'strong' stand by their rights, their freedom to do what they believe is not wrong; rather, he asks the 'strong' not to offend the weak or cause them to go astray (8:7-13). He recommends sacrificing personal freedoms for the community's sake (9:19-22; 10:23-33).

By this Paul is not endorsing some form of patriarchal, hierarchical unity, which is hegemonic and oppressive.[129] As Mitchell and others have noted, Paul takes up a common metaphor of his day (the body)[130] and uses it to promote unity, but adapts the model. Rhetoricians typically used the body analogy to speak against revolt and urge the lower classes to submit to their social superiors. But "strikingly, Paul's use of the argument moves in precisely the opposite direction. He urges the strong (probably the well-to-do) to give more honor and respect to the weak, and so cease *their* factious behaviors."[131] Instead of considering themselves independent from the lower-status persons in the church, Paul reminds all Christians, including the few of relatively higher status, that "God has deliberately made the members of Christ's body interdependent so that all would have concern for the others (v. 25)."[132] God's people reflect God's triune nature, so they too are called to respect each other's differences while maintaining unity in Christ.[133]

Further support for Yamsat's reading of unity-with-diversity comes from Bruce Hansen's examination of the baptismal formula in 1 Cor 12:13, Gal 3:28, and Col 3:11. Hansen notes that "the formulaic affirmation that unity in Christ overcomes the social divisions, Jew versus Greek and slave versus free, etc., is arguably the most prominent refrain in the Pauline corpus. Not only is this formula universally recognized in the three aforementioned verses, many also suspect its influence on the phrasing of Rom 3:9; 10:12; 1 Cor 1:22, 24; 7:18-22; 10:32; and Eph 6:8," and no other Pauline

---

129. Yung Suk Kim correctly diagnoses problems with Gerd Theissen's picture of 'love-patriarchalism' in the church (*Christ's Body in Corinth*, 16-17). Ben Witherington III likewise argues that Paul's approach in 1 Corinthians "represents a strong attempt to reform certain kinds of patriarchal and hierarchical structures in society. Paul seems to have been more of a reformer, within the Christian assembly, of existing power structures than Theissen seems to think" (*Conflict and Community*, 29).

130. Mitchell mentions various possibilities with regard to the background of the body metaphor (Stoic, gnostic, OT, Christian eucharist, rabbinic speculation on Adam's body), and recommends Hainz's *Ekklesia* for further study (*Paul and the Rhetoric of Reconciliation*, 157 n. 554).

131. Witherington, *Conflict and Community*, 254, italics in original.

132. Ibid., 261.

133. 1 Cor 12:4-6 contains what Witherington terms an "implicit trinitarianism" (ibid., 257).

tradition occurs as frequently and as widely.[134] However, prominence does not equal clarity; thus Hansen explores "what Paul wishes to alter about the named statuses . . . as well as what sort of unity he envisions."[135]

First, Hansen observes that the formula "turns on the implied tension between unity and diversity" in a way that "emphasizes its social effects," suggesting that the "tension implicit in the formula may be between social inclusion and exclusion, between social privilege and social marginalization."[136] While Daniel Boyarin argues that Paul seeks to create a generic, universal human by suppressing differences, Hansen counters that Paul is not "erasing particularity" but instead "rejecting dominance and marginalization in a socio-culturally diverse church."[137] Hansen's case fits with Yamsat's argument and echoes the concerns of Elochukwu Uzukwu, Paul Mbandi, and others in the next chapter. So what sort of relationship exists among these diverse people?

David Horrell proposes that the unity Paul envisions involves a religio-ethnic type of solidarity, where loyalty to Christ is the "new primary loyalty" and identity. Building upon Horrell's proposal, Hansen further specifies that "in each epistle where the formula occurs . . . it supports an ethnic vision of ecclesial unity wherein cultural conflict is to be governed by appeal to *imitatio Christi*."[138] The formula "supports Paul's construal of the believers as a new ethnic group patterned on the identity of Israel as re-envisioned through Christ," and Paul takes up "both the vocabulary and special logic of kinship in order to persuade his audience."[139] The apostle continually refers to common ancestors, a common homeland, familial terminology, and a common cult: in Paul's world, these derive from kinship. For instance, Paul continually appeals to God as their father, as a result of their identity with Jesus. Christians share common ancestors in the faith—Abraham, Israel, and so forth—and Paul addresses them as 'brothers and sisters.' In other

---

134. Hansen, "All of You Are One," 1, 2.

135. Ibid., 4.

136. Ibid., 7.

137. Ibid., 11–15. Hansen also examines a range of possible sources from which Paul could have drawn his formula: Hellenistic philosophy, Gnosticism, and Judaism. Regardless of which source(s) Paul drew from, what matters most is what he did with these opposing pairs, and what sort of community he envisioned for them 'in Christ.'

138. Ibid., 25.

139. Ibid., 31, 32. By 'ethnic,' Hansen means an identity that is socially constructed, flexible, and mutable; it is not about actual biological descent (though it is ascribed at birth), but is actually a subjective perception (34–35). Ethnicity gets at a person's most basic identity, a presumed (common) origin; in like manner, "we find the identity urged in each Pauline epistle . . . to constitute a foundational identity, trumping other loyalties, and expecting difficult social reorganization" (38).

words, Paul uses 'ethnicity markers' when describing Christians. It is "on the basis of their presumed kinship [that] Paul urges familial concord," directing Christians to show mercy, care for the weak, and so forth—all of which "reflect an ethos that in antiquity would be appropriate only within the family or clan."[140] Like a clan, they share a common story of origin, are to marry only certain people, and eat together. These and other markers in Paul's letters indicate that Paul may envision an ethnic type of solidarity. In particular, Paul's body analogy in 1 Corinthians 12 "participates in the typical symbolism of ethnic unity," and other recent works "have demonstrated the frequent use of the body metaphor in antiquity to picture the ideal of fraternal harmony."[141]

The body metaphor ties in with a concern of the previous chapter: how previously existing communal identities relate to the Christian identity. There is a great difference between a universalizing, homogenizing unity and a unity that integrates diversity without 'flattening' it. Applying the work of D. Horowitz, Hansen notes that there are two types of integration into a new group: either incorporation—group A adopting group B's identity—or amalgamation, where group A and group B form a new entity, group C. Amalgamation does not require one group to renounce its own history and communal identity, but creates a larger identity within which both groups can live in harmony. Paul, facing a church divided by class, cultural background, and more, does not advocate that Gentiles live by Jewish rules, or that all persons within the church must play the same roles. Instead, these diverse identities can exist within the church as long as their first priority and loyalty is to the Christian communal identity. Thus Paul is willing to follow Jewish custom for himself (Acts 18:18), but later speaks of being 'like' a Jew to the Jews, and 'like' a Gentile to Gentiles, becoming all things to all people (1 Cor 9:19–22). Paul's statement that in Christ there are no distinctions is hyperbolic in the sense that Paul finds these distinct identities less important than their common bond in Christ. However, as the rest of his actions and words make clear, distinctions do continue to exist among Christians, and differences are not inherently bad; these distinctions only become problematic when they result in a unloving, judgmental attitudes toward others and communal divisions. Not incidentally, Paul's use of the body metaphor supports the arguments of theologians in Africa that African identity need not be excluded from Christian identity.

Hansen thus rejects Boyarin's interpretation that Paul attempts to erase particularity, noting that Boyarin "can account for only one social identity at

140. Ibid., 46, 47.
141. Ibid., 49.

a time," whereas social scientists—and Paul—"make abundantly clear that maintaining multiple, overlapping social identities is the norm."[142] Hansen proposes that Paul does not allow "indices of other identities to cause division within his churches," raising the question, What aspects of Christian identity "does Paul consider inviolable and thus to be norms before which conflicting indices of other identities must cede?"[143] Based on 1 Corinthians 12 and 13, it is not hard to see why Hansen concludes that "social (ethnic) solidarity in Christ and Christologically-defined other-regard are the core of Paul's ecclesial vision."[144]

At the opening of chapter 12, Paul gestures to a pre-Christian past, when they were "pagans," or rather, ἔθνη (v. 2). "Here Paul can unproblematically refer to their former status as ἔθνη, as if they have now become covenant insiders," because through Christ who has united them the Corinthian Christians are now identified as the singular people of God.[145] All have been baptized into one body and share the Spirit in common (v. 13). With different pasts, roles, and social statuses, each person is necessary (v. 21–22). The members are to appreciate and honor each other, taking care of each other (v. 25–26). The contrasts in v. 13 followed by the declaration of unity in one body "concisely asserts [Paul's] conclusion that the unity of the body alters understanding of ethnicity [and other differences] in the church."[146] By contrasting former communal identities with their new identity, Paul implies that the Christians now compose an alternate group.[147] In other words, what Paul hopes to change about these other identities is their level of relevance.

Paul's goal is a reconciled community "comprised of members who were formerly socially alienated."[148] In sum, unity "in their new identity as God's people is a sign of the new thing that God is doing through the cross and resurrection of Christ."[149] Representing the new creation means reflecting Christ's cross by displaying sacrificial, other-focused love. Because visible unity and harmony are vital to Christian witness (John 17), Paul asks the Corinthians to avoid activities that offend others, placing loyalty to

---

142. Ibid., 61–62.
143. Ibid., 63.
144. Ibid.
145. Ibid., 116.
146. Ibid., 119.
147. Ibid., 125.
148. Ibid., 128.

149. Ibid., 129–30. In the next chapter, we will see that Mbandi's ecclesiology affirms this same point, particularly in his study of Ephesians 2.

Christ and love for God's people before personal freedom (1 Corinthians 9–10). Thus, while diversity is vital for the church's life, Paul places it in its proper context of Christian unity here, due to the Corinthian problem of factionalism. At the same time, the legitimate diversity described in the chapter cannot be forgotten: diversity of gifts and roles—and thus diversity of perspectives—brings richness and health to the body. Paul does not forsake diversity; rather, he highlights that God-given diversity lovingly makes the united body healthy.

Galatians 3:26–28

Nigerian Bernard Onyebuchi Ukwuegbu identifies these verses as the climax of Galatians 3, and also as the climax of Paul's argument in the book.[150] However, contrary to such readings of the implications of 1 Corinthians 12, some scholars read Galatians 3 as suppressing differences in the Christian communal identity. Accordingly, we need to consider what they teach with respect to differences within the united Christian identity.

Like Ukwuegbu, Bruce Hansen understands "all of you are one in Christ Jesus" as showing that social unity is Paul's concern in this chapter.[151] From Paul's viewpoint, a separation between Jewish- and Gentile-background Christians would be a ministry failure, because "a united church . . . is for Paul the essential goal of the gospel."[152] Ukwuegbu argues that because reconciliation 'in Christ' grounds Paul's message, "when it comes to compromising on this principle, on what in his language is the 'truth of the Gospel,' he is ready to fight. . . . His conflict with Peter over table-fellowship between Jewish and Gentile Christians in Antioch shows how far Paul is ready to go in defending the practical consequences of the common identity 'in Christ.'"[153]

Paul preaches Christ, the reconciler between God and humans, and among humans. From issues Paul deals with in the letters historically attributed to him, it is clear that ethnicity, social status, and gender were not eliminated within the church, nor did Paul believe that these factors were irrelevant in the church's functioning.[154] Yet Jewish- and

---

150. Ukwuegbu, *The Emergence of Christian Identity*, 308; cf. Hansen, "All of You Are One," 67.

151. Hansen, "All of You Are One," 67.

152. Ibid., 69.

153. Ukwuegbu, *Emergence of Christian Identity*, 324.

154. Some scholars suggest that Paul fails to be consistent on this point (for example, in comparison with 1 Cor. 12:12–13), others try to harmonize the passages,

Gentile-background Christians were called to share table fellowship, showing that the gospel must produce social effects; it cannot be relegated to the realm of the 'spiritual' or 'theological' alone, as some have disingenuously argued (assuming that such a dichotomy between social and theological realms were even possible).[155]

Accordingly, Ukwuegbu and the ecclesiologies of chapter 5 argue that Paul's goal is not to repress or destroy differences. Rather, Paul's concern is that no one group should dominate in God's people; there should be no social exclusion and marginalization.[156] Pauline theology bears the imprint of the cross; hence Paul often refers to dualisms: in the cosmos where there are competing powers, and in terms of two distinct ages divided by God's judgment. In Galatians, Paul emphasizes that the Christian identity means participating in the new creation. Participation in the new creation requires a decisive break with the old creation. Thus, "the binary social divisions expressed by the formula fall on the cosmos side of the Christ-versus-cosmos duality. Conversely, 'all of you are one in Christ Jesus' (3:28d) corresponds to the new creation" marked by reconciliation and unity, not alienation and division.[157] Unity among previously alienated groups indicates the new creation at work in the Galatians.[158] There is only one gospel, one way to God, and hence all who embrace that unique gospel join the singular community it produces.[159]

Gal 3:26–28 emphasizes that identity in Christ is a Christian's first and foremost allegiance: all other loyalties are relativized alongside this new

---

and still others suggest Paul did not intend to be systematic and consistent. Ukwuegbu rejects these options, and here agrees with Daniel Boyarin, who resolves this apparent paradox with the reminder that Paul wrote these two passages from "different discursive political contexts" (*Emergence of Christian Identity*, 319, citing Boyarin, *A Radical Jew: Paul and the Politics of Identity*.

155. For example, Troy W. Martin finds these verses simply verifying that all are allowed entry into God's people ("The Covenant of Circumcision," 111–25).

156. Aune, "Galatians 3:28," 164, and Hansen, "*All of You Are One*," 73. Hansen suggests that the reason why Paul refuses to force Gentiles to live like Jews is "that capitulation would enshrine the boundary markers of one particular culture as normative for the church." Hansen further argues that the logic of the cross supports Paul's argument, as seen in 2:14c–21, where "the pattern of Christ's self-giving for the redemption of others suggests that in settings of differential power or privilege, the privileged members ought to be the ones who sacrifice their status for the sake of unity" (79). Thus the other-focused, self-denying love revealed on the cross compels Christ's followers to selflessly love others and deny their own privileges and power as much as possible.

157. Hansen, "*All of You Are One*," 85.

158. See John 17.

159. Hansen, "*All of You Are One*," 86. Regarding solidarity among God's people in the Galatian epistle, see Manus, *Intercultural Hermeneutics*, 55–66.

identity.[160] Christians are one in Christ, belonging to him, together God's children by participation in Christ, jointly heirs of God's promises. Congolese Mulago described this divinely created union as "far more sublime, far more beautiful than the *Bantu vital union* . . . and at the same time more mysterious."[161] Paul makes the case that "God's covenant with Abraham has been fulfilled uniquely in Jesus Christ and that only those identified with him may share in it. Moreover, this singularity of Christ has negated all other criteria for participation, including, most prominently, the [Jewish] law," so "nothing from the cosmos side of that duality must be allowed to undermine what God is doing in Christ, which is precisely forming a new people identified with him."[162]

God's people share a collective identity that Paul describes in kinship terms: they are offspring and heirs of God. The term 'ethnic' can be substituted for 'kinship'; Paul affirms that all God's people are one new people in Christ.[163] Hansen justifies this conclusion by asking, What 'one' thing do people become? Because the other adjectives in verse 28 refer to different social groups—Jew, Greek, slave, free, male and female—Hansen concludes that Paul expects his readers to supply the term 'people.' The 'one' thing they become are "one kind of people," "a collective new humanity."[164] Because Paul's goal in Galatians is to help God's people realize the unity of their new identity, here he does not explain how to handle differences within the church. Buell and Hodge agree that Gal 3:28 "can be seen as an attempt to define a communal vision in terms of ethnicity—not over against ethnicity."[165] Ethnicity and religion are "intertwined and mutually constituting," so that "religious practices both produce and reinforce kinship ties."[166]

---

160. Ukwuegbu, *Emergence of Christian Identity*, 311. Aune quotes Troels Engberg-Pedersen, who notes that those in Christ focus on the characteristic they all share, their incorporation in Christ, which is a communitarian (not modern individualistic) understanding of self-identity ("Galatians 3:28," 175).

161. Mulago, *Un Visage africain*, 193, italics in original; cf. Mulago, "Nécessité de l'adaptation," 40.

162. Hansen, "All of You Are One," 89, 90. Thus Paul "does not need to ban law observance per se, but only law observance as essential to identification with Christ" (95). The law and other cultural or social group markers are permitted, if they do not conflict with Christian identity and are not imposed as a requirement upon other Christians, since Christ has fulfilled all God's requirements and is heir to all the promises.

163. Ibid., 98–99.

164. Ibid., 101.

165. Buell and Hodge, "The Politics of Interpretation," 238. They advocate that Paul employs "ethnic reasoning," which entails various strategies used to "construe collective identity in terms of peoplehood."

166. Ibid., 243. Ukwuegbu comments that the Jew-Greek divide "was national in

In Christ people take on a new ethnicity, in a sense: they are now God's children in Christ.

Chinese Lung-kwong Lo too argues that Gal 3:28 is wrongly interpreted if the reader thinks that Paul urges unity in Christ "by erasing diversities of ethnic identities."[167] Lo rejects the idea that Paul desires to abrogate differences between Christians. Rather, Paul calls for "a new social value system that implies a new nature of an existing social relationship which eventually will transform the social reality."[168] According to Lo, Paul's goal in Gal 3:28 is the destruction of hostile relationships between these groups, which would mean that ethnic differences and other differences (gender, social status, socio-economic) may remain "but not the value judgment" of them.[169] Ukwuegbu believes that when differences cease to provoke divisions and hegemonic impulses, when "men and women treat each other as true brothers and sisters in Christ regardless of their social standing, then the power of such distinctions is broken and a basis is laid for social change."[170] Equality across social lines is Paul's as-yet-unrealized hope for the Galatian Christian community.

Nigerian Chris Ukachukwu Manus interprets the verse similarly, arguing that Paul's letter to the Galatians was occasioned by the pressure for Gentile Christians to conform to Jewish practices. So, when reading Gal 3:28, it must be understood that it "opens on the larger purview of freedom from any form of human alienations and structures that imperil the development of the real *humanum*."[171] Situating Galatians 3:28 in the framework of other Pauline writings, he notes how Paul treats the socially differentiated groups of Gal 3:26–28 in other contexts. For example, Paul elsewhere articulates views that rest on women being distinct from men, indicating that he does view men and women as possessing relevant differences, or else he would not argue so strongly about it. Likewise, Paul approves of Jewish Christians who wish to continue certain Jewish religious practices—hence his willingness to take a vow in the temple (Acts 21:26) and have Timothy circumcised

---

many respects, but the depth of feeling (at least from the Jewish perspective) came from the fact that it was also religious" (*Emergence of Christian Identity*, 317). Ukwuegbu seems to be working, then, with an implicit idea of nationality and ethnicity being linked to some extent, at least for Jews.

167. Lo, "'Neither Jew nor Greek,'" 26. Lo differentiates quite sharply between race and ethnicity, and believes the issue in Galatia was a problem of ethnic division (ibid., 28 n. 15).

168. Ibid., 29.

169. Ibid., 31–32.

170. Ukwuegbu, *Emergence of Christian Identity*, 318.

171. Manus, "Galatians 3:28," 20.

(Acts 16:3). According to this logic, then, Paul is not inconsistent when vehemently protesting an attempt to circumcise Titus (Gal 2:3) and rebuking Peter for withdrawing from eating with Gentile Christians (Gal 2:14). For Paul, such behavior contradicts the gospel itself, because Christ frees Christians from the bonds of their past, and their new primary loyalty is not to inherited traditions or anything else, but to Christ.[172]

Both Ukwuegbu and Manus interpret 'there is not man *and* (kai) woman' as an allusion to Gen 1:27, which stresses equality of male and female before God as bearers of the divine image. Manus concludes, then, that Paul "does not encourage the suppression of the natural difference [between the genders] but that 'in Christ' the difference is immaterial," or not of first importance, as Oduyoye too argues.[173] So the 'one' thing that Christians become in Christ is one person or body. When Gal 3:26–28 and 1 Corinthians 12 are compared, it is clear that "the coming into being of this one family in which all barriers of tribe, culture and social status are broken down is the wonder which fills Paul's vision."[174] Applying Gal 3:26–28 to Nigeria, Manus presses the reader to acknowledge that "ethno-tribal," socio-political, and gender differences

> and discrimination should have no place in our midst. Justice demands that no one group holds the power to exploit another. Though not immediately mentioned in the text under study, Paul's cherished concept of the *adelphoi*, brethren, should guide and motivate all our interpersonal relationships and no longer the natural and the ontological basis of our being Hausa or Fulani, Ibo or Yoruba, etc. First and foremost, we are Christians, Nigerians, then Hausa, Yoruba or Ibo, etc. Certainly for Paul, tribal or racial differences like those of sex are a matter of nature,

---

172. The situation of modern-day Christians coming from non-Christian backgrounds and ancient Jews who became Christians is not an exact parallel. Jewish laws are based on divine revelation from YHWH. Modern-day Christians in Africa who come from an African religious background, however, are a different story. Their cultural and religious practices do not have the same level of authority. However, the situation of modern-day non-African Christians forcing their cultural expectations upon African churches is similar to the Judaizing problem Paul confronts, in that it is an attempt to force one culture to abide by another's practices as if they were sacrosanct in the gospel, when to the contrary in light of Christ those practices are not to be considered requirements for a Christ-follower. Thus the concern of Galatians with legalism stemming from cultural hegemony is pertinent as ever.

173. Manus, "Paul's Attitude towards Ethnicity," 23.

174. Ibid., 24.

immutable and irreversible, but in Christ and as Christians the differences are inconsequent.[175]

So Manus, Ukwuegbu, Lo, and others argue that one's priorities and values are re-ordered when one becomes God's child and enters God's family. Being 'in Christ' does not erase differences, which explains Paul's diametrically opposed responses to the issue of circumcision depending on the circumstance: Paul discerns an appropriate response based on each unique situation. In Galatia, Paul opposes forcing the law upon Gentile Christians, but he does not deny Jewish Christians the opportunity to observe their traditions, provided those traditions are secondary to their loyalty to and freedom in Christ.[176]

Bernard Ukwuegbu maintains that "the Christian message eschews any possibility of the hegemony of one culture" over another in the Christian community.[177] In his opinion, post-Constantinian Christianity became locked into a single cultural form: that of Hellenistic culture. Thus, when missionaries came to Africa centuries later, "the fact that the preaching of the gospel was so closely associated with the spread of colonialism made it unavoidable for the Church to become an agent for cultural imperialism."[178] For Ukwuegbu, a proper reading of Paul views the Christ-event as the "decisive eschatological act of God," which brings freedom and new life, seen in the church. Aspects that formerly caused separation and division

---

175. Ibid.

176. This interpretation opposes the position taken by Wayne A. Meeks in "The Image of the Androgyne" 165–208. Meeks believes that Paul draws upon Gnosticism, and the idea of erasing sexual differences. He concedes that Paul adapts this imagery somewhat, and concludes that Paul's instructions about women in worship therefore reflect "solely the *symbols* that distinguish male from female," and, in Corinth, a concern "with *order*" (201, 203, italics original), without inconsistency on Paul's part. The African theologians here agree that Paul is not inconsistent, but they differ with Meeks that Paul aims to erase differences, or that he envisions uniformity for God's people. For an analysis of Paul's possible reliance on Rabbinic literature, see Uzukwu, "Gal 3:28," 370–92. She also frames her study of Rom 16:1–16 with Gal 3:28, reading Romans 16 as a "practical response" and fulfillment of Gal 3:28 ("The Oneness of the Believers" 779). She reads Rom 16:1–16 in this way because it mentions "26 names which include Christian Jews, Greeks, slaves, free men and women, male and female, [which] illustrates Paul's message that the believing community is a community where racial, social and gender distinctions are overcome" (780). Gal 3:28 speaks about how the Christian community should be composed of people from various groups "because the privileges attached to their differences are overcome" (781). This qualification clarifies that the concern is not the distinctions themselves, but divisions, special privileging, and power differences in the community.

177. Ukwuegbu, "'Neither Jew nor Greek,'" 305.

178. Ibid., 306.

among people "are no longer decisive," though differences still remain; "Paul does not seek to 'erase' or 'eradicate' cultural specificities, but to *relativise* them."[179] These identities continue to exist; what Paul does away with is dominance and hegemony in the Christian identity. "Paul succeeds in *affirming* both Jews and Gentiles in their cultural particularities, while at the same time *humbling* them in their cultural hegemonic or absolutist pretensions."[180] Ukwuegbu understands equality in Christ as a theological and social reality, based on factors such as Paul's call for ecclesial table fellowship. Envisioning this type of Christian identity, Ukwuegbu describes Christians relating "to each other in the midst of our many differences with mutuality and equality."[181] Christians need not—and ought not, per 1 Corinthians 12—seek to disregard or remove all their differences; God does not ask that distinctions in the church be ignored or done away with, and indeed the Pauline corpus as a whole indicates that God values differences and incorporates them into Christ's Body so that it will function properly.[182]

To draw these threads together with an additional, extensive study of Galatians 3, we turn to Senegalese Aliou Cissé Niang's *Faith and Freedom in Galatia and Senegal: The Apostle Paul, Colonists and Sending Gods*.[183] Niang compares Galatians 2 and 3 with the historical and sociological traits of his own people, the Diola of Senegal, arguing that Paul is "a sociopostcolo-

---

179. Ibid., 308, italics in original. Samuel Ngewa's popular-level commentary on Galatians makes a similar point. Although Ngewa initially states that the differences that divide people "should cease to exist in Christ," this may be somewhat hyperbolic language, or simply imprecise choice of words, for he goes on to discuss the issue of discrimination's presence in the church, claiming that "anything that divides believers into two groups is not of God. We, as sinful people, may maintain such distinctions, but God sees all of us as his children and so as one family" (*Galatians*, 118). It would be more helpful if Ngewa clarified that division is the problem, not distinctions. The other African scholars here might argue that a Christian does retain distinguishing characteristics (gender, language, ethnicity, etc.), but ought not to behave in divisive, hegemonic ways. Differences do not necessarily equal divisions, and differences are not inherently problematic.

180. Ukwuegbu, "'Neither Jew nor Greek,'" 308, italics in original; cf. Ukweugbu, *Emergence of Christian Identity*, 324 for a similar declaration.

181. Ukwuegbu, "'Neither Jew nor Greek,'" 309. He insists that valuing differences does not remove a concern for stability and structure in the church; this position simply insists that 'the truth of the gospel' is the highest concern (311).

182. Obviously the focus here is on Christian communal identity; due to space constraints, I cannot explore the significance of the baptismal echoes in this passage nor the phrase 'into Christ.' However, theologically that phrase is tremendously important. An essay on baptism into Christ, which explores the phrase in more detail, making significant use of Galatians 3 and 1 Corinthians 12, is Bernard Onyebuchi Ukwuegbu's "Baptism 'Into Christ,'" 129–53.

183. Niang, *Faith and Freedom*.

nial hermeneut who acts on his self-understanding as God's messenger in order to create or form through faith in the cross of Christ free egalitarian communities."[184] Niang details the parallels between the Gauls/Galatians who were being compelled to adopt Jewish ways, and the Diola people who were forced to become French. Both peoples were colonized, their communal identity trampled and denigrated, and portrayed by the colonizers as vanquished barbarians.[185]

The Gospel "frees and empowers the colonized to reclaim their true and equal human status and identity in God"; it breaks down social boundaries and dehumanizing forces, building an egalitarian, inclusive community.[186] Paul offers the Galatians what the Diola, too, desperately need: a new identity that frees and transforms their self-perception and social lives, while allowing them to remain Diola. Niang views this transformation as central to Paul's gospel:

> As far as Paul was concerned, table-fellowship between Judeans and other people symbolizes the kind of community created by revelatory faith in Jesus Christ. Faith gave them a new identity, freed and transformed them from being savage beasts and adherents of the imperial cultus, to Christ-followers and Children of God (Gal 3:26–29). They received this life-changing religious experience through τὸ εὐαγγέλιον τὸ εὐαγγελισθὲν, 'the good news announced' by Paul (Gal 1:11).[187]

Disagreeing with the idea that Paul intends to abolish differences, Niang instead argues that Paul is emphasizing equality among various groups within the church.[188] Baptism into Christ has socio-political effects

---

184. Ibid., 2. Niang provides vivid examples of the way in which nineteenth-century missionaries to Senegal brought both Christianity and their own civilization to the Diola, and he notes, as an aside, that the lack of respect for Diola infrastructure was in part a result of "a rampant individualism" and "privatization of faith" that flowed from Enlightenment thinking (3). Niang insists that this Enlightenment individualism affects biblical exegesis to this day; in his view, Paul "shows that boundaries between him and Christ are removed—giving rise to a new community in which Christ is present. The immanence of Jesus Christ in the community shapes the identity of its members (Gal 3:28)" (3). Again, note his insistence that Paul's message is not an individual, privatized, 'spiritual' one, but rather one with particular social effects: it forms a community and identity.

185. Niang lists other parallels (ibid., 65).

186. Ibid., 7, 8. Here he echoes Oduyoye's concerns with equality among humans due to the common *imago Dei*.

187. Ibid., 103.

188. Ibid., 104 n. 40. This position agrees with that of Ukwuegbu and Manus, that previous identities continue to exist within the overarching Christian identity.

that cannot be denied; it is entry into a community free from oppression, so "the baptism ritual of putting on Christ (Gal 3:1, 10–13; 26–29) is central to Paul's identity and community formation."[189]

Niang's statement in his concluding chapter integrates his study of the Diola and Gaul/Galatian situations, while keeping Christ and the new creation at the center. Niang avers that Paul's experience of the cross and resulting new creation

> freed and empowered him [Paul] to proclaim the continuous power of the cross-event to crucify Graeco-Roman binarism that legitimizes colonization, repression, oppression, derogatory labeling, exclusivism of the kind of James' emissaries, the 'false believers,' and French claim to supremacy.... Paul was not constructing an exclusive Christian community, 'separate from the Jewish community.' Rather, as a diaspora Judean, Paul was debating some of his fellow diaspora and Palestinian Judeans insisting that the cross of Christ universalizes or internationalizes Judaism.
>
> It does so by faith through love shaping Christocentric people into *other-centered* people—a project through which Greeks, Romans, diaspora and Palestinian Judeans, French, Diola and other peoples would change the world. This way of creating communities does not *ethnocentricize* but contextualizes or inculturates with a view to universalizing the Christian message.[190]

All people are received at God's table, if they will reconcile with their former enemies and fellowship as equals. Niang's work demonstrates that Christ's message has always been intended to have sociological effects, as it offers freedom, community, and a new identity through the power of the Holy Spirit who joins people to Christ and his Body.

Summary

Once the importance of communal identity and its place in the biblical texts is comprehended, stark individualism is measured and found wanting. Also, specifying what type of identity is being discussed (chapter 3) and fleshing out its biblical bases and nature more fully (chapter 4) helps advance ecclesial discussions (chapter 5). The value of employing precise terminology in theologizing should not be underestimated: it adds intelligibility and

189. Ibid., 108. He proceeds to critique all colonizing, dominating efforts.
190. Ibid., 132.

lucidity to the topic under examination, and hopefully in this instance can make these identity concerns and discussions more understandable and applicable to non-Africans.

Acknowledging that cultures are dynamic and emphasis on corporate personality may vary, Letlhare still reaffirms the Motswana proverb *motho ke motho ka batho*, 'A person is a person through people' or 'A human being is a human being through human beings.'[191] Thus she concludes that while traditional mindsets have less hold in many areas of her country than they once did, the proverb still serves as a vital reminder that the one voicing it "is worthy of respect because he/she is a person, that is, a member of the largest of all groups, that of humanity. Paradoxically, at the largest level of corporate personality, we find we have come full circle and that corporate identity becomes individual worth."[192]

Furthermore, it is not difficult to discern how these biblical passages assist in rooting and deepening the understanding of Christian communal identity. They show that God's aim for humanity is communal in nature, and demonstrate that the communal identity 'God's people' should be one's primary identity. This identity is based on and analogous to Trinitarian communion in certain (limited) ways, and is an identity embodying divine love toward others. Indeed, this unified social identity admits, even requires, appropriate diversity. Appreciation for diverse ethnicities, various spiritual gifts, and gender differences within God's people results in a healthy, unified body that prioritizes that communal identity over other identities. This prioritizing of communal identity does not negate individual responsibility or an individual's differences. The cultural and gender differences that also play a role in self-identification must not be given too great a priority, overwhelming the most important identifier of membership in God's people, united with God and others 'in Christ.' Participation in the Godhead through union with Christ and the new creation fundamentally re-defines God's people individually and corporately, so that they must learn how to clothe themselves in this new, foundational identity from then on.

The African scholars here continually reveal a pragmatic focus in their hermeneutics, and emphasize the communal nature of Christian identity. The biblical texts that are used to support their arguments for a communal perspective and for a focus on communal identity specifically affirm their arguments and show that a communal perspective has biblical, not just cultural, bases. The texts they employ show a firm, consistent biblical basis for this perspective. This identity, which values diversity and incorporates

---

191. Letlhare, "Corporate Personality," 477.
192. Ibid., 477, 479, 480.

previous identities rather than suppressing them, is of great importance in their contexts: gender, ethnicity, role in the church, and other difference all are integrated into the primary identity, 'people of God.' The present chapter's interweaving of non-African scholarship helps to demonstrate that these African concerns are not contextually foisted onto these biblical texts but emerge from their own practical concerns. As the non-African scholarship on these passages also increasingly shows, a properly diverse unity is of great importance in every church context; non-Africans are beginning to recognize that. There is a need to value both the individual and the community of which they are part, and simultaneously emphasize that the Christian communal identity should be a person's most important identifier. African scholars accordingly warn against attempts to dominate or marginalize others, whether these attempts are by African church leaders or non-Africans in their treatment of African Christians.

What, then, is the way forward for ecclesial identity in Africa? If African theological appeals to the Bible are any indication then Christian identity, it seems, must embrace healthy differences rather than seeking to repress them or to dominate others. The concern with solidarity and communal identity will also prompt discussions on the appropriateness of familial ecclesial models. Hence the explicit ecclesiologies examined in chapter 5 will be focused on ecclesial identity in African contexts, its solidarity, and the appropriate response of that identity to those who are 'other.'

Chapter 5

֍

Ecclesiology in Africa

Chapter 4 examined how communal notions of identity were grounded in Scripture, describing the nature of the solidarity characterizing God's people. These texts are ones used to reinforce theological arguments in Africa about the Christian communal identity's nature, and in particular the unity of God's people in its relationship with diversity. The texts studied emphasize that the communal identity of God's people should be a person's primary identity, but not one that destroys other social identities. Instead, the 'in Christ' identity requires and incorporates diversity and individuality within itself, overcoming previous social divisions and creating a new, pre-eminent identity. This communal identity values individual 'voice', agency, and responsibility: the individual and corporate aspects of identity are both important and mutually reinforcing. This identity is marked by equality; valuing diversity; and godly, other-focused love.

How, then, do African ecclesiologies further hone the nature of the Christian communal identity? Few ecclesiological surveys have been written, aside from Charles Nyamiti's, and none that I am aware of explicitly surface the priority and nature of Christian identity.[1] Therefore it is a particular contribution of this work to examine major written ecclesiologies, focusing almost entirely on "primary" sources since the relevant secondary literature

---

1. Nyamiti, *Contemporary Models*. The majority of the ecclesiologies Nyamiti surveys come from Roman Catholic theologians, so this book is less helpful to those interested in Protestant or AICs (African Instituted/Initiated/Independent Church) ecclesiologies. For example, he includes a scant page on ecclesiology in the AICs, and has roughly two pages dedicated to Manas Buthelezi, a South African Lutheran. This lack indicates another contribution of this work: further analysis of Protestant ecclesiologies.

is understandably minimal.[2] Yet, beyond providing this basic analysis, I will demonstrate that these ecclesiologies, despite their differences, describe Christian identity markers, particularly solidarity, in quite similar ways. This is somewhat surprising, given the proliferating variety of churches and complexity of theologies across the continent.[3]

Some might suspect that identity would be less explicitly addressed because its animating concerns are a matter of the past, relevant only for a previous generation of scholars. For example, Elochukwu Uzukwu's examination of second and third generation theologians in Africa convinces him that "leading young African theologians today are concerned more about the wholesome appropriation of the historical self-disclosure of God in Jesus Christ than questions of identity."[4] These younger theologians, like Augustin Ramazani Bishwende, focus upon God's self-communication in Christ, rather than beginning with apologetic defenses of African theology or African Christian identity as Kwame Bediako and Fabien Eboussi-Boulaga did.[5]

In like manner, Valentin Dedji's assessment of Kä Mana notes that "Kä Mana appreciates the pioneering work achieved by 'identity' theologians in establishing a genuine dialogue between African world views and Christ. However, considering the harrowing realities of human beings in contemporary Africa, 'identity' theologies are no longer a priority for African Christians." Dedji lists Kwame Bediako as an example of an 'identity' theologian, for whom identity is a "preeminent theological concern," in contrast to Kä Mana, who focuses first upon social transformation, believing that success in this arena is required before Africans can have a dignified Christian identity.[6]

Yet in fact these examples reveal that identity concerns have shifted in, not disappeared from, theologies in Africa. Identity in a defensive sense is not the first concern of many theologies today, but arguments about transformation and reconstruction of African societies with the end result of producing a 'dignified' Christian identity indicate that identity remains an important concern. The concern for identity is implicit in ecclesiological concerns about what the church must *be* and *become* in facing contemporary crises. Who the church is—its mission and character—and how it ought to

---

2. To mention one obvious reason, African scholars have fewer opportunities to write and publish than their Euro-American counterparts.
3. Dedji, *Reconstruction and Renewal*, 1.
4. Uzukwu, "Trinity in Contemporary African Theology," 23.
5. Ibid., 23, 25, 26, 29.
6. Dedji, *Reconstruction and Renewal*, 95.

respond credibly to social issues, is a question of communal identity. These discussions assume that African Christian identity exists in principle, and the debates now are generally about the shape of that identity.

Since identity concerns remain, we will examine select but fairly representative ecclesiological models with interest in how they construe ecclesial identity. It is important to determine some particular traits that characterize Christian communal identity, clarifying the nature of the community's solidarity. Concomitant with the concern for unity is a persistent concern with the embrace of diversity in this identity. Each ecclesiology studied here continually reiterates that unity cannot truly exist without diversity; Christian identity inherently joins together elements that are different or distinct in some way. Here it is helpful to recall Mulago's suggestion that universality requires particularity, and particularity displays or proves Christian claims of universality. Unity/universality and diversity/particularity together compose a healthy ecclesial identity.

The theologians in this chapter argue that ecclesiology requires certain traits if it is to produce healthy, stable Christian communities and communal identities able to meet the challenges of the African context and integrate past, present, and future. Some, such as Uzukwu, describe this united church using family imagery, while others, like Ande, insist that ecclesial identity should not be linked to familial language. But the animating concern in both cases is a Christian identity that can sustain healthy communal life. Thus, for example, emphasis on solidarity indicates concern for a common Christian identity that transcends social barriers of ethnicity, gender, and so forth.

So leaving behind the apologetic stage regarding African Christian identity does not necessarily entail jettisoning identity questions and the African emphasis upon communal identity's importance. After all, as Kwame Bediako insisted, Christian identity is a properly theological concern. On the primacy and solidarity of the communal Christian identity there is general accord across the generational and geographical spectrum, despite differences on more specific points. In order to demonstrate the extent to which this concern permeates African ecclesiology, the authors examined here come from various backgrounds—from Nigeria, the Democratic Republic of Congo, and Kenya; Roman Catholic and Protestant; some writing in French and others in English. The works are arranged chronologically, indicating the persistence of the concern.

Another indicator and concrete example of the communal identity concern is the debate over applying 'family' language to ecclesiology, which reflects a preoccupation with communal identity in a way that non-African models typically do not. Proponents of familial language argue that such language best describes the origin, nature, and mission of the church—in short, its identity. Such familial imagery predominates in Roman Catholic ecclesiologies, at least in part because it received endorsement at the 1994 African Synod and from the pope in 1995.[7] Yet because familial models of the church were employed before this date, this theme is neither a novel concept nor is its prominence entirely attributable to the 1994 Synod. Other possible reasons for the popularity of familial ecclesial models in Africa include African cultural emphases of communitarianism and familial ties, and its perceived rejection of dangerous Western individualistic extremes. Again, while the final ecclesiology examined here rejects this metaphor, still it strikingly describes a similar Christian identity, with a high degree of solidarity.

Accordingly, despite a difference of opinion over familial terminology, common themes pervade all these ecclesiologies: (1) a persistent concern for contextualization of Christianity, (2) inclusion of equality and diversity in ecclesial unity, and (3) an interdependent, relational view of God and humans.

Elochukwu E. Uzukwu

The first ecclesiologist to examine is Elochukwu E. Uzukwu (b. 1945), a Nigerian Roman Catholic in the Spiritan tradition who studies liturgy in African churches. He is a prolific author and professor, and his work has earned him a place on Bénézet Bujo and Juvénal Ilunga Muya's list of pioneers of African theology.[8] Uzukwu's book *A Listening Church: Autonomy and Communion in African Churches* was first published in the mid-1990s, shortly after Bediako's *Theology and Identity*.[9] Uzukwu's volume is often referenced by other theologians, particularly those writing about ecclesiology, and he continues to write and teach at his current position at Duquesne University in Pittsburgh, PA.

---

7. http://www.vatican.va/holy_father/john_paul_ii/apost_exhortations/documents/hf_jp-ii_exh_14091995_ecclesia-in-africa_en.html#top

8. Bujo and Muya, *African Theology in the 21st Century: The Contribution of the Pioneers*, originally published as *Théologie africaine au XXIe siècle—Quelques figures*.

9. Bediako, *Theology and Identity*. The book was the result of lectures given in Tübingen and Rennes (Heijke, "Review of *A Listening Church*," 86). One reviewer described it as exciting, a fresh approach to ecclesiology in Africa that moved "out of the realm of mere theological speculation into the real world of pastoral concern" (Donders, "Review of *A Listening Church*," 131–32. Gabriel Mmassi's article draws inspiration from Uzukwu's book, which Mmassi describes as a "groundbreaking essay on ecclesiology" (Mmassi, "Palaver," 173 n. 1).

Contextualization

One major concern of *Listening Church* is contextualization. For instance, the book shares common themes with many other theologies in Africa, themes that have been identified as prominent traits in African cultures: valuing relationality, community, and a holistic view of life. Secondly, Uzukwu chooses his resources (Christian history and African culture) and method (inculturation) at least in part because they aid in properly understanding and contextualizing African Christian identity. Uzukwu employs the inculturation method because it "considers the totality of African culture, ancient and modern, as the context of theology. Inculturation theology is first and foremost a reaffirmation of African culture and identity, denied by Western colonialism and Christian missionary evangelism."[10] Note that inculturation theology, the method of Uzukwu, and before him Mulago and Bediako, begins with cultural (communal) identity.

By contrast, the cumulative effect of colonizing forces in the last few centuries was decimation of African cultures.[11] Uzukwu argues that "retrieval and modernization of our African cultural matrix is the necessary route toward healing the political, economic, social and religious misery of Africa."[12] He envisions the African church being re-built using indigenous resources and Christian tradition, producing a church that is independent and deliberate opens out toward other communities—thus exhibiting the gospel's transformative nature.[13] The church must be contextualized, yet also distinct. Another way to say this is that one crucial aspect of life transformed by the gospel is communal identity: a new nature, given by God, developed in the community of God's people, who behave in distinctive yet loving ways that do not isolate them from others. This new communal identity displays the gospel power.

---

10. Uzukwu, *Listening Church*, 5.
11. Ibid.
12. Ibid.
13. Ibid., 7–8. Crucially, by 'autonomy' Uzukwu does not refer to a lone individual. Rather, he uses autonomy in reference to the relationship of the African church with the Western church, and the sense that the African church is perceived as lesser, subordinate in this relationship. Bernard Ukwuegbu, discussing autonomy and identity in the African church, points to Bénézet Bujo and Elochukwu Uzukwu's works in this regard. Ukwuegbu too refers to the "challenge of self-understanding and the assertion of autonomous identity of the African Church," seen for example in the centralization of power that Uzukwu critiques ("'Neither Jew nor Greek,'" 310–11). With regard to the gospel's transformative nature and the expectation that the church will address social issues, see Ilo, *The Church and Development*.

Given the vastness and complexity on the continent, are there any shared traits that ecclesial identity in Africa should manifest? Acknowledging the multiplicity of ethnic groups and traditions across the continent, Uzukwu argues that there are nevertheless commonalities, notably African communitarianism.[14] Studying African societies, Uzukwu notes that many have democratic elements, with the leader's authority restrained by others. The well-being of all members of the community is the leader's responsibility, and a leader who misuses power can be removed. The tendency in present-day African leaders "toward tyranny and the denial of democratic and humane living" he attributes to slavery and colonialism, both of which tore the fabric of traditional values, and birthed inhumane, demoralizing methods of governing society and church.[15] True, healthy communitarianism should be one aspect of ecclesial identity, and he specifies some aspects of communitarianism in Africa that should be part of the church; he contextualizes ecclesiology.

Uzukwu does not propose a contextualization that assumes all that is African is good and worthy of inclusion in the church. On the contrary, he envisions an "African theology drawn fully from a radical listening to the gospel . . . , and interwoven fully with a critical retrieval of our cultural traditions."[16] Another example of his 'critical retrieval' and contextualization is his adoption of the Manja peoples' totem for the chief: a rabbit with large ears. We will examine what this symbol expresses below. The point here is that Uzukwu adopts a method focused on contextualization, explicitly affirms the need for retrieval of cultural resources, and provides specific traits from African cultures that should be utilized in ecclesial models.

A Community of Solidarity, Diversity, and Equality

Describing the church, Uzukwu envisions a community marked by a high degree of solidarity, respect for diversity, and equality. For one, the ecclesial identity should possess these traits, particularly unity, because the church reflects the Trinity. Through Jesus, reconciler of relationships, the church is born and receives Spirit-produced unity, "breaking down thereby the artificial barriers erected by groups and people."[17] Acts 10–11 is an illustration

---

14. Uzukwu, *Listening Church*, 14.
15. Ibid., 19, 22–24, 29–33.
16. Ibid., 149.
17. Ibid., 49.

of the Spirit breaking down socially erected barriers to unite Christians, presumably thereby giving them a new overarching identity.[18]

Unity, however, does not equal uniformity; the church fathers held that each local church has independence and equality.[19] Uzukwu cites Cyprian: "The Petrine privilege is the symbol of the one priesthood. . . . However, all the bishops are equal, and each is answerable to God for his ministry."[20] Uzukwu laments that the confusion between "unity and uniformity was sealed in the eleventh century" and eventually local churches came under Rome's control so "the idea of the multiplicity in the one church was totally lost."[21] He criticizes Rome for maintaining this inequity today, especially in relations with Africa.[22] In other words, Uzukwu seeks a particular type of ecclesial identity, marked by diversity.

As the previous quotation indicates, Uzukwu also envisions ecclesial unity as characterized by equality among the diverse members, and hopes that the metaphor of church as 'family of God' will produce a church characterized by caring, non-dominating relationships.[23] The chief obstacles to the equality involved in this "new way of being church," in Uzukwu's estimation, are clericalism and an overemphasis on autocratic power. A monarchical, centralized structure maintains inequality, thus preventing true unity.[24] Hierarchicalism makes equality difficult; so too does prioritizing other identities. The 'church-family' claims priority over a Christian's other loyalties, since it reaches "beyond the frontiers of blood relationship, clan, ethnic group, or race. A primordial uprooting is needed in order to be admitted to membership in this new family."[25] Here Uzukwu seems to view solidarity as revealed in treatment of marginalized people. This 'church-family' overcomes old barriers, bestowing a new communal identity that should not contain division or domination. Presumably an ecclesial identity that radically includes diverse 'others' will shift in some ways over time as new viewpoints are included and as the context continues to evolve. Ecclesial identity must create equality and overcome divisions without erasing differences: other identities are retained, but their importance diminishes.

18. Ibid., 50.
19. Ibid., 51–55.
20. Ibid., 53.
21. Ibid., 57.
22. Ibid., 59–65.
23. Ibid., 66–67.
24. Ibid., 121–22.
25. Ibid., 67.

As mentioned previously, Uzukwu employs a paradigm from the Manja people in the Central African Republic: the totem for their chief is a rabbit, because it has big ears and the chief should be known above all for listening to his people. Hearing every person requires patience and time, yet respects freedom of speech for all.[26] This paradigm inspires his suggestion of the means by which the church can learn to welcome diversity and maintain equality. The church must patiently listen, encouraging free speech by all, with the result that all persons are treated as valuable and as part of the whole.[27] Uzukwu cites Teresa Okure's emphasis on Jesus's leadership style as caring and mothering, "best displayed in the context of the Eucharist, where he nourishes or feeds his flock" by giving himself.[28] Listening to and serving all persons requires giving equal voice to the marginalized.[29] Christianity's core is sharing in Christ's life through love, evidenced in listening and dialogue, which strengthens solidarity.[30] The many social divisions mentioned previously—such as ethnicity and gender—can only be overcome by love, which unites by creating a more basic common identity. Listening and dialogue are means to respect diversity, strengthen unity, and recognize others as equals.

Uzukwu holds hope for Africa's future if the church shows a new way of living:

> African theology drawn fully from a radical listening to the gospel . . . , and interwoven fully with a critical retrieval of our cultural traditions energizes us to propose a way or ways of hearing the Word of the Spirit, of feeling the Wind hovering over our dry bones. . . . New life will be created![31]

Among other things, living this way requires identities that are dynamic rather than static, allowing people to embrace and adjust to this new life.[32] Hence "the church in Africa may project onto the world church issues of listening and hearing the other, issues of being related to the other:

---

26. Ibid., 127–28. Charles Nyamiti states that Uzukwu's most important contribution in this book is "the emphasis on the exercise of Church authority as a *listening process*" in which authority is not monopolized but every member has a contribution to make and a voice that will be heard (*Contemporary Models*, 77).

27. Uzukwu, *Listening Church*, 129–33.

28. Ibid., 133–34.

29. Ibid., 139–41.

30. Ibid., 141, drawing on Mwoleka, "The Two Forms of Evangelization," 173.

31. Uzukwu, *Listening Church*, 149.

32. Uzukwu's language echoes the parable of new wine in new wineskins; cf. Luke 5:37–38.

Mmotho ke mothoka batho ka bang (A church is a church because of other churches)."[33]

Relationality and Interdependence

The proverb just cited raises two closely related themes: relationality and interdependence. For contemporary African societies to reconstruct themselves so as to recover communitarianism, these traits play crucial roles. Uzukwu identifies two key points: "(a) The relational notion of the human person should control the exercise of democratic and human rights, and (b) the full respect of rights and freedoms within the local and universal church is the highest testimony of the transformation of human societies."[34] By the first, he means that people must be understood as relational creatures, whose personhood is shaped and upheld in ongoing relationships with others.[35] Relational ties have harmed Africa at times but *Listening Church* refuses to jettison this value. Instead, Uzukwu wants to expand relational ties to include people beyond one's ethnic community, religious group, and so forth.[36] In his mind, to reject such interdependence and relationality would mean falling into the deadly trap of Western individualism.[37] By the second point, then, Uzukwu means that the church's own global practice must manifest true interdependence consistent with the human relationality it promotes. Uzukwu judges that these traits are key aspects of being truly human, and therefore vital in Africa and beyond.

As mentioned previously, a relational anthropology is foundational for these claims: "In most African societies the individual human is described in terms of a complexity of relationship."[38] Relationship is "the essential element of 'personhood,'" and a person "is human because of others, with others, and for others."[39] Uzukwu demonstrates this principle at work in biology: systems biology defines an organism as alive "when all the interconnections which make it up are active."[40] He wants to apply this view of life to all creation, which is interdependent and connected.

---

33. Uzukwu, *Listening Church*, 152–53.
34. Ibid., 35.
35. Ibid., 36–37.
36. Ibid., 38–40.
37. Ibid., 41–44.
38. Ibid., 36.
39. Ibid., 37.
40. Ibid.

This anthropology produces an ecclesiology that values each member's participation and contribution, and deliberately seeks relationships with other communities.[41] Uzukwu argues that viewing a person—or, presumably, a local church—as an autonomous being whose freedom is self-serving logically implies that society is optional, or at best not strictly necessary. Thus Euro-American ecclesiologies and societies face the same quandary: they are viewed as voluntary and secondary. A 'utilitarian' or 'expressive' individualism undervalues communal responsibilities and anything beyond individual rights.[42] Alternatively, viewing humans relationally unites individuals to communities.[43]

A relational perspective, and a unified-yet-outward looking church, can "reeducate the West in particular . . . to correct the excesses of radical individualism" and challenge structural evils.[44] Euro-American Christians can also learn from Africa that a relational view of personhood does not destroy the individual, but rather "promotes individual gifts for the benefit of the community" and freedom as service.[45]

Twice Uzukwu references 1 Corinthians 12. When he cites it near the book's conclusion, he weaves it into his image of the interdependent, outward-facing Christian.

> Each baptized Christian is endowed with the gift of the Spirit as the Spirit wills. Each charism is a way of giving internal coherence to each Christian. It is a way of liberating each Christian from being closed within the self, so that he or she may be fully involved in the service of the community. As the church does not exist for herself but for the Kingdom, the gifts of the Spirit given to each Christian are for the purpose of propagating the same Kingdom (cf. 1 Cor 12:4-11).[46]

Christian freedom is not freedom for self in isolation, but freedom for service and living together with God's people. Freedom and identity are defined in the context of relationships.

Church leaders need to create an atmosphere in which each person contributes to the community.[47] In treating each other as family, African Christians will learn to respect and care for each other, and thus solve

41. Ibid., 7.
42. Ibid., 41-46.
43. Ibid., 46.
44. Ibid., 72-73.
45. Ibid., 78-79.
46. Ibid., 108-9.
47. Ibid., 105.

their own problems—perhaps another example of interdependence, of a particular kind.[48] The Spirit gives different gifts and simultaneously knits the community together into a whole: these gifts break the individual's isolation, bringing them into relationship with and service in the community.[49] The result would be a church with a collegial, collaborative structure, as in Cyprian's day.[50]

Church History

One trait that sets *Listening Church* apart from many other African ecclesiologies is its use of church history: in particular, Uzukwu references the deeds and theology of early church theologians, such as Tertullian, Origen, and Cyprian, in making his argument. For example, he appeals to Cyprian when arguing for the equality of the African church in its relationship to the church in Rome. In this appeal, Uzukwu adds another basis for his argument by showing historic precedents from church history, precedents, not incidentally, set by African theologians from early church history. Appeal to African theologians from the early church also highlights that Christianity is not foreign to or new in Africa, and also shows that Africa has contributed to the global church.

Yet Uzukwu's work is not without potential concerns. First, he references the Bible fairly minimally and second, he does not fully describe means of implementing his model. Thirdly, the doctrine of the Trinity is used to support his view of humans as relational, equal, and interdependent.[51] But some theologians argue that Trinitarian theology supports a hierarchical church system, and Uzukwu's failure to address this interpretation weakens his case. A fourth concern regards his attitude toward the past. His model of the 'listening church' depends upon his audience adopting the type of community suggested by the Manja paradigm, in which the leader ultimately exists to listen to the people and guard the sacred 'Word.'[52] While this metaphor may appeal to some, it might be less likely to resonate with the youth or more modernized, globally influenced urbanites who might

48. Ibid., 69–71, 94–101.
49. Ibid., 108–12.
50. Ibid., 124–25.
51. Ibid., 42. Tanzanian theologian Charles Nyamiti concludes that Uzukwu's position in the book can be summarized in two words: "*autonomy* of the (local) African church and *dialogue* as an essential quality of leadership and authority in the church." Further, in the book Nyamiti understands Uzukwu as pleading for "an African Church that is aware of its identity, personality, and autonomy" (*Contemporary Models*, 77).
52. Uzukwu, *Listening Church*, 127–28.

find this imagery antiquated. Nor is it a metaphor that would be familiar to most, since it is apparently particular to the Manja people. Whether Uzukwu's model can overcome this generational and cultural gap remains to be seen. This imagery may also indicate that his method is too focused upon the past, without sufficient dialogue with present culture and an eye toward the future.

In summary, Uzukwu's ecclesial vision is marked by a concern with contextualization yet without neglecting the church's longer history; communitarianism; a relational anthropology linked to communal interdependence; a kind of unity that, imitating the Triune God, is marked by diversity; and a call for equality. Drawing on the relational anthropology of African communitarianism, Uzukwu presses forward to an ecclesiological distinction between unity and uniformity. This distinction is repeated within his book, and by other theologians, from which we may infer it is central in properly understanding the nature of the ecclesial identity envisioned.

Rephrasing Uzukwu's argument, Christian identity—which is inherently communal—must be the elemental identity of a Christian. This claim implies that identity is intended to be communal and relational, as opposed to being individualistic and isolated. This is a judgment on any viewpoint that would begin with or prioritize an individualistic, isolationist type of identity. This judgment is based on the Triune God, not on cultural bases alone. The Holy Spirit creates the community of God's people; the Gospel transforms a person, and in so doing gives them a new, specifically communal identity. So not only is Uzukwu arguing for the preeminent nature of Christian communal identity, he is arguing for the foundational nature of communal identity for all humans, based on the fact that humans are created as relational beings, in God's image. Sin led to isolation, but this tendency toward isolation and separation does not destroy the divine design.

Uzukwu chose the inculturation method in part because it addresses African identity.[53] His repeated references to a "new way of being church" are another way of saying that his concern is specifically with African ecclesial identity, of traits and habits that should be central to the church's life.[54] This would explain, at least in part, his rejection of a monarchical, hierarchical church structure. The problem is not structure per se, but structures that are contrary to the church's defining, core features. Though Uzukwu does not explicitly say so, I surmise that the Christian communal identity should be primary, at least in part exactly because it begins to restore the *imago Dei*, the original relational definition of humanity, reuniting the bonds that sin

53. Ibid., 5.
54. Ibid., 8, 9, 11, 34, 118.

destroyed. Indeed, human depravity has affected human identity in a fundamental way. The fact that African cultures have retained a communitarian emphasis (though not without its flaws) would then provide an illustration of church doctrine that the image has been warped but not destroyed. Employing communal identity language also makes overt why solidarity is such a concern: a communal identity is by definition an identity shared by a group. The factors that define it, uniting its members and setting them apart from other groups, are the very factors that must be highly valued by those in the group if it is to possess a significant degree of solidarity. Like Uzukwu, the next author similarly advocates an outward-looking church marked by a similar type of solidarity.

Agbonkhianmeghe E. Orobator

A second African ecclesiological figure is Agbonkhianmeghe E. Orobator (b. 1967), a Nigerian who is the provincial superior of the Eastern Africa Province of the Jesuits. He lectures at Hekima College Jesuit School of Theology in Nairobi, Kenya, and has authored several books. One feature distinguishing Orobator is his dedication to using the social sciences in theology. In J. J. Carney's opinion, "Moving beyond both ill-fitting Western models and romanticist inculturation paradigms, African ecclesiologists are turning increasingly to social context as the key dimension for understanding the church's mission in the 21st century. . . . Jesuit priest A. E. Orobator is one of the most promising contemporary voices in this movement."[55] Orobator's methodology has been explicitly adopted by American Protestant Gregg Okesson in the published version of his own doctoral dissertation in African theology, and the Jesuit theologian holds a prominent place in Charles Nyamiti's survey and assessment of ecclesiologies in Africa despite Nyamiti's disagreement with him on many points.[56]

Contextualization

Orobator's concern with context is clear. He has published two books explicitly concerned with ecclesiology.[57] In these, he observes that few African ecclesiologies seriously address the church's social context and outreach,

55. Carney, "Review of *From Crisis to Kairos*," 311.

56. Okesson, *Re-Imaging Modernity* and Nyamiti, *Contemporary Models*. Orobator is a former student of Nyamiti's.

57. Orobator, *The Church as Family*, based on his MA thesis; idem, *From Crisis to Kairos*, the published version of his doctoral dissertation.

and in his estimation this failure leads to a lack of "creative and relevant" ecclesiologies.[58] Focusing on social mission, he utilizes the social sciences, believing that "*if one finger brings oil, it soon soils all the others*.' The socioeconomic and political problems which soil the humanity and identity of Africans do not spare either their faith or their church."[59] In both books, context, ecclesial mission, and ecclesial identity are closely linked, so his methodology includes Christians' current experiences; theologizing in this manner is "theology as critical reflection *informed* by empirical investigation."[60] In other words, theology done well must examine the whole context in which the church finds itself.

The 1994 Synod of Bishops proposed the model of 'church-as-family,' partly over concern that the church's context in Africa was one where identities were being "crushed."[61] This quotation expresses concern with African identities, suggesting the church's call to protect these; *Church as Family*'s focus on the ecclesial mission, its *raison d'être*, further suggests that communal identity specifically is at stake. *Crisis to Kairos* does not explicitly employ the family analogy, which indicates methodological adjustment.[62] Instead, it elucidates how the church in Africa responds to three specific crises—HIV/AIDS, refugees, and poverty—and the church's solidarity with the suffering: again, a concern with communal (ecclesial) identity. This book

58. Orobator, *Church as Family*, 9; idem, *Crisis to Kairos*, 13.

59. Orobator, *Church as Family*, 9. Ferdinand Nwaigbo commends Orobator's analysis of the political crises in African nations (106). Nwaigbo explores two tendencies in Africa that encourage terrorism: "unbridled materialism" and politicians employing "absolute force and radical violence" (Nwaigbo, "Church-as-Family," 97).

60. Orobator, *Crisis to Kairos*, 17, 28, 30, italics original. Orobator says that mission touches on the function, meaning, and theology of the church. According to Nyamiti, *Crisis to Kairos* displays Orobator's rejection of the inculturation method as 'inadequate and irrelevant,' and his turn to the Latin American liberation method "which consciously avoids metaphysical speculation" and relies mainly on social sciences. Nyamiti perceives this approach as anti-metaphysical, dismissive of the supernatural, critical of orthodox dogmatic ecclesiologies, and an approach "from below," which lacks grounding in the deeper nature of the church (*Contemporary Models*, 149). Nyamiti later characterizes liberation theology's approach as reductionistic, secularistic, and superficial in its treatment of traditional cultural elements (152–54, 161).

61. Orobator, *Church as Family*, 11–12. The model was also chosen because of its affinity with African cultural values of life, solidarity, and service—values Orobator affirms (138).

62. Despite serious disagreement with Orobator's methods and attitude toward inculturation and the like, Nyamiti gives *Crisis to Kairos* "extended treatment" for two reasons: firstly because he diagnoses Orobator with methodological problems "but also because he is currently perhaps the one who has studied the subject of African ecclesiology more extensively than any other author known to me" (Nyamiti, *Contemporary Models*, 146).

is also a specific example of Orobator's concern for a thoroughly contextualized ecclesiology. Orobator proceeds from the implicit ecclesiology of the church's self-understanding and actions to explore the "theological vistas" of this ecclesiology, moving from description to prescription.[63]

Since ecclesiology must account for context, Orobator rejects attempts to meld "African traditional cultural concepts and values" and "received notions of the church"[64]; they falsely assume that ideas can be directly translated from one context to another.[65] The result is "non-critical ecclesiology with little or no bearing" on struggles the church faces.[66] Orobator argues that social sciences ground reflection in historical reality for the sake of thoroughly contextual theology.

Yet he refuses to view the church as "any other social group," and prefers a socio-historical understanding, which locates the church in time and place, but does not preclude divine elements in its composition.[67] As mentioned before, focus on the church's understanding and mission reveals a concern with ecclesial identity, particularly the nature of its solidarity, as will become clear. His thesis in *Church as Family* is that,

> given [the African] social context, the church-as-family at the service of society embodies a community of solidarity at the service of life. This church can lay claim to credibility and relevance only when it becomes attentive, sensitive and responsive to the predicament of Africans and contributes concretely to the transformation and renewal of the African society.[68]

63. Orobator, *Crisis to Kairos*, 14, 247.

64. Ibid., 74. As example of such failure, he points to works of Bénézet Bujo, Charles Nyamiti, and Oliver Alozie Onwubiko (74–83). Although Nyamiti criticizes his former student, Orobator, in several regards, Nyamiti affirms that Orobator's research on these three areas is "detailed, well-researched," and with regard to these issues "Orobator's dissertation will remain a useful reference book for a number of years" (*Contemporary Models*, 155–56).

65. Orobator, *Crisis to Kairos*, 83–84. Nyamiti responds that use of different methods does not mean that the inculturation method fails to study its context. He retorts that Orobator acts as if African traditional cultures have no relevance, which reveals a lack of knowledge and maturity as to what is valuable in life. Nyamiti delivers a scathing judgment on the younger theologian: Orobator probably thinks that "African culture begins only with the time of Western colonization," but in holding such views, "he is implicitly denying his own authentic humanity" (*Contemporary Models*, 159).

66. Orobator, *Crisis to Kairos*, 84–85.

67. Ibid., 47–50.

68. Orobator, *Church as Family*, 13. Nyamiti characterizes Orobator's approach here as "predominantly pragmatic or functional" and lacking in speculative and systematic theology (*Contemporary Models*, 113). In the elder theologian's opinion, the pragmatic approach contains serious flaws, but he concurs with Orobator's focus on

This statement shows a recurring concern that theologizing take context seriously. Thus, *Church as Family* situates the church in its social context, treating 'church-as-family' as a framework (as opposed to a rigid, prefabricated model), and acknowledging the complexity and vastness of Africa.[69] It draws mainly from official Roman Catholic sources in Nigeria, Kenya, and South Africa, regions that have undergone 'representative' crises and where the church claims an active social role.[70] Although the approach bears similarities to liberation theology, Orobator is loath to claim the label because he rejects the dichotomy between inculturation and liberation theologies, proposing a new way.[71] He avoids what he terms "speculative generalizations and exhortations" in favor of concrete proposals, emphasizing the visible church, finding hope in signs of contextualization such as inculturated liturgies and in current ministries of the church.[72]

Whereas *Church as Family* explores ecclesial identity based on official church documents from Nigeria, Kenya, and South Africa, *Crisis to Kairos* focuses on Uganda, Tanzania, and Kenya, while widening its sources, examining various ways in which the church as a whole—both formal hierarchy and laity—responds to significant challenges in this setting: HIV/AIDS, refugees, and poverty. Again, *Crisis to Kairos* shows Orobator's concern that ecclesiology engage prominent issues in its context. He cites the 1994 Synod, which asserted that African cultures are in "serious crisis."[73] Orobator agrees: Africa faces "a major humanitarian crisis with many causes

---

life, a prominent aspect of traditional African thought (113–14), though "unfortunately, [*Church as Family*] limits this category" by examining only the earthly, material dimension of life and ignoring the vertical dimension, the "supraterrestrial world of the Supreme Being," while neglecting the hierarchical dimension of the Church (114).

69. Orobator, *Church as Family*, 13–14. Nyamiti criticizes Orobator for failing to study the traditional African family as a starting point for his reflections on the church as God's family (*Contemporary Models*, 114).

70. Orobator, *Church as Family*, 76.

71. Ibid., 17 n. 1. He argues that this "division appears artificial and irrelevant outside the context of pedagogical convenience. Emmanuel Martey succeeds in proving this point and reconciling both orientations." On the other hand, Orobator derides approaches such as inculturation theology that act "as if society and church operate on parallel tracks, with no points of convergence" (ibid., 108; cf. idem, *Crisis to Kairos*, 74, 84). This critique suggests that inculturation theology does not sufficiently engage society: its contextualization is inadequate and partial. Charles Nyamiti categorizes *Church as Family* as liberation theology (*Contemporary Models*, 112–14).

72. He finds hope despite negative assessments of the church from Adrian Hastings, Elochukwu Uzukwu, and Mercy Amba Oduyoye; their critiques pinpoint two issues the church faces: relevance and credibility (Orobator, *Church as Family*, 20–22; cf. idem, *Crisis to Kairos*, 221, 230–31).

73. Orobator, *Church as Family*, 49.

which requires many different responses at once."[74] The emergencies often have underlying structural factors, such as the socioeconomic crisis. Unfortunately "a significant percentage of the total African population presently live in absolute poverty. This [poverty] . . . is concentrated in sub-Saharan Africa."[75] Poverty is concomitant with the refugee situation and the HIV/AIDS crisis.[76] The many crises result in marginalization of and despair among Africans.[77] "Ultimately, socioeconomic and political problems bear serious consequences for the way Africans understand themselves and actualize this self-understanding."[78] What can nurture a positive (communal) identity where life flourishes?

In Orobator's estimation, one tool that aids in engaging the church's social context is social analysis, which identifies resources with which the church can fulfill its mission and "guarantees the important contribution of the grassroots population."[79] A second tool, theology, addresses the church's social role. African theology is called to reconstruction: it must include a contextually relevant, interdisciplinary focus, critical solidarity with society, and practical strategies. Orobator does not explicitly pursue this thought to its logical conclusion: the somewhat dynamic nature of ecclesial identity.

When context is not critically examined, theology can become skewed. South African apartheid vividly illustrates how far theology can be co-opted and twisted to support political aims, how sin and evil can be institutionalized, and how Christian communal identities can be warped. Unsurprisingly, "no social institution or structure, the church included, could insulate itself from the severe and ubiquitous effects of apartheid."[80] A pivotal moment for the Roman Catholic church was 1977's *Declaration of Commitment* that identified black South Africans as "oppressed," declared apartheid "intrinsically evil," and thus chose to seek liberation.[81] This moment provides "an example of a church that had to relocate from . . . hierarchical preoccupation with peripheral issues of ecclesial self-preservation to a level of commitment to the arduous process of social transformation. This relocation involved a theological process, because it allowed the church to rediscover its proper locus" and mission: in other words, it recovered

---

74. Ibid., 51, quoting from John Prendergast, *Crisis and Hope in Africa*.
75. Orobator, *Church as Family*, 53.
76. Orobator, *Crisis to Kairos*, 35.
77. Orobator, *Church as Family*, 67.
78. Ibid., 74.
79. Ibid., 118–19. How social analysis 'guarantees' this result is not altogether clear.
80. Ibid., 97.
81. Ibid., 100–101.

its true identity.[82] A church that engages its context well should not affirm everything in it, but transform it. Here we may infer too that solidarity is key to ecclesial identity: when the church chose solidarity with the oppressed it rediscovered its calling, so to speak.

A Community of Solidarity, Diversity, and Equality

We have seen Orobator's concern with thorough, transformative contextualization. What is the nature of the ecclesial identity he envisions? Certainly it entails a high degree of solidarity, as will be seen. Indeed, he identifies one tool of the church as "prophetic witnessing," or solidarity with the poor, marginalized, and oppressed and aiding people in "recognizing, naming and opposing" unjust social structures.[83] It is the gospel that compels the church to confront injustice. The church's mission requires "actualizing the liberating potential of the Kingdom of God embodied in the Gospel."[84] Orobator concludes that the church must offer a vision of and take steps toward a society of justice and righteousness, implementing kingdom principles.[85] More importantly, we see here that for Orobator, the church's mission arises from its identity, rooted in the gospel. Thus his mentions of the church's mission implicitly refer to solidarity in its divinely given identity.

Due to this concern for a high degree of cohesion in the church, Orobator criticizes Nigerian church leaders for neglecting the majority of churchgoers and for not showing solidarity with the poor and oppressed. Overall the Nigerian church manifests "social passivism and numbing resignation"[86] and has not displayed its transformative nature. By contrast, Kenyan church leaders keeps their members well-informed, and employs protests, shows of solidarity, and alliances with other groups to effect change.[87] Thus, Orobator concludes that unlike Nigeria, in Kenya the Catholic Church has a credible voice and active presence: its members are united, involved, and dialoguing

---

82. Ibid., 105–6.

83. Ibid., 123–24; idem, *Crisis to Kairos*, 236.

84. Orobator, *Church as Family*, 110. "Liberation means freedom from all extrinsic influences that dominate and alienate, and freedom for an authentic African relationship with God" (Cook, "The African Experience of Jesus," 689). Describing the common view in African theologies of the church as a community of life and a socially responsible group of people, Cook offers *Church as Family* as an example of a socially engaged ecclesiological model (689–90).

85. Orobator, *Church as Family*, 115, 117.

86. Ibid., 87.

87. Ibid., 92–94.

together. We could say that its ecclesial identity displays respect for unity with diversity, a trait that is central to its mission.

Solidarity is again a major concern in *Crisis to Kairos*, which studies Kenya, Uganda, and Tanzania, focusing particularly on major issues there. AIDS ravages Africa, and "the devastating vortex generated by this epidemic has further weakened the politically and socio-economically battered countries of sub-Saharan Africa."[88] Individuals and groups have responded in a multitude of ways; these responses highlight that the church must be a place of solidarity and acceptance for persons with HIV/AIDS, "a church that is not too far; not too busy; a church that does not wait for the people, but goes out to the people, to meet them where they are, to offer compassionate care and solidarity."[89] Most of the responses to the crisis come from laity, which for Orobator raises the question of who is the church: Is the church the hierarchy, or all God's people?[90] Finally, AIDS highlights that the church must be a place of welcome, healing, hope, and reconciliation: a community of solidarity which welcomes all.[91]

The refugee situation too brings the need for a high degree of cohesion to the fore. Africa and Asia "jointly generate and host the largest population of refugees," not including IDPs and other "people of concern"; within Africa, the East African region is a major host and generator of refugees.[92] Interviews with refugees and their neighboring churches indicate that the church offers refugees a sense of security, familiarity, and ownership; it is as close to home as they can get without physically returning to their homeland.[93] Complications include ethnic tensions and questions of how much and what type of assistance local churches should provide: some offer material assistance, education, and advocacy, while others limit the church's role to "pastoral care."[94] Orobator notes that a church that chooses solidarity with refugees puts itself at risk. What he does not explicitly surface is that the church offers a stable identity when other identities are threatened; unfortunately, it seems that many refugees still prioritize other identities, and/or misunderstand the nature of the Christian identity when they seek to reconquer their homelands.

---

88. Orobator, *Crisis to Kairos*, 87–88.
89. Orobator, *Church as Family*, 105.
90. Ibid., 109, citing an interviewee.
91. Orobator, *Crisis to Kairos*, 140–41.
92. Ibid., 145.
93. Ibid., 151.
94. Ibid., 154–63.

HIV/AIDS, poverty, and the refugee situation are "out-of-the-way issues. To become involved in them, the church would have to deliberately embark on a journey," not simply being near, for, or with people facing these, but being a church *of* the marginalized and needy, intimately identifying with and seeking liberation for these people.[95] At the same time, social involvement should not cause the church to "lose its face as a visible instrument of transformation and salvation, convoked to facilitate the advent of God's reign in the world, which reign brings justice, peace, and freedom."[96] Solidarity with the marginalized goes hand in hand with seeking transformation.

For Orobator, "As a general ecclesiological principle, *diakonia* [to the needy] presupposes *koinonia*. The church cannot be at [their service] . . . without forming one body with them."[97] The main theological basis for this stance is the Incarnation, in which God becomes human and dwells among his people; the church likewise must have unity among its members, sharing and engaging in each other's struggles, extending Christ's presence everywhere.[98] As Christ became human and lived among 'the least of these,' so too the church must be in solidarity with 'the least of these' in order to represent Christ.[99] Context "marks out the area where mission takes root, grows and bears fruit," and hence this mission is dynamic in response to its context.[100] Different situations explain why some particularities of ecclesial identity vary. Mission in turn shapes the church's being and what it is called to become: it "reveals the identity of the 'faces' of the church as healer, refuge, agent of development, advocate" and more in the Kenyan, Tanzanian, and Ugandan contexts.[101] Solidarity marked by diversity is central to the church's (dynamic) identity.

Orobator also criticizes structures and mindsets that damage solidarity or repress variety; ecclesial solidarity should include diverse voices and roles. Methodologically, listening and dialogue are means of including the full range of diverse voices, particularly those often marginalized (e.g., women) and as a way to root theology in a specific context.[102] Hence he prefers

95. Ibid., 229, 232, 234.
96. Ibid., 233.
97. Ibid., 236.
98. Ibid., 239–43.
99. Ibid., 248.
100. Ibid., 244–45.
101. Ibid., 247.

102. Orobator, *Church as Family*, 31–32. Peter Assenga seconds the importance of listening and dialogue in the church, and the social sciences' aid in this process. Assenga also cites *Church as Family* as an illustration of a theology that demonstrates

the palaver model of Bénézet Bujo and Elochukwu Uzukwu, which is based on extensive listening and dialogue. These practices reiterate that ecclesial identity should respond to difference (internal or external) not with repression or insistence that it is unimportant. Rather, differences should enrich, although not becoming of primary importance in, the church. Indeed, of seven ecclesiological problems identified in *Church as Family*, the majority involve exclusivism and hierarchicalism—improper, unhealthy responses to difference. It is clear that the treatment of diversity is critical in this ecclesial identity.

It is also with regard to solidarity with diversity that the 'Africa' question arises. Orobator rejects approaches that ignore the African church's diversity: he supports Ivorian Efoé-Julien Penoukou's argument "that a mosaic pattern, rather than a monolithic framework, best exemplifies the reality of life in Africa," because it encourages contributions from different perspectives.[103] Amidst rich diversity, commonality can be found, Orobator argues: "Instead of finding the basis of commonality or interconnectedness within the so-called pure cultural forms and expressions, it may be more fruitful . . . to argue that more pressing socioeconomic and political issues abound on the basis of which one can truly speak of a profound '*Africanness*,' albeit disfigured and faced with annihilation."[104] African countries share a history of recent colonial rule, which has contributed to present socioeconomic and political crises. Extreme poverty (anthropological and material), the prevalence of AIDS, and ongoing refugee situations are common.[105] Orobator concludes that "objective poverty" is the "most visible and tangible thread running through the complex diversities and divergences prevalent on the African continent."[106]

There is one aspect of diversity that Orobator appears to overlook. *Church as Family* emphasizes that the notion of 'family' is dynamic, not a "static pre-fabricated reality"; there is always more to say about the 'church

---

these traits ("The African Family Spirit," 69 n. 45).

103. Orobator, *Church as Family*, 26–27, 29. In *Crisis to Kairos* the approach widens to include the voices and ministries of laity, producing a fuller, more holistic picture of ecclesial identity, as well as more consistently applying his emphasis on the necessity of listening to all persons in the church, especially the marginalized.

104. Orobator, *Church as Family*, 29.

105. Ibid., 31, citing Cameroonian Engelbert Mveng as well as Ghanian Kwame Bediako. For more on anthropological poverty, see Mveng, "Églises et solidarité," 199–213. Anthropological poverty refers to humiliation and poverty on a social and cultural level, not just material, measurable poverty; objective poverty refers to the latter form of poverty in Africa brought about by economic and socio-political factors.

106. Orobator, *Church as Family*, 31.

as family."[107] However, it does not provide an in-depth analysis of various ways 'family' is understood in Africa: this omission is a failure to conscientiously, thoroughly contextualize ecclesiology and show multiple perspectives on the term. Thus, when Orobator states that ecclesiology must be based on an African view of family, it could sound as if there is a single definition of family in Africa. Potentially even more problematic is the very assumption that such a view of family should be the basis for ecclesiology; it is not clear whether Orobator means that cultural understandings can critique and override biblical and church teachings, or whether he is more modestly suggesting that cultural views of family provide a starting point for contextualizing ecclesiology.

Ethnocentrism threatens the ecclesiology Orobator envisions, because it promotes a solidarity that rejects diversity, or at best views those who are different as lesser, not as equals. Orobator does not explore ethnocentrism though he acknowledges that it poses "serious problems to the metaphor of church-as-family," and demands that ecclesiological models must find a way to be local yet not exclusivist.[108] While he briefly mentions that ethnocentrism threatens the 'church-as-family' and admits that the notion of 'family' must be deconstructed, he spends no time actually doing so. Accordingly, his use of family concepts in his account of communal solidarity contains some loopholes.

Crisis to Kairos stresses the importance of diversity, portraying a church offering multiple ministries to assist the suffering.[109] These "multiple ministries emerging from the core of the church in the time of crisis represent the gifts and charisms of the Holy Spirit, and confirm the church's identity as a community empowered" by Christ's Spirit.[110] Emphasizing these different gifts reiterates that every member has a place and a contribution to make, and that the laity, the numerical majority of the church, carry a great many of its burdens: they ought to be respected. Further, the diversity in the ecclesial identity is God-given. The Spirit's role highlights that the church is a community empowered by and flowing from the divine, with a unique mission.[111] The church must be a catholic community that is present with the suffering and encourages full recognition of and participation from

---

107. Ibid., 172.

108. Ibid., 36. Ande too repeatedly stresses the need for a local and inculturated, yet not exclusivist or inwardly focused, church (e.g., *Leadership and Authority*, 145, 154–57).

109. Orobator, *Crisis to Kairos*, 221.

110. Ibid.

111. Ibid., 222.

all its members.[112] 'Identity' is employed here to describe both the church's nature and resultant deeds.

The church's call is to be a catholic community, as seen in the biblical theme of a "universal assembly," and including all those 'in Christ' implies treating refugees as people with something to contribute to the church, not just as those with needs the church must meet.[113] Again the church must be for refugees a refuge that offers dignity, protection, and hospitality.[114] Finally, the church should provide a pastoral presence, advocacy, and hope.[115] So these crises require an ecclesial identity with a high degree and particular type of solidarity.

A third problem, poverty, raises questions about equality. In its collectivity, structural elements, and association with Africa, poverty has taken on a new face.[116] By any definition, West, Central, and East Africa rank first; it is a region where "*not* to be poor is the exception."[117] Responses of the church include socio-economic assistance, income-generating activities, relief charity, and advocacy.[118] Orobator expresses concern that relief aid can perpetuate poverty and create dependency, and that the church might externalize or manipulate the poor.[119] Still, he challenges the church to be an inclusive community that reflects Jesus Christ, who welcomed the needy.[120] The church must assist in liberating the poor and view them as equal members because Christ's body has an "organic unity" in Paul's thought.[121] The "paradox of authenticity, self-reliance and (inter) dependence"[122] also haunts such a church, which is fragile and not as self-determined as it would like to be, relying as it does on external resources.[123] Orobator does not minimize these problems or suggest that he has full solutions; yet the dangers do not outweigh the importance of solidarity among the equal-yet-diverse members.

---

112. Ibid., 225–26.

113. Ibid., 168–70.

114. Ibid., 170–72.

115. Ibid., 174–77.

116. Ibid., 221, 180.

117. Ibid., citing Kwabena Donkor, "Structural Adjustment and Mass Poverty in Ghana."

118. Orobator, *Crisis to Kairos*, 189–200.

119. Ibid., 195, 197.

120. Ibid., 204.

121. Ibid., 209–10.

122. Ibid., 212.

123. Ibid., 212, 214.

Emphasizing a church marked by equality among members, Orobabor rejects a pastoralist ecclesiology: it perpetuates a hierarchy wherein leaders monopolize authority and demand that their "'sheep' should be known principally for 'unwavering obedience.'"[124] This ecclesiology leads to authoritarianism, quietism, and an irrelevant laity.[125] Orobator observes that Nigerian bishops generally link ecclesial identity to church leaders, as opposed to all members: this creates a church with inequality.[126] This church sees its mission as dependent on ecclesial authority, and thus responds to problems by issuing statements. I conclude, then, that if the church is 'family' here, it is a family with a patriarchal identity that functions by domination; it does not view all members as equals and respect their different, necessary roles.

Relationality and Interdependence

In line with this emphasis on solidarity, Orobator, like Uzukwu, has a relational emphasis. Thus he advocates the church employing structures of initiatives that could erase the missionary legacy of an "emphasis on individual, privatized devotions aimed at facilitating the salvation of one's soul"; such an individualist view of salvation produces a quietism and isolationism that is deadly.[127] Christianity and the salvation it proclaims is not individualistic but relational; it reconciles a person to God and other humans, and creates a community of God's people.

Indeed, God too is clearly relational in nature; hence construals of the 'church-as-family' often link 'family' to the Trinity, the foundation of that model. In other words, this paradigm relies on a relational understanding of both God and humans. This familial account of relational identity presses toward solidarity that honors life: typically the family nurtures and protects life, so the "church-as-family should also become that place of communion and solidarity where life, threatened as it is by myriad forces, can find protection."[128] The emphasis on life further links ecclesial identity to

---

124. Orobator, *Church as Family*, 141; he claims that such imagery focused on the hierarchy is not only dangerous but an inaccurate representation of the ecclesial reality (idem, *Crisis to Kairos*, 217).

125. Orobator, *Church as Family*, 142–43.

126. Ibid., 81–82.

127. Ibid., 128. Orobator critiques definitions of the church's mission based on "narrow individualistic terms" or "an innocuous proclamation of blissful but delayed compensation in the hereafter. The resulting situation of social isolationism or passivism" is unacceptable (46).

128. Ibid., 151. Two pages later, Orobator defines life: "Life is understood here in the Johannine sense as 'eternal life' which encompasses and transcends earthly life. See

liberation because life comes from God, and Jesus came to bring life and liberation (Luke 4:16–21, John 10:10).

Because life is understood relationally, it makes "sense primarily in the communal context"; life is "*a shared experience*,"[129] which is why ecclesial identity must manifest solidarity: the church is a united community of people who actively work together, not merely live in proximity. Solidarity also links back to creation and incarnation, where God makes human life dependent on his life, and promises to be among his people.[130] To develop a healthy relationality, Orobator appeals to J. N. K. Mugambi's "principle of reciprocity" where "the individual and community have mutual obligations."[131]

Relationality also explains why service is essential to ecclesial identity and mission. A 'servant church' enters into relationship with the secular world and dialogues with it. Orobator suggests that his model is confirmed by biblical concepts of *diakonia* and *kenosis*, *koinonia*, and the command to love one's neighbor.[132] The relational emphasis applies to those outside, not just those inside, the church. Indeed, "only in a flawed ecclesiology does the church stand by itself, alone, insulated and isolated from the rest of society. We could not agree more with Jean-Marc Ela that 'what we need in our churches is a Christianity with 'dirty hands'—one that will abandon its ghetto mentality and commit itself to the down-to-earth questions that decide the future of a people.'"[133] This type of church could potentially renew Africa: it would encourage ethnic reconciliation, and address issues of mission, authority, ecumenism, ministry, dialogue, and the role of women.[134] So the call to service is here a call to engage the church's context and to think relationally and realize the church must distinguish itself but not separate itself from society: ecclesial identity and societal identity are in some ways interrelated.

Relationality is intertwined with interdependence: not only are people shaped by their relationships with others, they rely on others who in turn rely on them. For instance, the complexity of AIDS requires what Orobator

---

John 3:16, 36; 4:14, 36; 6:32–66; 11:25–26; 14:6; 20:31."

129. Ibid., 154, italics in original.

130. Ibid., 158. He supports this position with African proverbs and biblical passages such as John 1 and 1 Corinthians 12 (159); Cf. *Crisis to Kairos*, 239–41, 243.

131. Orobator, *Church as Family*, 156, drawing on Mugambi's *From Liberation to Reconstruction*, 200–201.

132. Orobator, *Church as Family*, 162; idem, *Crisis to Kairos*, 236.

133. Orobator, *Church as Family*, 169, citing Jean-Marc Ela, "Christianity and Liberation in Africa."

134. Orobator, *Church as Family*, 170–71.

terms a "multi-sectoral" response. Orobator concludes that no one group studied exhausts the meaning of 'church,' and each contributes something to who the church is and how she functions.[135] A multi-sectoral church learns from others, integrates various responses to AIDS (here he references 1 Corinthians 12) and must be "mobile," going out to people.[136] AIDS highlights that the church is a servant community where all persons have a role to play, and also that the church must be firmly committed to solidarity with the marginalized.[137] Clearly, then, Orobator remains concerned that diverse roles and ministries in the church relate interdependently in order to fulfill the church's mission.

Social Sciences

As we have seen, Orobator repeatedly insists that the social sciences are a vital means by which church comprehends its context and thus is better prepared to engage it. The social sciences also ground theology in the concrete details of daily life, keeping theology from becoming abstract speculation, as Orobator phrases it. Though he does not use these words, what he seeks is a complete and comprehensive contextualization of theology, an ecclesial identity that is rooted in and responsive to the strengths and challenges of its context while bringing to it the transformative Gospel message. If the church does not engage or address major challenges in its context, its message will seem irrelevant and its people uncaring or uninformed.

Incorporation of Marginalized Voices

Use of the social sciences assists the church in listening and dialoguing with its context. With regard to listening to all persons, and especially those who are usually marginalized or voiceless, Orobator focuses on the voiceless, vulnerable, and marginalized persons, specifically victims of HIV/AIDS, refugees, and the poverty-stricken. Also, in *Crisis to Kairos*, he takes care to include the ministries and voices of laity, not just recognized church leaders and professional theologians. The contributions of these people shape his conclusions in significant ways, and show that listening and dialogue are an integral part of his own theologizing. The inclusion of lay voices is clearly a strength of Orobator's ecclesiology, a trait others

135. Ibid., 125.
136. Orobator, *Crisis to Kairos*, 126–28.
137. Ibid., 134–36, referring to E. Uzukwu's 'listening' church model.

would do well to emulate. Indeed, it displays an ecclesial identity displaying gentleness and respect to all.

In summary, Orobator prevents his works from being solely sociological in nature by providing theological analyses throughout, as well as concluding *Crisis to Kairos* with a theological interpretation of ecclesial identity. Perhaps, then, Orobator's repeated criticism of some theologies as too "abstract" and speculative means that they lack social specificity, not that they should neglect thinking Christianly about God and God's people. Yet Orobator's attitude toward Christian doctrine does seem somewhat odd for a theologian. Because he does not delineate whether 'doctrine' is used broadly, including dogma, or more specifically applies to elite theologies and *adiaphora*, in places he seems to view doctrine as relatively unimportant. For example, at one point *Church as Family* states that theologies in Africa must avoid "becoming preoccupied with sterile debates about intraecclesial and doctrinal niceties."[138] A few pages later, he again rejects "any tendency to weigh down the ecumenical project with theological and doctrinal intricacies."[139]

He previously stated his desire to fill a lacuna in ecclesiological studies. Perhaps, then, Orobator is simply suggesting that there are times to put aside differences of belief in the interest of common problems and urgent needs, or perhaps he thinks that others have laid the dogmatic groundwork that allows him to give his attention to other areas of ecclesiology. On the other hand, given that his statements about doctrine are negative here, it could be assumed that he does not value dogma.[140] To dismiss it altogether

---

138. Orobator, *Church as Family*, 121.

139. Ibid., 125. In response, Nyamiti charges Orobator and other ecclesiologies with "*superficiality* in theological reflection, and a strong tendency towards *secularizing* the Church's mission and *reducing* it to its involvement in human temporal or terrestrial well-being" (*Contemporary Models*, 116).

140. To balance out this lack—or simply complicate the picture—Orobator has written a book introducing basic church doctrines to laity. Scott Clyburn praised it as "wonderfully creative" ("Review of *Theology Brewed in an African Pot*," 583). Each chapter opens with a passage from Achebe's famous *Things Fall Apart*, linking that passage to a key doctrine in Roman Catholic teaching, and ends with questions and a prayer or hymn, some composed by Orobator. Clyburn celebrates that "these explorations satisfy the author's seductive overture: 'This book offers an invitation to drink, savor, and celebrate theology in an African context. It is palm-wine theology—the kind that is brewed to be sweet, refreshing, and enjoyable' (p.10)" (583). Casely B. Essamuah also praises the book as a "masterful treatment," and detects the "strengths of both of [Orobator's] identities—African and Christian" ("Review of *Theology Brewed in an African Pot*," 211). Essamuah concludes that Orobator comprehends "the continuing relevance of the Gospel and Culture debate in Africa," and in this book "adds a great deal to the ongoing self-discovery of African Christians" (212). The Essamuah quotations specifically foreground identity concerns.

would smack of self-contradiction. Yet at the very beginning of *Church as Family*, he describes his understanding of the 'church-as-family' framework: "The church does not appear as a set of carefully formulated *a priori* doctrinal propositions in need of application."[141] He contrasts the idea of an interpretive framework with that of a model, "a designation which evokes a static pre-fabricated reality," while a framework or hermeneutical paradigm suggests room for innovation and adaptation.[142] A one-size-fits-all, rigid model would be harmful in certain ways; yet one could ask Orobator whether, just as he finds commonalities that unite the vast continent, there might appropriately be common dogmatic teachings around which Christians are united.

Oroborator's concern with 'abstract' theology is clear. Perhaps another way to state this is that he is concerned that Christians may affirm abstractions, or principles, without acting upon those principles in daily life. From my own perspective, what some view as 'abstract' theology or general principles are often drawn from biblical material, particularly the Gospel story. When seemingly abstract statements and principles are rooted in scriptural teachings, then I would argue that the problem is not in the truths; the problem is failing to concretely or properly appropriate these truths. For example, two central commandments are the call to love God and neighbor (Luke 10:25–28). I agree with Orobator that ecclesiology in Africa is called to respond to the crises it faces; the question is *how* to best love those who struggle with HIV/AIDS and so on. Theologians, then, would aid the church by examining principles, 'abstract' truths and doctrines, and exploring various ways in which they might be applied. From this angle, Orobator's concern with thorough contextualization is addressed without disparaging doctrine.

Despite methodological developments, there is a high degree of continuity between *Church as Family* and *Crisis to Kairos*, and several key similarities with these and the other ecclesiologies in this chapter. Unsurprisingly, a constant refrain is solidarity: acting like a family, sacrificially committing resources, time, and energy to caring for the needy. Rather than waiting for persons in need to arrive at the church, God's people should seek them out, which is a demonstration of God's love forming their identity into that of a catholic, welcoming community. This solidarity requires welcoming all persons with the assurance that in this place they belong, can rest in security, and have something particular to contribute. In this regard, Orobator references 1 Corinthians 12 multiple times because

---

141. Orobator, *Church as Family*, 13.
142. Ibid., 172.

it supports the need for diversity of ministries and gifts within the very nature of ecclesial unity.[143]

This type of solidarity can be perceived as a coin: one side of the coin is unity, noted above, while the other side is diversity. The diverse persons whom the Spirit has united in one body each have a part to play and a particular perspective to share. Orobator highlights women, and people dealing with poverty, refugee status, and HIV/AIDS, but the broader point applies to all marginalized persons. For a church seeking to combat such deadly plagues, the 'multi-sectoral' approach is both a pragmatic move and reflects a core theological value.

His theology could be strengthened by providing more theological nuancing regarding solidarity. For example, Paul notes that humans are united in sin and rebellion against God (e.g., Rom 3:9–18). Human solidarity is also based on the shared *imago Dei*. Within God's people, solidarity arises from union with Christ. Orobator affirms that the church must be in solidarity with society, yet does not describe the nature of ecclesial solidarity with non-Christians. It would strengthen his arguments if Orobator would root his discussions on ecclesial solidarity—both with those in the church and with those in society who are not part of the church—more deeply in the Bible and theological bases.

Overall, he shares much in common with other theologians in Africa. For example, his characterization of ecclesial solidarity resonates with Uzukwu's. Life and solidarity are major elements in many theologies, and are key building blocks for Uzukwu's ecclesiology. Furthermore, Orobator clearly argues that ecclesial identity must embrace solidarity, and this solidarity embraces diversity and equality. He also emphasizes a relational, interdependent view of those in the church; on this point he parallels Uzukwu. Unlike Uzukwu, Orobator does not endorse the inculturation approach per se. But he shares the values of contextualization, perhaps even extending them farther with his interest in listening via the social sciences—to promote, again, a genuinely Christian identity marked by solidarity that values diversity and equality, relationality, and interdependent views of persons.

Augustin Ramazani Bishwende

A third ecclesiologist, Augustin Ramazani Bishwende (b. 1964), is a Congolese Catholic priest who teaches at the University of Ottawa and the University of Saint Paul in Ottawa, Canada. He also holds the position of director of the Fraternité Mondiale pour le Développement and co-founder of the

---

143. Cf. Orobator, *Crisis to Kairos*, 128, 130, 210.

Centre des Recherches Pluridisciplinaires sur les Communautés d'Afrique noire et des Diasporas.

By way of background, *Église-famille de Dieu dans la mondialisation: théologie d'une nouvelle voie africaine d'évangélisation*—one of three books Bishwende has authored on this subject—advocates an interdisciplinary approach to the model 'Church-Family of God.'[144] He integrates history, sociology, theology, and more as he examines his proposed model from various angles. His interdisciplinary approach proposes to negotiate three concerns: "Christian churches between Christianization and Africanization; African churches between communion [and] society; the Church in Africa seen as simultaneously Eucharistic and pneumatic community" viewed from a Trinitarian perspective.[145] Examining the challenges of particularity amidst homogenizing globalization, he balances these concerns with a stress on openness to others. He critiques, then nuances and deepens, the term inculturation, as well as carefully defining terms like family and communion. This work shares themes with the previous ecclesiologies: a relational, communal view of persons, and concern for solidarity. Identity concerns arise repeatedly.[146] Bishwende perceives the struggle to define one's own identity as ongoing in an ever-changing world where the Spirit is at work, which means that identity is a theological issue for all Christians, not just Africans, as Bediako argued.

---

144. Bishwende, *Église-famille*, 7. The book is based on his 2005 PhD dissertation. He mentions at one point that the term "people of God," as opposed to church, highlights the continuity between Israel and the NT church (166). However, the terms "people of God" and "church" are used interchangeably in his work, as in my own. His first book on the topic of 'Church-Family of God' was *Église-famille de Dieu: Esquisse d'ecclésiologie africaine* (Paris: L'Harmattan, 2001), followed in 2006 by this book, and in 2007 by *Ecclésiologie africaine de famille de Dieu: Annonce et débat avec les contemporains*. The latter two are the result of his thesis at l'École Pratique de Hautes; for a concise summary of these, see Mbenga, "Review of *Église famille*," 209–10.

145. Bishwende, *Église-famille*, 8.

146. E.g., Bishwende, *Église-famille*, 49, 51–52, 58, 61–62, 66, 71, 77, 82, 130, 242. Elochukwu Uzukwu comments, "Second and third generation sub-Saharan African Christians [such as Bishwende] may not be as preoccupied with issues of identity that dominated African theology in the 1950s. They live the postcolonial reality. It is a long way from the seminal *Des Prêtres noirs s'interrogent*" (23). Furthermore, Bishwende and his colleagues tend not to begin with defensive (or in Uzukwu's words, 'negative') apologetics (26, 29) ("Trinity in Contemporary African Theology"). However, there is a distinct difference between less apologetic stress on, and lack of liberating concern with, identity. While the younger generation of theologians may approach identity from a different angle, they are still addressing it, albeit in different ways and in the postcolonial context.

Contextualization

In order to situate and explain his own approach, Bishwende sketches the last century of African Christianity. Missionaries viewed African cultures as pagan and evil; the missionary role was to bring the gospel and to civilize, or Westernize, Africans.[147] The missionaries conveyed a hierarchical view.[148] Colonization's effects persist today, as African churches are still "defined by a state of subordination and submission" to the West.[149] Eventually inculturation theology arose, addressing differentiation for African identity and affirming God's work in all cultures.[150] However, inculturation theology tended to focus on the past and did not seriously engage modernity.[151] Next came liberation theology, seeking means of deliverance from domination.[152] It criticized inculturation theology for ignoring the present and failing to address all areas of human life; liberation theology has a broader scope.[153]

The third movement in African theology is reconstruction, a synthesis of the first two that identifies means with which to reconcile past and present as well as build for the future.[154] In other words, he agrees that contextualization is vital; his quarrel with these movements is that they fail to offer complete contextualization: they are not sufficiently and comprehensively inculturated. To Bishwende, all of these movements underscore the need for dynamic, full inculturation of the Gospel, which is both a means to convey the Gospel story, and a core trait of the Gospel itself.[155] Because Bishwende works to integrate these streams into a single rich, holistic theology, presumably he would want to address identity in some way, as it is a major concern for inculturation theology.[156] Furthermore, for the church to be fully inculturated—successfully engaging culture and bringing liberation and reconstruction—it must first know its own identity and God-given mission.

---

147. Bishwende, *Église-famille*, 24–25.

148. Ibid., 25–27.

149. Ibid., 28. When not quoting others, English translations of Bishwende here are my own.

150. Ibid., 44, 49.

151. Ibid., 48–49.

152. Ibid., 50.

153. Ibid., 53–54, 55, 58.

154. Ibid., 61–62.

155. Ibid., 63–65.

156. Ibid., 69–70. He describes the three streams as, respectively, self-understanding (thesis), self-appropriation (antithesis), and engagement (synthesis) (72–83).

Aware of the reality of being contextually shaped, Bishwende notes that ecclesiological models too are human creations.[157] To address his own context, he weaves the Trinity; ecclesial structure and mission; and solidarity that welcomes alterity, dialogue, and globalization into his ecclesiology, delineating a complex network of issues.[158] Charles Nyamiti identifies one of Bishwende's major ecclesiological contributions as this web that unites "history and eschatology, identity and otherness, African identity and Christian identity, tradition and modernity, anthropology and theology."[159] Ecclesiology that addresses these concerns is both contextual and, I argue, concerned with communal identity, specifically a dynamic identity since it involves ongoing debates and ultimately an eschatological identity. Bishwende is noticeably concerned with both solidarity and alterity in ecclesial identity: for example, one danger of globalization is the possibility of smothering or downplaying difference, making it harder for African churches to find their own identities. His concern, then, is that contextualization has been inadequate and incomplete; he seeks to correct this problem both in his method and the resulting ecclesiology.

A Community of Solidarity, Diversity, and Equality

Like Uzukwu and Orobator, Bishwende is concerned that the church in Africa develop a high degree of solidarity. He scrutinizes the model 'Church-Family of God,' exploring its various bases. For Bishwende, Trinitarian communion highlights divine solidarity. The church is based on the Trinity, and so churches too must display a noticeable solidarity. And, despite changes in Africa, family relationships remain important, indicating that solidarity is key for African cultures, as well as among the three Persons of the Godhead. There are multiple reasons, then, that ecclesial solidarity is vital for Bishwende.

His own ecclesiology arises from a post-Vatican II context, when Roman Catholic ecclesiology formally moved from a juridical concept of the church as "institutional, monarchical, and societal" with "excessive centralization" to an emphasis on church as communion.[160] He seeks to continue the renewal prompted by Vatican II and find a compromise between the various ecclesial models, applying "the relational and communal Trinitar-

---

157. Ibid., 84.

158. Ibid., 280, 282, 289.

159. Nyamiti, *Contemporary Models*, 79, referring to Bishwende's *Église Famille de Dieu: Esquisse d'ecclesiologie africaine.*

160. Uzukwu, "Trinity in Contemporary African Theology," 27.

ian image of the Church that is non-hierarchical."[161] Bishwende's contrast between ecclesial models demonstrates his concern that ecclesial identity be marked not by hierarchy but by equality, where each one has a place and is respected.

Attempts to downplay ecclesial diversity or to dominate those who are different harm ecclesial unity. Without diversity, the church will be damaged and fall short of God's intentions for it. The need for diversity within ecclesial solidarity explains one reason why Bishwende is concerned with Christian churches being fully Christianized and Africanized: Christianity must not erase diversity, or promote homogenization, like globalization does. The church is both global and local, and her diversity should be a strength.

Bishwende also addresses both particular and universal aspects of ecclesiology in light of the Trinity. Since the "church is a local eucharistic community constituted of believers with a unique history," ecclesiology is contextual and responds to contextual challenges.[162] At the same time, churches belong to the Christian tradition, and each church is an icon of the Trinity, so each local church has a universal aspect.[163] Bishwende claims that his model can give African Christianity its 'true face'—its true identity.[164]

Equality is also central for ecclesiology; we could reframe this to say that equality is a key marker of ecclesial identity. Equality among churches and among church members in a particular church is one basis of Bishwende's assessment of the 'communion' versus 'society' debate in Catholic ecclesiology. He repeatedly states concerns about hierarchical, centralized ecclesiologies, and believes that 'Church-family-of-God' can provide a way forward in this debate, though it is neither perfect nor the sole solution.[165] Vatican II described the church as communion as opposed to a hierarchical society in which all are not treated as equals; Bishwende would like to apply the 'communion' perspective even further.[166]

Église-Famille de Dieu also fears replicating hierarchical elements in African societies remaining from colonization.[167] Neither larger society

---

161. Bishwende, *Église-famille*, 16; Uzukwu, "Trinity in Contemporary African Theology," 27.

162. Bishwende, *Église-famille*, 258–59. Note his ongoing concern with contextualization, yet not to the extent that a church would become isolated from the global church.

163. Ibid., 259.

164. Ibid., 261–62.

165. Ibid., 89–90.

166. Ibid., 110–11, 117.

167. Ibid., 240–41.

nor the church has yet found a fruitful synthesis of traditional and modern influences; this conflict must be resolved before a healthy ecclesiological model can become a reality.[168] Bishwende fears a church that is leaning toward becoming hierarchical, patriarchal, or clan-like. Each of these paths is marked by domination and inequality. He even describes Église-Famille de Dieu's model as a 'utopia,' an ideal not an ideology, in that Bishwende understands an ideology as a static model characterized by a dominating, absolutizing authority that attempts to force all elements into a single unchanging mold: it rejects diversity and equality in favor of conformity.[169]

Bishwende proposes means that will move the church toward the envisioned community. For one, he underscores the role for dialogue, which enlarges an imperfect grasp on truth and generates solidarity.[170] God's self-revelation is also dialogical, and ethically, dialogue inculcates the Gospel precept of love.[171] Yet there are topics on which the church in Africa fails to dialogue well: money, power, and women, for example. Walls between races, cultures, and ethnicities must be torn down: these barriers further hinder the church from realizing its identity.[172] By contrast, dialogue strengthens unity and equality, which would presumably enhance an overarching sense of Christian identity. Removing barriers within the community without eradicating God-given differences is key to this Christian identity, where godly unity incorporates diversity—and dialogue aids in achieving this goal.

Other means of creating a church ethos marked by equality and dialogue include giving local churches more decision-making power, dividing the Apostolic patriarchy of the West and creating new patriarchies, and respecting the independence of certain Christian denominations "while integrating them into the *koinonia* of the *oikoumene* without absorbing them."[173] Bishwende also imagines an "ecclesiastical ministry of the laity without clericalizing and sacerdotalizing the laity," in which laity are treated as equal with but distinct from clergy.[174] His basis for these ideas is the Trinity, which emphasizes diversity in the unity of equals, interdependence, and relationality.[175]

---

168. Bishwende, *Église-famille*, 242.
169. Ibid., 250, 258.
170. Ibid., 283, 284, 286, 287.
171. Ibid., 290–91.
172. Ibid., 299. African values of relationship and orality also support dialogue.
173. Ibid., 307–11, 317–26.
174. Ibid., 169–71, 336.
175. Ibid., 263–65.

Relationality

A relational perspective of God and humans drives Bishwende's ecclesiology. First and foremost, the Trinity helps Africans comprehend that the church's essence is communion.[176] Trinitarian communion is the model for ecclesial communion, in which all participate as equals, different yet united; this communion among equals militates against centralization, uniformity, and dependency on Rome, as mentioned previously.[177] Like others here, Bishwende views God's relational nature as highly relevant for ecclesiology. Indeed, the 1994 African Synod chose 'Church-family of God' as the fundamental ecclesiological paradigm for Africa, linking this image to the Trinitarian communion of love.[178]

Bishwende emphasizes that Trinitarian communion is the basis of this ecclesiology, not any human model of family.[179] Its particular 'face', or the points that most quickly resonate with certain local churches, is colored by human culture, but the face's basic contours have a divine basis that is inextricably relational. In a similar way, he lays out the values and pitfalls of solidarity in African cultures, and defines ecclesiological solidarity by the Trinity. The way in which he employs the doctrine of the Trinity suggests that it is the foundation for other theological elements; furthermore, that a relational perspective is key to ecclesial identity.

Bishwende describes ecclesiology as formed first and foremost by Son and Spirit; in my own words, they are foundational for ecclesial identity.[180] Intriguingly, he regards the Spirit as the entryway into 'Church-Family of God,' but he continually underscores that African ecclesiology must be Trinitarian, not emphasizing any one member of the Trinity over the others.[181] Identifying the involvement of each person of the Trinity refers back to and adds more support for his case that a Trinitarian-based ecclesiology

---

176. Ibid., 14.

177. Ibid., 114–15.

178. Ibid., 165–66.

179. Nyamiti lists Bishwende's clarification on the term 'family' as one of the Congolese theologian's special contributions to the field of ecclesiology in Africa (*Contemporary Models*, 79).

180. Bishwende, *Église-famille*, 246–47. Elochukwu Uzukwu identifies this starting point in God's nature as "dependence on evangelical theology whose insistence on the absolute uniqueness and incomparability of the Word of God addressed to humans is well known" ("Trinity in Contemporary African Theology," 36). Uzukwu sees this "dependence on evangelical theology" as one trend among younger African theologians; a second commonality he notices among Bishwende and his Roman Catholic contemporaries is an ecumenical perspective and imperative (23, 26, 29, 36).

181. Bishwende, *Église-famille*, 19, 264–65.

requires unity with diversity and interdependence. Indeed, Église-Famille de Dieu develops the Trinitarian roots of ecclesiology more than the other works here.[182]

To this divine basis for a relational, communal perspective is added the African emphasis of the human as a relational being. Yet this African anthropology can never be equated with the Trinitarian communion that shapes Christian identity. The divine relationship is primary and definitive; thus, 'Church-family of God' must be marked by communion because it participates in the Trinity.[183] Following this line of thought, if the divine relationship defines God's people, then it ought to have more 'weight' than other relationships or identities. Presumably other identities—such as gender or ethnicity—are not destroyed, since Bishwende makes it clear that the Christian identity values diversity.

The Triune nature of God and African cultural values are not the only warrants for using relational language to describe the church. Bishwende points to Paul as a biblical example: the Apostle refers to Christians as 'house of God', where the term 'house' has to do with family and household.[184] Notably, Bishwende clarifies that language like 'family' is symbolic and metaphorical.[185] If the family model becomes an ideology, there is danger of absolutizing structures, of fostering domination, and of stifling the Spirit.[186] The Church needs structures, but they are provisional and only means to loving ends; the critique on ecclesial structures reflects back to his concern for an ecclesial solidarity with diversity and equality, focused on God's mission.[187]

At the same time, Bishwende identifies weaknesses in African and biblical families—authoritarianism, enmity, gerontocracy, and the like—which should not be part of the church. These traits militate against the solidarity with diversity and equality which churches should display, indicating that he uses 'family' and relational emphases in a nuanced way, and not necessarily in simplistic accord with common cultural usage.[188]

182. Ibid., 111, 114, 165–67, 180, 210, 212–13, 254–57, 266–68, etc.

183. Ibid., 255–56.

184. Ibid., 207–14. He notes that other biblical passages support this language, while at the same time repeatedly affirms that 'family' is not to be understood in a patriarchal or paternalistic sense; both Jesus and Paul rejected such positions (207–8).

185. Ibid., 218.

186. Ibid., 229.

187. Ibid., 230–31.

188. Ibid., 273. Nyamiti identifies this same emphasis in Bishwende's *L'Église-famille de Dieu: Esquisse d'ecclésiologie africaine*: "Bishwende indicates how the attitude of Jesus and his disciples towards consanguineous kinship relativizes the family, in the sense

Accordingly Bishwende evaluates other African ecclesiologies in terms of properly understanding the church in light of the Triune God. For instance, Mulago's model highlights communion, life, participation, and the human as an interdependent being in relationship with others.[189] Yet Bishwende diagnoses Mulago's 'stepping-stone'—or adaptation—method as problematic and characterizes Mulago's ecclesiology as clan-like and hierarchical.[190] Bénézet Bujo's Eucharistic ecclesiology views Christ as "Proto-Ancestor" and founder of a "new clan" who receives Christ's life communicated through the Eucharist.[191] Yet a clan model too creates a hierarchical, authoritarian church.[192] Église-Famille de Dieu rejects such models, arguing that they result in churches that do not properly imitate the Trinity: the church should mirror the reality that the unified divine persons are equals. If the church fails to model equality of members, its ability to image God is deeply damaged. As can be seen, these critiques reflect Bishwende's concern with the nature of ecclesial unity: its divinely based identity models a community marked by relational perspective of God, the church, and humans.

Eschatology and Eucharist

Église-Famille de Dieu describes a model that is an 'ideal,' not an ideology: an ideal is dynamic, seeking an as-yet-unrealized future. Thus, unlike ideologies, ideals improve life contexts. For Bishwende, an ideal links to an eschatological vision that motivates and empowers renewal in the present.[193] This eschatological goal toward which the Spirit leads God's people also prevents the church from being overly rigid, closed in upon itself, or limited to the visible realm.[194] The eschatological pull distinguishes the Christian utopia of the future from perspectives that seek only present liberation.[195] The

---

that although the latter is not suppressed, it is opened to a larger and more fecund kinship" (*Contemporary Models*, 78). Nyamiti agrees with Bishwende that the church cannot be called 'family of God' "unless we transcend the biological sense of the family and embrace the symbolic sense, namely of the family understood as communion of grace in God's love which brings it about and structures it. Moreover, this image of the family must be joined to that of kinship in Jesus Christ in union with the Holy Spirit. This implies that the Church as God's family is the icon of the Trinity" (79).

189. Bishwende, *Église-famille*, 178–80.
190. Ibid., 180–83.
191. Ibid., 187–89.
192. Ibid., 190.
193. Ibid., 249, 261.
194. Ibid., 249, 332.
195. Ibid., 68–69.

eschatological goal reinforces Bishwende's point that identity is not static but dynamic and developing: it must be capable of changing in response to particular contexts.

Further relating the universal and the particular, as well as the *eschaton* and the present, Bishwende visualizes an ecclesiology that cannot be formulated apart from the Eucharist: the two have an "essential and ontological relationship."[196] In celebrating the Eucharist, the local church indicates that it is a manifestation of the kingdom because of God's presence among this community, while simultaneously pointing to the universal church. This meal is communal, sacrificial, and memorial, remembering the death and resurrection of Christ until he returns. "With the Eucharist, the universal is manifested and revealed in the particular."[197] It also shapes the church's engagement with the world.[198]

The Eucharist unites Christ-followers, "inaugurating a new way of being church," a way of loving service.[199] The union and participation in a common life that church members share is Eucharistic, both in source and in nature. This meal displays the church's reliance on Christ for life, and is where Christians receive the Spirit who creates the communion.[200] Even more relevant for this work, Bishwende specifically links the Eucharist with Christian identity: the Eucharistic meal leads the Christian toward love of neighbor, the Other who affects one's own identity.[201] It also reminds Christians of the not-yet-final nature of their identity, which will be revealed by God. In this way the Eucharist is also eschatological, as it anticipates Christians' full communion with Christ in the future.[202] This eschatological and Eucharistic way of framing the church is a distinctive of Bishwende's work, and deserves further exploration.

I suggested previously that ecclesiology discussions in Africa tend to revolve around the character and key marks of ecclesial identity; in that case, Bishwende's work is significant for several reasons. First, he addresses dangers of globalization, noting its homogenizing tendencies, which is significant in a situation where there has already been a lengthy fight for recognition and valuing of African identity. Globalization, like hierarchicalism, urges conformity and threatens to run roughshod over diversity. It might

196. Ibid., 267.
197. Ibid., 268; see also 312.
198. Ibid., 271, 273.
199. Ibid., 270–73.
200. Ibid., 168, 265.
201. Ibid., 77–78.
202. Ibid., 19–20, 168, cf. 333ff.

be worth exploring whether globalization also contains resources that could strengthen the African church, such as facilitating connections with other minority voices in the church. Regardless, Bishwende's intentional address of globalization's effects on theology in Africa is helpful.

More important for my own argument is his eschatological thread that runs throughout the book. Many works in Africa have sought to demonstrate how past cultural traits can influence present-day theology, such as Uzukwu's *Listening Church*. Other theologies explore present-day challenges that African theology must address, such as Orobator's *Church as Family* and *Crisis to Kairos*. What Bishwende repeatedly highlights is the eschatological nature of the church. The church's eschatological serves as a reminder that the church of the present, in any location, is a sign of God's kingdom, but that the fulfillment has not yet arrived. What are some implications of this move for ecclesial identity?

The as-yet-unfulfilled and incomplete nature of the church must not be overlooked. The church seeks to represent her sovereign Lord, whose plans will come to pass. Part of that commission involves relying on the promises of God, and acting in light of them in the present. What glimpses God has given of the future ought to shape the paths chosen in the present, just as much as present challenges do, if not more. For instance, Rev 5:9–10 proclaims the victory of the Lamb, a promise that strengthens churches to endure despite persecution and hardship; it could also urge the church in a particular context to hold fast in a particular ethos and practice that does not seem to be succeeding, with a reminder that faithfulness to God is more important than immediate, measureable 'success' and that despite evidence to the contrary, God and God's people will triumph in the end.

The eschatological emphasis also reinforces that ecclesial identity is 'in process,' it is becoming what it will one day be. This is not to say that there are no constants by which to identify God's people; however, there is a dynamic, progressive element in the identity of God's people as they approach the eschaton (e.g. 1 John 3:2; Rom 8:18–19; 1 Cor 15:35ff). The dynamic aspect of Christian identity must militate against any attempts to present a static or comprehensive ecclesial identity. Presumably, this eschatological element might also serve as a reminder to non-African churches that attempting to impose their own contextually shaped and limited models upon others is rather short-sighted and presumptuous, at best.

In sum, Bishwende's Église-*Famille de Dieu* ties ecclesiology tightly to the Gospel and the economic Trinity, and in the latter finds a theological basis for inculturation, a plumb line for defining family and community, and theological justification for the necessity of ecclesial unity with equality and diversity.[203] Fraternity in Christ through the Spirit balances out diversity with a reminder of the equality and unity of Christians. The church is above all a community drawn into the Trinitarian communion, so ecclesial structures must serve the church's mission. Bishwende's synthesis of various streams results in an African theology that is in ongoing dialogue with dynamic cultures and various resources.[204] Neither ecclesial structures—nor, by inference, ecclesial identities—are absolute or final at this time.

Finally, by way of transition, another noteworthy aspect of ecclesial identity is its treatment of alterity. The Trinity suggests that community can be tightly woven, interdependent and united, yet simultaneously welcoming to others. Indeed, Bishwende suggests that alterity plays a key role in defining Christian identity: both one's differences from others, as well as similarities with them, shape the continual process of one's self-definition.[205] After all, the Gospel is a story of reconciliation with others and God, birthing the history of the church.[206] With the next theologian, we switch to a Protestant ecclesiology, and the diversity and alterity in question are that of ethnic identities.

Paul M. Mbandi

Paul M. Mbandi (b. 1962), a Kenyan ordained by the Africa Inland Church, has written one of the few Protestant ecclesiological works by an African. He has taught at Scott Christian University and other schools in Kenya, as well as offering leadership training. Mbandi has published comparatively little; however, by far, the majority of African ecclesiological works are authored by Roman Catholic theologians while there are notably fewer from Protestants, so Mbandi's contribution to the field is helpful.[207]

---

203. Ibid., 76, 79, 81–82, etc.

204. Ibid., 17–19.

205. Ibid., 76–78.

206. More than any other work here, Bishwende explores the ramifications of Trinity for ecclesiology, particularly a relational, communal, and non-hierarchical view of the Trinity. Uzukwu also notes Bishwende's commitment to the Gospel and the Trinity. Bishwende and his colleagues "show that the local can be brought into constructive dialogue with the global for the transformation of the African. But they all insist (and who will disagree?) that it is the God revealed as Triune in the Crucified and Risen Jesus who addresses the therapeutic word that redefines the African, in the event that is the Spirit-filled Church, for the transformation of the world" (Uzukwu, "Trinity in Contemporary African Theology," 40).

207. Other than the published dissertation, it appears that his only other academic writing involves an MA thesis.

A Theology of the Unity of the Church in a Multi-Ethnic Context: Toward a Theological Understanding of the Unity of the Church in Relation to Ethnic Diversity addresses ecclesial solidarity in light of ethnicity.[208] Unlike the other works examined in this chapter, this book devotes a significant amount of discussion to biblical texts. On the other hand, its discussion of sociological and other extrabiblical resources is comparatively scant, and there is relatively little substantive engagement with other African theologians.

Contextualization

Mbandi displays his concern with contextualization by his focus on the relationship of ethnic identities to ecclesial unity. Ethnicity and ethnic identities are a major force in his own Kenyan context. Ethnocentrism is not limited to the church, of course; Stanley Mutunga's research revealed "that ethnicity is a factor in every political election" in Namibia, Nigeria, Rwanda, and Tanzania.[209] Ande's research supports Mbandi's point that ethnicity continues to loom large in African contexts. Given the widespread influence of ethnicity and ethnic identity, *Unity of the Church* makes a significant point: both in many biblical texts and in many African cultures, ethnic groups are first and foremost about kinship and common ancestry, which often results in shared cultural traits or phenotypical characteristics.[210] These groups provide a high degree of solidarity in a shared, communal identity.

Like poverty, ethnicity is an omnipresent reality for most Africans; but, unlike poverty, ethnicity can be a source of strength and cultural wealth. Ethnicity is a complex force the church cannot afford to ignore or treat naively. So while Mbandi does not significantly engage other African theologians, he is exploring a concern arising from his context. He focuses more on critiquing the Church Growth Movement's "homogeneous unit principle," also known as HUP, than on constructing a new model.

Because social context affects theology, Mbandi affirms that theology must integrate data regarding socio-ethnic issues, while subjecting it to biblical, theological claims.[211] Mbandi follows Kevin J. Vanhoozer's critical hermeneutical realism, in which meaning resides in the text rather than the reader, thus minimizing "the chances of reading or using biblical texts to promote sinful social-cultural beliefs and practices" such as ethnocen-

---

208. Mbandi, *Theology of the Unity*, based on his 2004 PhD dissertation.
209. Ibid., 6.
210. Ibid., 1–3, citing Sparks, *Ethnicity and Identity in Israel*, 1, 3, 4, 5, 16, 18, 19, 21.
211. Mbandi, *Theology of the Unity*, 9.

trism.²¹² Perhaps with this surprising twist that seeks to combine biblical authority with social concern, Mbandi's work can be a platform for future theologians to build upon, providing a more biblically based starting point to spur on creative endeavors. The biblical work engages a neglected area, yet the comparative inattention to sociological and other constructive resources indicates an area for further growth. It is clear in his work is that context is a resource for theology, while being subordinate to biblical teachings.

A Community of Solidarity, Diversity, and Equality

Like the ecclesiological works of Uzukwu, Orobator, and Bishwende, Mbandi's work argues for a high degree of solidarity in the church, detailing the nature of ecclesial solidarity with regard to ethnic diversity. *Unity of the Church* examines the unity of God's people in the OT, Christ as basis for unity in the NT, and multiple ecclesiological models addressing unity with regard to ethnic plurality.²¹³ Mbandi's stance is that ethnicity is not sinful, but ethnocentrism and ill treatment of 'outsiders' threaten the gospel message itself.²¹⁴ Because he argues for inter-ethnic unity within the Christian identity, he focuses mainly on the visible, local church, echoing a common tendency of ecclesiologies in Africa.²¹⁵ Based on the Trinity and pneumatology, Mbandi argues for "integrative heterogeneity," meaning "'differentiated unity' characterized by a mutual embracing and edification of one another, regardless of different socio-ethnic identities."²¹⁶ His main sparring partners on the issue of socio-ethnic diversity as it relates to ecclesial unity are C. Peter Wagner and Donald A. McGavran, advocates of the HUP.

The book's biblical survey begins by examining the OT description of the unity of God's people and their treatment of 'aliens' who worshipped YHWH, moving somewhat cursorily through several passages in order to show the theme's continuity and prevalence.²¹⁷ The *imago Dei* establishes humans in a special relationship to God, and designed for relationships with

---

212. Ibid., 43.
213. Ibid., 10.
214. Ibid., 3–4, 126, 138, etc.
215. Ibid., 4.
216. Ibid., viii.
217. Mbandi emphasizes the connection between Israel and the church, based on "many New Testament passages that understand the church as the new Israel or new people of God" (ibid., 45–47). His emphasis on the connection may account for his significant use of OT passages, whereas other ecclesiologies rely only or mainly on NT passages.

each other. Gen 2:24–25 further indicates that God intended close kinship and unity among humans. Such familial language is found throughout the OT and NT, describing God's relationship with God's people and God's people with each other. However, sin's entrance into the world sounded the death-knell for familial harmony.

Israel's election began the work of repairing and re-creating the lost solidarity. To achieve this restoration, God commanded Abraham to leave his people: the bond to God held priority over all other ties. What, then, was the basis for the solidarity among God's people? Mbandi notes some scholars' claim that in Deuteronomy the name 'Israel' focuses on their bond to YHWH, so the tribes' unity here was "not grounded on blood relationships (ethnic bonds), rather it was based on faith in Yahweh."[218] This solidarity is religious in nature. Correspondingly, the NT demonstrates that Christian unity is found in Christ, by the Spirit's indwelling of God's people, Jew and Gentile. It is God who unites God's people, and their shared relationship to God and each other takes priority over any other bonds.

As the progression of revelation has made clear, Christ is the one who provides reconciliation with God and other people, uniting Christians of various backgrounds. The divinely given unity with Christ, by the Spirit, is a trait that should be manifested and maintained by God's people. Phil 2:1–8, particularly v. 2, depicts "a person whose entire disposition is unity. Thus, Christian unity is not only to be expressed in terms of confessions, but also in terms of mutual and visible services of believers to one another."[219] Unity requires humility and self-denial, indicating that legitimate differences continue to exist; the real threat to Christian unity is self-centeredness.[220] The Incarnation also reveals that solidarity does not require homogeneity; Christ did not lose his divinity by becoming human.[221] Like the other theologians here, Mbandi affirms that Christian solidarity requires a particular ethos marked by love for others and respect for diversity, not attempts to repress or destroy differences. To rephrase this point in communal identity terms, assuming a new identity requires assessing the importance of a former identity but not necessarily relinquishing that former identity.

Hints of the importance of diversity have already been revealed above. More explicitly, the OT notes that Abraham's blessing would extend to other peoples, signaling that God's plan was always catholic in its reach: its global

218. Ibid., 63. Deuteronomy also stipulates that non-Israelite converts have equal treatment and full access in worship of YHWH, alongside those of Israelite blood (69), indicating that "the unity of God's people transcended their ethnic differences" (70).

219. Ibid., 84.

220. Ibid., 84.

221. Ibid., 86–87.

solidarity would include ethnic diversity. Rahab is one example of how God's people included non-Israelite YHWH worshippers, demonstrating that they "always constituted people from diverse ethnic groups."[222] Restoration prophecies also mention a day when people from other nations will join Israel in worshipping YHWH.[223] For example, Ps 102:18–22 points to Christ's kingdom, inaugurated and partially visible in the church, implying "that local churches are the primary places where the visible unity of God's people, which goes beyond ethnic differences [sic] is to be manifested."[224] This concern with an ecclesial identity marked by unity-with-diversity, already surfacing from the OT, resonates with the emphases of the other theologians in this chapter. I would like to make explicit what Mbandi leaves implicit here, that solidarity in Christian identity is specifically prioritized over, but does not destroy, ethnic identities.

NT support for this view of solidarity amidst ethnic diversity is seen in the resolution of the Jew-Gentile conflicts. The early church struggled to understand how Jewish and Gentile Christians were to relate and which laws Gentiles must keep, but the church did not decide that the way to resolve their struggles was to worship separately. Rather, they continued worshipping together, visibly displaying unity, because to do otherwise would deny the gospel message. The Jerusalem Council concluded that a Jewish Christian could observe the law as a way to "express his or her piety, but not as a means of salvation for either Jew or Gentile," and thus it was not a way of life to impose upon Gentile Christians.[225] Diversity of ethnicity and even religious observances was acceptable within the Christian identity.

Unity of the Church also addresses 'problem passages' that might seem to counter Mbandi's arguments on behalf of ethnic diversity within God's people. Regarding Christ's attitude toward Gentiles, Mbandi examines Jesus's encounter with the Samaritan woman and the conversation with the Roman centurion, concluding that Jesus prioritized Jews during his earthly ministry in order to fulfill God's plan and demonstrate God's faithfulness to his promises.[226] At the same time, Jesus introduced the "centrifugal aspect of mission" in the NT, displaying the gospel's universality: "No doubt this tension is reflected by the tension between Jesus' particularistic statements

---

222. Ibid., 62.
223. Ibid., 71, 74–75.
224. Ibid., 79.
225. Ibid., 133.
226. Ibid., 99.

towards Gentiles and his acts of compassion toward Gentiles."[227] For Paul, this plan demonstrates God's mercy to non-Jews (Rom 15:8–9a).

Mbandi identifies the realm of the 'new creation' as the locus of Christians' primary identity. Passages like 1 Cor 12:12–30 discussing spiritual gifts reinforce that diversity within unity is God's plan for people and a reflection of God's Triune nature. Relationships—and hence prior communal identities—are transformed in this realm. Reconciliation does not remove difference, but creates a realm where the differences may function in harmony. "Paul's claim that 'there is neither Jew nor Greek, slave nor free, male nor female' also raises the issue of how the Christian is to define her/his identity."[228] Christians are members of God's household, and that identity transcends all others, as Jesus's words in Luke 14:25–33 indicate.[229] In short, it is critical according to Mbandi for the church to preserve alterity while reprioritizing other identities within the overarching Christian identity.

The book of Revelation affirms that the consummated, perfected church will be fully and authentically multi-ethnic. Mbandi focuses on Rev 5:9 and 7:9–10, which have the "fourfold formula (tribe, language, people and nation)" referring to God's people, which "clearly depicts the ethnic and cultural diversity of the consummated church worshipping God in unity around his throne."[230] In the eschaton the damages of sin are reversed, and harmony between God, humanity, and creation is restored. Harmony clearly does not mean uniformity, as the eschatological gathering proves. God's people point to that future age by their present visible unity. So not only have God's people in the past and present displayed a solidarity with diversity, but God's eschatological goal for God's people is that they include socio-ethnic diversity.

Given his biblically based case that God's people were always intended to be a unity-with-diversity, it becomes clear why Mbandi rejects the HUP. Not only does it over-value pragmatism, in Mbandi's estimation, but perhaps more importantly it views diversity within truly Christian unity as secondary in comparison with other goals. The HUP situates Christians within a homogeneous church broadly reflecting their culture, failing to place Christian identity first, actually compromising the gospel message and prioritizing sociological, cultural values over biblical claims. Mbandi also rejects the assimilative model, which views differences as something to overcome and remove; the dominant group in a church will thus impose

227. Ibid., 97.
228. Ibid., 112.
229. Ibid., 115.
230. Ibid., 135.

their ways on all other groups, producing uniformity. This view does not acknowledge that diversity is a divine gift, nor does it admit that viewing one's group as the best or only credible lifestyle is a failure to love and respect others. His emphasis on valuing and accepting differences, not seeking to dominate other groups and force conformity on them, also demonstrates that while diversity is the main concern of this work, within the group the diverse persons and groups are to be treated as equals. The employment of the Trinitarian analogy confirms this reading: in the Trinity, each person is fully God, equal with each other person. In short, Christian solidarity must be marked by diversity and equality among persons and groups.

Relationality and Interdependence

Unity of the Church argued earlier that the *imago Dei* establishes humans as relational creatures. As mentioned earlier, Israel's election was intended to being the process of restoring broken relational ties. Christ is the source of restoration. Furthermore, the peace Christ brings is not individualistic but communal: peace that heals and brings people into relationship with God and God's people. Eph 2:19 reveals that "Christians are to define their identity not only in terms of ethnicity, nationality, or socio-political associations, but also in terms of their relationship with God and the fellow members of the new community."[231] Mbandi emphasizes that "the reconciliation between Jewish and Gentile Christians [in Ephesians 2] is grounded on their new identity as participants in the new creation, rather than eradication of their ethnic differences."[232] Mbandi views humans relationally, as do the other theologians, though he emphasizes a divine source rather than a cultural basis for this standpoint.

This book echoes Miroslav Volf in claiming that the church reflects the Trinity.[233] The Triune nature of God is the basis for humanity's relational nature. Not only does Mbandi view God and humans as relational, he also emphasizes the interdependent nature of both. For the church to reflect its relational, communal God, ecclesiology should model "'integrative heterogeneity,' [a term] to describe a complex (creative) interaction between Christians of different ethnic groups that result [*sic*] in mutual interdependence. Such integrative unity is also redemptive (missiological) in the sense that it demonstrates to the world the wisdom and power of God in Jesus

---

231. Ibid., 114.
232. Ibid., 106.
233. Ibid., 153.

Christ."[234] Of course the Trinity and church are analogous, not identical, Mbandi emphasizes. Whereas divine unity involves *perichoresis*, ecclesial unity and interdependence have as their source the Spirit who indwells, gifts, and unites Christians; the resulting unity witnesses to God's presence, echoing John 20:21 and Eph 3:6, 10.[235]

Maintaining Spirit-given unity, and living in a way that values diversity and interdependence, require certain postures and practices. In Eph 4:1–6, Paul exhorts the Ephesians to live in harmony, exhibiting humility and patience, attitudes

> essential for accepting the 'others' in their uniqueness, and allowing each person to contribute to the spiritual formation of the whole body of believers. In this context, 'patience' seems to have the sense of forbearance or tolerance of one another's weaknesses and differences. These virtues are essential for communal living in any society, but they are more essential for integrative heterogeneity.[236]

Mbandi concludes that diversity is originally blessed and intended by God. Human sin led to a curse that "results in the disunity of humans, which produces social conflicts. This implies that socio-ethnic affiliations are not sinful" per se; in fact Spirit-wrought diversity-in-unity testifies to God's work and reflects God's Triune nature.[237] In his model of ecclesiological unity incorporating alterity, the Spirit transforms relationships rather than obliterating differences.[238] These specifics clarify how ecclesial identity, shaped by the Trinity, the Incarnation, and the Spirit, is unique.[239]

---

234. Ibid. He uses John 17:1–26 as support.

235. Ibid., 156, 158–59.

236. Ibid., 160–61.

237. Ibid., 167.

238. Ibid., 112, 139. Mbandi elaborates on Ephesians 2, citing O'Brien: "Nothing less than a new creation, an entirely new entity, was needed to transcend the deep rift between the two [Jews and Gentiles]. It was effected through Christ's death, and *the result is not an amalgam of the best element of the two, but a new person who transcends them both.* The new humanity is not achieved by transforming Gentiles into Jews, or vice versa" (O'Brien, *The Letter to the Ephesians*, 200, emphasis mine, quoted in ibid., 106).

239. Mbandi, *Theology of the Unity*, 84, 86–87, for example.

OT and NT Foundation of 'People of God'

In this extensive biblical work lies one of Mbandi's contributions. Uzukwu, Orobator, and Bishwende devote little space to biblical research. *Leadership and Authority* by Titre Ande, whom we study soon, is largely sociological and historical, although the final chapter delves into the biblical basis (mainly NT) for his model. On the other hand, Mbandi devotes over fifty percent of his book to studying the biblical evidence for the nature of God's people: one chapter on the OT, and one on the NT. Thus, *Unity of the Church*, more than any other work here, has shown the broad sweep of the 'people of God' throughout the OT and NT, demonstrating that the theme is found in various genres, time periods, and portions of the biblical storyline.[240]

He repeatedly affirms and demonstrates that the Bible uses familial language to describe God's people. *Unity of the Church* also affirms the viewpoint that ethnicity is understood first and foremost as a language affirming common origin and kinship: it is analogous to extended family.[241] "Primarily rooted in genealogical characteristics, ethnic identity includes the idea that members of the same ethnic group share a common ancestry."[242] Mbandi agrees with Sparks that ethnicity is primarily an issue of "genetic perception," though often linked with other socio-cultural identities; it is only secondarily "instrumental," a tool of socio-economic manipulation.[243]

However, given his own concerns with ethnocentrism, and its influence in his context, it is more than a slight problem that Mbandi avoids directly addressing the dangers of using familial language for the church. If ethnocentrism results in an attitude of superiority to and exclusion of 'outsiders,' what is to prevent ecclesial identity from developing similar characteristics? Mbandi argues that Christian identity is intended to include ethnic diversity, and that Christian identity ought to be a person's primary identity. However, these affirmations do not address concerns that Christian identity might develop its own 'ethnocentric' tendencies in relationships with non-Christians. He also does not engage with other African theologians advocating for or critiquing familial models of the church. These omissions are significant.

Mbandi describes his model's foundation as Trinitarian and pneumatological; like Miroslav Volf, he affirms that the Trinity's unity is grounded in *perichoresis*, "their *mutually interior being*. 'By the power of their internal

---

240. In regard to the NT, he draws heavily, though not solely, upon Pauline texts.
241. E.g., Mbandi, *Theology of the Unity*, vii, 1–3, 57, 59, 63, 115 fn. 461, 167 n. 660.
242. Ibid., 2.
243. Ibid., 2–3, citing Sparks, *Ethnicity and Identity in Israel*.

love, the divine persons exist so intimately with, for, and in one another that they themselves constitute themselves in their unique, incomparable and complete union.'"[244] Further, by conceiving the Trinitarian relations as "complementary" and mutual, rather than "unilinear hierarchical relation," one can envision a vital correspondence between the unity of the triune God and the unity of Christians.[245] Like the Trinitarian persons, ecclesial persons "are constituted as independently believing persons . . . [but] they manifest and affirm their own ecclesial personhood in mutual giving and receiving."[246] The unity of Christians is based not on mutual interiority, but on the indwelling Spirit.

Describing the mutuality among the divine Persons, and the mutual, uniting Spirit among Christians, Mbandi evokes a communal, relational perspective with equality of being. He clearly rejects any 'unilinear hierarchical relation' for the Trinity and presumably God's people. However, ontological equality does not rule out functional subordination; if Mbandi wants a Trinitarian foundation that rules out this possibility, he needs to provide a deeper description of the Trinity.

Furthermore, Mbandi does not provide steps to move a church toward "integrative heterogeneity" or examples of what governance and structure would most closely correspond to this. Would this model move far afield from any hierarchical structure, or could a Trinitarian, pneumatologically based church take various forms? Would one particular form be more appropriate in his own context? The point is that Mbandi provides an initial step, but has not gone so far as to provide a full model with details, or discuss implications and applications of his thesis, leaving the reader metaphorically dangling.

Like the previous theologians, but drawing more explicitly on counter-cultural biblical texts, Mbandi argues emphatically that ecclesial identity must reflect a particular character. Concerned with divisions and longing to see church unity that embraces ethnic diversity, he too utilizes a relational view of humanity, and envisions integrative, interdependent churches that treat outsiders with godly love. In contrast the next theologian, Titre Ande, refuses to countenance familial language being applied to the church, even as he again identifies similar traits as key to ecclesial identity: solidarity marked by diversity, equality, and interdependence, building on a relational view of God and humans.

---

244. Mbandi, *Theology of the Unity*, 155, citing Volf, *After Our Likeness*.
245. Ibid., citing Volf, *After Our Likeness*.
246. Ibid., 155–56, citing *After Our Likeness*.

Georges Titre Ande

The fifth ecclesiology profiled, the second Protestant one, comes from Georges Titre Ande (b. 1960), who has experience as Anglican Bishop of Aru in the Democratic Republic of Congo (DRC), and as a lecturer and principal at the Institut Supérieur de Théologie Anglican in Bunia (incorporated into the Université Anglicane du Congo in 2011). He has published articles, chapters and books in both French and English, and his most extensive work, *Leadership and Authority: Bula Matari and Life-Community Ecclesiology in Congo*, is noteworthy for two reasons in particular.[247] First, in Africa the majority of ecclesiological works, and theologies as a whole, are written by Catholic theologians, whereas Ande is Anglican. Second, the most common ecclesiological model in Africa appeals to family, variously defined, whereas Ande unequivocally rejects familial terms and models in his ecclesiology.

Leadership and Authority concentrates on showing how one particular conception of authority has influenced church structure, unity, relationship to political powers and culture, and general ethos, before proposing a different view. Ande explores multiple forces that have influenced the Église Anglicane du Congo (EAC): colonialist models of government, negatively reinforced by cultural values, the history of Christianity—particularly Anglicanism—and shoddy usage of biblical texts. Ande then describes the EAC's self-understanding, contrasting it with the ecclesial identity that should exist.

Contextualization

Ande's book opens by discussing the seemingly hopeless situation of Africa, illustrated by the DRC political context since 1960. The EAC's state is assessed in light of former president Mobutu's leadership.[248] Ande delineates his approach—"postcolonial liberation theology, which recognizes the value of the local culture but adopts a critical attitude towards modern society"—and his key terms: power is ability to carry out one's wishes, and authority is legitimized, institutionalized power.[249]

---

247. Ande, *Leadership and Authority*.

248. Anthony Balcomb concludes that the book is thoroughly researched, but ultimately depressing in regard to the EAC's state. He finds Ande's vision inspiring, but "his attempt to finish on a note of hope does little to bring one out of the growing sense of despair" ("Review of *Leadership and Authority*," 92).

249. Ande, *Leadership and Authority*, 2, 5–6; his definition of power draws on Pobee, "Take Thou Authority," 189–90.

Leadership and Authority judges inculturation theology to be an incomplete approach, not sufficiently re-orienting the church as a life-impacting, supra-ethnic community.[250] The present context of crisis in the DRC is a "kairotic moment," a time of "judging injustice . . . [as well as] providing opportunity to redeem," which requires commitment to thorough analysis of the situation, willingness to adapt, and courage to act.[251] The church must not be superficial or uncritical in its stance toward society—inculturation gone awry. Instead it must address economic, political, and social issues prophetically and with deep knowledge of their context.[252] So Ande wants more thorough contextualization and transformation of the context, not capitulation to it.

In line with this desire, he carefully critiques Congolese culture. Examining African societies in the DRC, Ande concludes that many saw authority as limited, and a means for serving the community.[253] The chief's main role was to listen well and seek consensus; his authority should provide security for the group.[254] Thus, authority in Congolese societies was a sacred gift to maintain harmonious, participatory unity and abundant life.[255] However, colonizing Belgians arrived, and after 1880 the term '*Bula Matari*' arose, describing "a force which crushes all resistance, or of European representatives as impersonal agents of domination. . . . It was alien, outside society but irresistibly imposed upon it."[256] In order to control Congo more easily, the Belgians heightened ethnic consciousness using colonial administration, trade, and the Catholic Church.[257] Mobutu Sese Seko seized power in 1965 and retained this centralized approach to power; the first democratic elections were not held until 2006.

Ecclesial history also has bearing on the current EAC situation. Church-state relations in post-colonial Congo have varied, with Protestants generally loyal to the regime.[258] Christianity originally arrived in Congo

---

250. Ande, *Leadership and Authority*, 154–56.

251. Ibid., 159–61.

252. Ibid., 161–67.

253. Ibid., 7–8.

254. Ibid., 8–9. This example from Congolese culture sounds similar to Uzukwu's description of African pre-colonial models of authority, fitting with the Manja paradigm.

255. Ibid., 10.

256. Ibid., 12. For Martin Conway '*Bula Matari*' signifies "totally autocratic, unquestionable dictators and their henchmen" ("Review of *Leadership and Authority*," 224).

257. Ande, *Leadership and Authority*, 15, 18.

258. Ibid., 55–57.

thanks to Baganda evangelists relying on British authority.[259] The Ugandan church in turn maintained a tight hold on its position, leading to the perception of Christianity as an ethnically linked power.[260] In light of this history, the EAC therefore understands authority as the power to do one's own will with accountability only to superiors, flowing from a sacred source (which makes office-holders likewise holy), and personally possessed by said office-holders.[261] Ande cites a group of bishops who tellingly agreed that the bishop "*is* the church."[262] Culturally, Ande notes that obedience to authority is valued, and obedience means "unquestioning submission," a view justified by a distortion of the scriptural image of Jesus as the good shepherd. In this flawed interpretation, a church leader (*muchungaji*, shepherd) gives commands to his sheep, Christians (*wakristo*), who should 'blindly' obey. The EAC leadership maintains power by making official documents vague or inaccessible, using ageism and even gender to control the church: in sum, the leaders are essentially invulnerable.[263]

A patronage system within the church inflames ethnocentrism as groups desire leaders from their own group, while the Bible is used to control and intimidate.[264] Missionaries added to the problem by working with specific ethnic groups, highlighting ethnic consciousness and an impression of denominations being ethnic.[265] As Ande describes it, the EAC is a church characterized by divisions, inequality, and forced conformity. Church members sense that their leaders do not stand in solidarity with or for them: "Once a Roman Catholic becomes a priest, he gives his life to others, while in our church, pastors want to conserve their lives, and there is no self-sacrifice."[266] In short, the church has adopted the *Bula Matari* model: it has adopted damaging, unChristian elements from its context without critically assessing them in light of biblical teachings.[267] This model is not contextualization done well; rather, it illustrates capitulation to context, which *Leadership and Authority* intends to counter. So Ande's

259. Ibid., 63, 65. The Baganda are the largest ethnic group in Uganda.
260. Ibid., 68–77.
261. Ibid., 81–82.
262. Ibid., 83, emphasis mine.
263. Ibid., 85–87, 97–104.
264. Ibid., 87, 89, 91–92.
265. Ibid., 93–94.
266. Ibid., 107.
267. Ibid., 109–10. Balcomb assesses the EAC situation, and concludes that the church's role "as a nexus of power in a failed and dysfunctional state such as the Congo takes on enormous significance in terms of provision of infrastructure and stability" ("Review of *Leadership and Authority*," 91).

goal is to contextualize, without submitting to context, and indeed move beyond contextualization to incorporate a global focus. His analysis of culture, local ecclesial history, and politics offers a richer, more complex picture of elements shaping the EAC.

A Community of Solidarity, Diversity, and Equality

The aim of *Leadership and Authority* is to offer a better ecclesiological model. One key aspect of the ecclesiology Ande envisions is solidarity of a particular type. He critiques African ecclesiologies based on clan or family models: they are exclusivist and tend to become ethnocentric.[268] Identifying the church as 'great family' results in including non-Christian ancestors, while the Catholic model of 'church-as-family' based in the Trinity leads to confusion between human families and the Trinitarian community, reinforcing paternal authority structures.[269] Yet, despite such major disagreements, Ande agrees with the other models that community and identity must be integrated, viewing solidarity as an essential aspect of ecclesial identity.[270] The issue is whether family models promote a genuine Christian identity and foster true communal solidarity.

Means of maintaining and strengthening solidarity are also addressed. In exploring the church's Triune basis, Ande in places moves away from ontological language to some extent, and instead mentions what might be termed one's manner of relating to others: intimacy, transparency, openness, and acceptance. Though he says that he is using Trinitarian ontology, I would argue that in actuality what he encourages the church to imitate is not so much God's being, but God's ways. Thus, only God can truly *be* love and fully experience perichoretic union, but God's people are commanded to love, being open to and intimately connected with their fellow Christians in a way that is like, yet distinct from and lesser than, the Trinity. So while at first Ande might be taken for a social Trinitarian, I will demonstrate that the label seems less applicable upon closer reading.

The basis for ecclesial solidarity should be the Triune God. Ande rejects the 'family' model (officially proposed by the 1994 Catholic Synod of Bishops for Africa) because of his concern that the church has become exclusivist toward other ethnic groups, while simultaneously becoming too

---

268. Ande, *Leadership and Authority*, 114–16.

269. Ibid., 116–20, 122–23. In Ande's judgment, Bénézet Bujo's proto-ancestor model commits the error of including non-Christian biological ancestors.

270. Ibid., 121.

inclusivist in regard to the ancestors.²⁷¹ By contrast, the Life-Community model locates Christ at the center, and the unity and equality of Christians in Christ result from "the fact that all members possess the same Spirit (1 Corinthians 12:13) with a diversity of function that does not exalt one group above others."²⁷² Due to the Spirit, God is simultaneously the source of solidarity and of diversity in the church (diversity of gifts and hence functions). Those who function as authority figures are intended to serve the other community members rather than to dominate or distance themselves from others.²⁷³ Leaders do not possess power in their person, nor are they elevated by said power; rather, they perform a particular ecclesial role.²⁷⁴ Ande distinguishes between role and status, stating that authority may come along with certain roles, but authority does not change status so as to set one above other Christians in a rigidly hierarchical structure.²⁷⁵

This last makes it clear that equality in the church is important. Since the Trinity is the basis for both ecclesial solidarity and diversity, this doctrine affirms the importance of equality among diverse persons. *Leadership and Authority* agrees with other African theologians that relational, communitarian life must be central in the church, and that a Christ-centered community of life based on the Trinity will be liberating for all types of people.²⁷⁶ Ande emphasizes that community must be based on the Trinity, not African cultural views.²⁷⁷ He appreciates the 'Trinitarian revival', which highlights communion, but insists that the Trinity has been misunderstood by those who think it reveals patricentric, ontological grading of persons.²⁷⁸ The reference to 1 Cor 12:13 highlights that diversity does not negate equality among persons in the ecclesial body. Furthermore, Ande notes that the NT use of *laos* indicates equality among God's people, Gentiles and Jews as well as leaders and laity; God grants an identity that should bring humility and dependence, not pride, since that identity is a gracious gift.²⁷⁹ The

---

271. Uzukwu, *Listening Church*, 47, refers to the Synod, and it is referenced in multiple places throughout Ande's book and the works of Catholic writers.

272. Ande, *Leadership and Authority*, 145–46. Mbandi too affirmed that Christian unity arises from the Spirit.

273. Ibid., 145–47.

274. Ibid., 149.

275. Ibid., 150–51.

276. Ibid., 135.

277. Ibid., 136–37. For example, he criticizes A. Okechukwu Ogbonnaya's *On Communitarian Divinity: An African Interpretation of the Trinity* for assessing the Trinity in light of African views of community instead of vice versa.

278. Ibid., 138–44.

279. Ibid., 145. Ande echoes Uzukwu's insistence that all churches are equal and

Spirit who gives diverse gifts also unites people as equals, showing a need for close interdependence.[280] Church structure should be dynamic, working cooperatively, rather than static or monarchical.[281]

Relationality and Interdependence

Leadership and Authority views solidarity, diversity, and equality as central traits of the ecclesial community. Having rejected ecclesial models based on 'family' or 'clan', Ande proposes understanding the church as "Life-Community, living the life of Christ in its fullness and sharing Christ's life with others."[282] This community focuses on service, and can effectively confront secular authority as well as "unmask the ideological use of theological and biblical concepts."[283] Ande insists that this model is uniquely—'properly'—motivated: rather than being politically, socially, or economically driven and anthropologically centered, the Life-Community model "is a theological concept mostly Christ-centered on a Trinitarian basis, with sociological, economic and political implications."[284] Thus Ande does not dismiss such concerns but re-orients their place in his model. He wishes to prioritize the Bible and the Triune God, instead of placing context in an authoritative theological position.

What is noteworthy here is that the 'Life-Community' model, with its Triune basis, rejects familial language, yet nevertheless retains a relational perspective of God and humans, and affirms the importance of interdependence in their respective communities. For example, the relational perspective can be seen in Ande's description of Christ and the life he gives. His ecclesiological construction begins with Christ. Life is from God, so the "supreme goal of human life is represented as sharing in divine life (1 Peter 1:4)."[285] The divine life is manifest in Christ, mediated by the

---

none should dominate over others, Orobator's insistence on treating the marginalized with respect and equality, and Mbandi's concern that ethnic differences do not lead a person to assume an 'outsider' is therefore inferior. In short, all of these writers are deeply concerned that differences not be allowed to divide God's people, to be interpreted as inequality, or to cause people to treat others without respect.

280. Ibid., 145–46.

281. Ibid., 146–51.

282. Ibid., 133. For more on Ande's Christology, see his "African Christology," 183–93.

283. Ande, *Leadership and Authority*, 133.

284. Ibid., 137.

285. Ibid., 144.

Spirit, and received by faith.[286] Thus, the life animating God's people is one that arises from a relationship with Christ and involves entering the divine communal life.

An emphasis on divine relationality, and human reception into this, lead naturally to a relational perspective on humans: divine and human relationality are interrelated. Christ's centrality means that his relationship to the Father and Spirit must be understood. Ande points out that the Triune persons have a relationship marked by sharing life, *perichoresis*, equality, and loving communion. This relationality and interdependence are part of divine and ecclesial life. Ande's attention rests mainly on communion, which

> implies intimacy, transparency of intention, and union of hearts, convergence of interests. This is what Life-Community intends for personal and social well-being, and it comes only from bonds of communion between all parts. Moreover, openness as a mark of Spirit is important to build a community. It implies feeling oneself referred outside oneself. Without this openness, there is no acceptance. Therefore, the Holy Trinity is not merely a society in the sense of a collectivity; God is communion of love and unbroken personal relationships. As the personal nature of God is fellowship, to have a personal relationship with God is "a question of being caught up into the fellowship of God which is always personal but never individualistic." The Trinitarian ontology helps us to appropriate something of the richness and openness.[287]

Ande here suggests that being 'referred outside oneself' is crucial in understanding God's nature and God's intention for God's people.

Does Ande's positive appraisal of Zizioulas and Leonardo Boff, using the Trinity as foundation for ecclesiology, indicate that Ande is a 'social Trinitarian'? Karen Kilby lays out three basic characteristics of social Trinitarians: (1) a certain definition of 'person,' (2) a particular view of the history of Trinitarian doctrine, and (3) a "tendency to wax enthusiastic when it comes to explaining how the three . . . can also be one."[288] The first point notes that social Trinitarians typically prefer to retain but refine or redefine the word while their opponents argue that 'person', as it relates to the Trinity, is a complex theological term that may need to be discarded. The second trait is that social Trinitarians typically distinguish sharply between

---

286. Ibid., 138–39.
287. Ibid., 144, quoting from the British Council of Churches' *The Forgotten Trinity*.
288. Kilby, "Perichoresis and Projection," 433.

so-called Western and Eastern views of the Trinity. The third trait is that social Trinitarians tend to treat what was previously a confusing, paradoxical doctrine as if it now provides particular clarity and insight.[289]

By these standards, how does Ande fare? He does not clearly define the term person at any point, or discuss the history of Trinitarian doctrine extensively. Noting the recent 'revival' in Trinitarian theology, he acknowledges that the doctrine has been understood and applied in various, sometimes directly conflicting, ways.[290] If it is difficult or well-nigh impossible to judge his fit with the first two traits Kilby proposes, the third is less problematic. Ande does not suggest that the doctrine is completely clear or simply a panacea. He pointedly notes differing ways the doctrine has been explained, but refrains from concluding that the Trinity is thereby useful only as a boundary marker of orthodoxy.[291] Instead, in keeping with his Christocentric model, he suggests, "A close examination of who and what kind of being Christ is in relation to God the Father and the Holy Spirit, and the rest of the human race is needed."[292] Ande returns to central themes of African theologies: relationality, life, and community. Life is "essentially relational and communitarian"; the problem Ande finds is that this view of life is anthropocentric and must be re-oriented toward the Trinity, the first and foremost example of communion.[293] In short, a relational view of God and humans created in God's image drives Ande, not social Trinitarianism in the usual, developed Western sense.

For his own ecclesiology, then, *Leadership and Authority* proposes that "Life-Community, contrary to African communion ecclesiology, should be built on Christ, the life and the source of authority."[294] Therefore, Ande studies the NT use of *zoe*, particularly in Johannine and Pauline literature, before discussing Christ as source of authority and Christ

---

289. Ibid., 433–35, 438.
290. Ande, *Leadership and Authority*, 141–43.
291. Kilby, "Perichoresis and Projection," 443.
292. Ande, *Leadership and Authority*, 143.
293. Ibid., 135.
294. Ibid., 137. In Martin Conway's words, the EAC system of authority "is not theologically in harmony" with what Christian authority is intended to be, nor does it meet the needs of Congolese Christians. He also points out that Ande places Christians under the authority of Christ, instead of ethnic ancestors ("Review of *Leadership and Authority*," 225).

understood in the Trinity.²⁹⁵ Citing John Zizioulas—"the nature of God is communion"²⁹⁶—Ande proposes Trinitarian communion as the foundation for Life-Community.²⁹⁷

Examining African theologians' discussions of community, Ande approves of the interdependence that is highlighted, but again judges the models problematic in that they are typically more culturally than biblically rooted, they include non-Christian ancestors, and they are deficient in their view of sin.²⁹⁸ He also critiques theologians such as Kwesi Dickson, John Pobee, and Laurenti Magesa who show that "community, relationality, and fundamental interconnections are still crucial to the African worldview" but fail to define 'community.'²⁹⁹ In sum, he appreciates that all these models place communion at the center of the church, emphasizing participation-sharing of all and leading through service, but he advises discarding the tie to biological family. Instead, he advocates emphasizing the centrality of Christ, that membership in Christ's body "should supersede [the Christian's] ties to his natural family."³⁰⁰ So the goal is to affirm relationality and interdependence in more biblically rooted and defined ways.

Rejection of Familial Language

One of *Leadership and Authority*'s contributions to ecclesiological discussions is its rejection of familial language applied to ecclesiology. Because familial models are prevalent in African theologies, it is helpful to have a different perspective on them, one that realizes the dangers inherent in such systems. Ande clearly supports contextualizing, as seen in his valuing of relational, communal perspectives; his focus on life; and more—but he wants to see contextualization that not only adapts to but also transforms the context, and which can see the danger of 'church as family' models. *Leadership and Authority* engages with and critiques what other African ecclesiologies

---

295. Ande, *Leadership and Authority*, 138–43.

296. Ibid., 144, quoting Zizioulas, *Being as Communion*. Ande also references Leonardo Boff's *Trinity and Society*.

297. Ande, *Leadership and Authority*, 135, 137, 143. Fellow Congolese Bishwende also builds ecclesiology upon the being and acts of the Trinity, arguing for the necessity of a Trinitarian ecclesiology that is dynamic, relational, anthropological, and cosmological (Mbenga, "Review of *Église famille*," 210). Bishwende emphatically affirms that human understandings of 'family' are flawed and potentially destructive. Thus, while he uses imagery that Ande rejects, their models share striking similarities.

298. Ande, *Leadership and Authority*, 124–28.

299. Ibid., 135–36.

300. Ibid., 130–32.

offer, and proposes a new model in its place; this proposal of a new model deserves attention.

However, in his desire to avoid the dangers of familial ecclesial models—problems like hierarchicalism and hostility toward outsiders—Ande goes so far as to argue that since a "Christian's membership in the body of Christ should supersede his ties to his natural family" (Mark 3:35), then "it can be argued that the New Testament avoids any kind of kinship imagery."[301] Though Jesus makes it clear that his followers must give their primary allegiance to him and the community he forms, it is difficult to read Mark 3:35 and other NT passages as if familial imagery is not applied to God's people. The Markan pericope finds Jesus discussing true family: Who are his relatives, those to whom he is most closely bound? Are they his biological kin? Jesus scans the upturned faces of his followers and declares them his siblings (Mark 3:34–35). Paul refers to God's people as the "household of God" (Eph 2:19; 1 Tim 3:15) and "the family of faith" (Gal 6:10). The author of Hebrews likewise addresses the people of God as "brothers and sisters," those who are also in the house—family—of God (Heb 3:1–6). Such familial language can be found in the Gospels, Pauline material, and the Catholic Epistles. Christians are those who "belong" to God (John 17:9), born by God's Spirit to become God's children and co-heirs with Christ, their elder brother (John 3:1–6; Rom 8:14–17; Gal 4:1–7; Jas 2:5 and 1 Pet 3:7 use the term 'heirs' as well). In addition, throughout the OT God alternately refers to Israel as God's child or bride, both terms involving close kinship bonds.

So Ande overstates his case in alleging that the NT avoids kinship imagery. Still, it would be unwise to ignore Ande's warnings of the dangers of family imagery being applied to the church. Ecclesiology needs to devote more careful attention to defining how 'family' when applied to the church differs from biological, ethnic concepts. Indeed, arguably familial language cannot be avoided while retaining traditional Trinitarian God language, but that connection again demonstrates the greater care needed for addressing the relation and distinction between divine community and human family.

Ande explores various facets of the EAC context, providing a full-orbed picture of forces affecting the church. Yet insufficient attention is given to doctrinal theology—the importance of Christology is gestured toward, and the Trinity is likewise mentioned as foundational for a proper ecclesiology, but neither is explored in sufficient depth.[302] Ande emphasizes a Christo-centric ecclesiology, Christ the liberator, and Christ as source of

---

301. Ibid., 132.
302. Ibid., 137, 143.

life and authority, but these sections total only seven pages in his own ecclesiological construction.

The Trinity, too, would benefit from more attention. Ande criticizes Trinitarian positions that suggest an ontological inequality among the divine persons and that are 'patricentric', having a rigidly hierarchical perspective.[303] He emphasizes that different roles among church members have no bearing on the equal status of all members, particularly critiquing leaders that view themselves as holier or in some way ontologically better than other church members. So he wants to be clear that functional differences—whether among human or Divine persons—do not affect ontological equality in the respective communities. Ande also rejects approaches that interpret the Trinity in light of African culture, instead of vice versa; he believes that A. Okechukwu Ogbonnaya falls into just such a trap.[304]

For Ogbonnaya, "ultimate reality" and hence existence is relational and social.[305] The African worldview is rooted in community, underscoring "the fundamental and irrevocable belief of the African in relationality," so much so that in the African context "belonging is the key to existence."[306] African unity is communal and respects difference while not sanctioning isolation and separation, as in the "modern" (presumably Euro-American) understanding of 'person.'[307]

Ogbonnaya describes God by drawing upon an African definition of community. Since 'ultimate reality' is fundamentally communal, God cannot be a singularity, alone and separate, but neither can the divine be described as 'polytheistic', since that emphasizes differences, not commonality.[308] Ogbonnaya concludes that "the Divine in the African context is a community of gods, or in Tertullian's terms, a community of persons"; contra both "separatistic" polytheism and singular, bare monotheism, "communotheism" best describes God.[309] The above brief sketch shows how Ogbonnaya prioritizes African worldviews, using them to 'define' God, hence Ande's rejection of Ogbonnaya's methodology.

To reiterate, three major concerns of Ande are equality among church members and among the Triune Persons, rejection of static hierarchical models, and interpreting culture in light of the Trinity (in other words,

---

303. Ibid., 143.
304. E.g., ibid., 136–37.
305. Ogbonnaya, *On Communitarian Divinity*, xviii, 8, 10, 11, 28, 77–79.
306. Ibid., 14, 28.
307. Ibid., 44, 85.
308. Ibid., xii, xiii, xvii, 1, 22, 26, 28, 38, 63, 77, 79, 89.
309. Ibid., 14.

prioritize biblical, theological claims over cultural perspectives and insights). All that being said, there still seems to be a degree of semantics in rejecting ecclesiology modeled on the Triune 'family' in favor of an ecclesiology modeled on Triune communion. Rather than straightforwardly rejecting the use of family language, it may be possible, realizing the tension between its biblical roots and destructive cultural connotations, to emphasize the traits God's people are to display while avoiding the term itself for a time (much as Jesus avoided the term "Messiah") until it can be heard differently.[310] In one sense, this appears to be what Ande does: he rejects family terminology by name, but goes on to describe a community that functions very much as a family ideally would. So perhaps he is simply seeking a neutral name—Life-Community—to refer to traits drawn from biblical uses of the imagery. Yet he does not develop such an approach explicitly, hampering his argument for a relational perspective.

In the end, despite concerns for the church in the DRC, Ande remains optimistic because of the Gospel's power to transform society, and concludes that the Life-Community model "relates not only to selfhood or identity but also takes seriously the local socio-political situation" which, like all things in this fallen world, must be changed by the "death, resurrection, and ascension of Christ."[311] Ande's ecclesiology describes Christian identity as given by the Triune God, an identity marked by solidarity, diversity, equality, and a relational perspective. Christ alone is the head of the body, and its parts are interdependent. The 'in Christ' aspect of identity is more foundational than any other. This model can orient Christians beyond local contextualization to a global mindset: this mindset moves "from ethnicism to inter-ethnic consciousness, and from contextualisation to vitalistic globalisation."[312] This shift happens when leaders help Christians root their new identity firmly in Christ, developing an inter-ethnic consciousness and the knowledge of belonging "to a 'new' . . . supra-ethnic community."[313] This language makes it clear that Ande envisions his ecclesiological model as offering an alternate communal identity for Christians: ecclesiology is the place wherein a person finds her primary communal identity, one which, through the Spirit, opens outward to embrace as equals those of differing ethnic identities and nationalities and differing ecclesial roles. In rejecting both the *Bula Matari* "dominer pour servir" and the cultural view of "sacred

---

310. This point draws on Donald R. Jacobs, "Conversion and Culture," 186–91.

311. Ande, *Leadership and Authority*, 169.

312. Ibid., 154. Conway praises Ande's book as "excellent theology which deserves careful reading in many parts of the world, by no means only in Africa" ("Review of *Leadership and Authority*," 224).

313. Ande, *Leadership and Authority*, 155.

hierarchy," the Christian identity refuses to dominate and instead invites "voluntary acknowledgement."[314]

Leadership and Authority centers ecclesiology on Christ and the NT before building from there. However, it does so with minimal exegetical discussion and without treating some of the biblical material on describing God's people in familial terms, as noted previously. Debates over family terminology aside, Ande shares many of the same concerns as other ecclesiologies: equality among church members, particularly with regard to non-dominating relationships between leaders and laity and between ethnic groups. This equality is based on valuing diversity of roles and gifts within Christian unity. Whereas Mbandi focuses on accepting ethnic outsiders as equals in the church, Ande displays some of the same concerns but approaches them from a Trinitarian angle and with an eye to Christ's ministry, which illustrates the ethos necessary to yield an atmosphere of humility, enabling others, and equal treatment of church members. Such an ecclesiology should promote life and communion in Christ, treating outsiders with love befitting the Gospel. And as Ande repeatedly notes, this ecclesiology explicitly addresses concerns about, and provides for, a stable communal identity.

Preliminary Synthesis

Among these authors are differences of church affiliation, theological era and approach, disciplinary method(s), language, and country of origin, as well as some disagreements about appropriate ecclesial terminology. Yet amidst all these differences, there is surprising, significant overlap. To repeat, the communal identity 'God's people' should be a person's principal identity, but it need not require relinquishing other communal identities. Instead, the 'in Christ' identity requires and incorporates diversity and individuality within itself, overcoming previous social divisions and creating a new, preeminent identity. In this communal identity, the individual and communal aspects of identity are both important and mutually reinforcing. This identity is marked by equality, valuing diversity, and godly, other-focused love.

How, then, do ecclesiologies more particularly address and further hone the nature of the Christian communal identity? For one, the debate over familial language is a concrete example of the continuing concern with communal identity. Despite substantial disagreement with many of his contemporaries on the suitability of familial language for ecclesiology, Ande's

---

314. Ibid., 6–7, 10, 12, 146–48, 152–54.

model too depends on a high degree of solidarity, a trait often associated with family. Though his basis differs, his description of ecclesial identity distinguished by equality and diversity in solidarity, and an ethos of love that welcomes those who are different from particular selves or communities, matches quite well with the other theologians here. He particularly emphasizes the importance of equality among ethnic groups in the church, and between leaders and laity. The Christian identity is also marked by humility and serving others in love, markers that differ significantly from what he sees in the EAC and Congolese culture.

To recap, the following themes arose in the ecclesiological identities envisioned here: firstly, contextualization. In order to contextualize, Uzukwu adopts the inculturation approach, employs church history, and draws on African cultures. He argues that Christianity is not foreign to Africa, and by extension, the communal Christian identity resonates in an African context. Orobator takes another root to contextualize more thoroughly (in his perspective) he draws upon the social sciences in order that theology will engage its context and be well rooted in it. He views the African context as united by common socioeconomic and political problems, and he too advocates listening and dialogue as a means to ensure equality and contributions from every church member. So in *Crisis to Kairos* the response of the church as a whole (leaders and laity) to HIV/AIDS, poverty, and refugees are examined. Bishwende's method is full, dynamic inculturation that incorporates and enlarges on previous methods in Africa. He examines specifically the challenges of maintaining diversity and particularity in the face of homogenizing globalization, while remaining open to others and allowing them to shape one's identity. His conception of Christian identity addresses the concern of globalization, and the imperative for Christian identity to welcome alterity in its ongoing process of definition.

Mbandi does not adopt any specific method of theology (inculturation, liberation, or reconstruction), but critiques the HUP model, providing a biblical basis for the argument that ecclesial identity must include ethnic diversity, an ongoing concern in Kenya and other African countries. Ethnocentrism reveals itself in politics, ecclesial life, and more, which is why Mbandi proposes an ecclesiology termed "integrative heterogeneity," based on the Trinity and pneumatology. Ande adopts the liberation method, and explores how the EAC has adopted the *Bula Matari* governing model, which does not view all in the church as equals, or respect the voice and contributions of laity. The EAC's uncritical adoption of contextual norms produces a church characterized by divisions and forced conformity. Also, Ande wants to contextualize, then move beyond this to a global perspective with an accompanying Christ-based, supra-ethnic identity.

The second theme explored with regard to ecclesial identity is solidarity: for Uzukwu, solidarity and communality are African values. The church should be marked by unity, as well as equality, both by members within a local church, and in the relationship of African churches to Rome: Uzukwu envisions an ecclesial structure that is collegial. Unity includes multiplicity (diversity), and should not be confused with uniformity; the Christian identity is intended to include diversity, not produce conformity. Because the church is analogous to the Trinity, the importance of unity's character properly reflecting the divine unity. Finally, ecclesial (Christian) identity should be a person's primary identity. Orobator views solidarity as essential to the church's nature. *Church as Family* explores and analyzes church unity through the way in which church leaders relate to laity. In other words, ecclesial identity should be marked by a particular type of unity, one where leaders and laity, mainstream and marginalized members, are committed to standing together. Solidarity with the poor and marginalized, treating them as equals with a voice, is of high importance to Orobator. Again, Orobator concludes that listening and dialogue are key in developing a true unity, marked by diversity and equality, in the church. He urges that the church must not just be with or for the marginalized, but identify fully with them, due to creation and Incarnation. Bishwende's desire is to continue Vatican II's trend of viewing the church not as hierarchical society, but as a communion of united, diverse equals based on the Trinity. A hierarchical church fails to reflect the Trinitarian communion, because it does not value equality and interdependence among members. He balances the local, particular aspects of ecclesiology with the universal aspects through the Eucharist, and advocates dialogue as a means of removing barriers, increasing equality and solidarity with diversity, and demonstrating love and welcome of others. For him, too, the Christian identity should be a person's overarching, preeminent identity.

For Mbandi, the Incarnation shows that solidarity does not equal homogeneity. Indeed, solidarity should be marked by love and respect for diversity, and equality; the Spirit creates a new identity where differences can function in harmony, and previous social barriers (and identities) are not destroyed but transcended by the common 'in Christ' identity. The church reflects the Trinity, so it must display a similar type of unity, and remember that the Spirit transforms relationships rather than destroy or suppress differences. Ande embraces claims that true solidarity is central to ecclesial identity, but prefers to ground such understandings of communion and unity on the Trinity and the Bible rather than culture, and develop an ecclesial identity that supersedes other identities and reaches out to others.

Third is relationality, another central mark of the ecclesial identities described. Uzukwu describes Africa as united (at least in part) by its various cultures' emphasis on communitarianism, urges the church to recover this value, becoming a relational, interdependent community. The church is analogous to the Trinity, which is understood relationally. Orobator roots his understanding of solidarity and relationality in creation and the Incarnation. So here Christian identity is determined in part by the commitment of church members to each other, by their loving treatment of each other. Bishwende imagines the church as a communion of diverse equals, based on the Trinity and relational values. God's relational nature speaks volumes for ecclesiology, revealing its centrality. Because of God's relational nature, hierarchical church models are judged as failing to faithfully reflect the Trinity, a major fault.

Mbandi approaches relationships from a biblical angle, emphasizing that God created humanity as a unity, and as relational. Here Christian identity is seen in one's response to those who are ethnically 'other': a Christian response is to welcome, love, and view as an equal the one who is different ethnically but equally committed to following God. In other words, Mbandi advocates a relationally defined identity. For Ande, like Bishwende, the Trinitarian basis of ecclesial identity is crucial. God's Triune nature is why relationality, equality, diversity of gifts and persons, and Spirit-given unity in Christ are central to the church. Leaders have a different role, but are not to be viewed as greater than or separated from laity, as if they were a separate caste: their common relationship 'in Christ' is more basic than their ecclesial roles. Furthermore, Christian identity is discerned in part by its treatment of others who are different from oneself, particularly in humility and a desire to liberate and enable others. Domination is no part of a truly Christian identity, perhaps because it inherently damages relationships and places the participants on unequal footing.

Finally, we noted that each theologian possessed certain unique aspects in their ecclesial models. Uzukwu particularly urges the practices of intentional listening and dialogue as aids in developing this godly unity, and incorporated ecclesial history in and as a defense of his construction. Orobator incorporates this 'listening' model, but chooses a different method. He formulates an approach that includes the social sciences, producing an ecclesial identity that includes laity voices. Bishwende's model reminds readers that Christian identity is eschatological: moving toward a divinely established *telos*, and thus a 'work in progress' in the present. Mbandi provides a much greater biblical basis for a diverse-yet-united ecclesial identity than the others, and this biblical work includes OT bases. Ande is unusual in rejecting familial language for the church, yet provides contextual reasons why familial language ought to be treated with greater care.

The distinct positions of these authors should not be downplayed. The ecclesiologies are arranged chronologically, from the mid-1990s to the last few years. They also diverge in method, ecclesial affiliation, and terminology applied to the church. While these differences are significant in certain respects, it does not seem to produce major differences in their descriptions of ecclesial identity. They do prioritize different sources in supporting their cases—culture, ecclesial statements, social sciences, doctrinal theology, and the Bible—and examine differing aspects of church unity (at the local level, as well as on the larger level of African churches relating to Rome and to the forces of globalization).

Yet, all of these ecclesiological authors in Africa share a fundamental concern with a Christian identity marked by a deep, true unity, over against ecclesial divisions caused by flawed concepts of authority, social status, ethnic differences, or other distinguishing marks of identity. All the authors insist that the personal and communal equality involved in Christian identity does not negate valid and valuable differences: unity in Christ is emphatically not uniformity. Unity in Christ provides an overarching identity that properly identifies—relativizes—the importance of differences within other identities. Entering the new community in which the new creation is inaugurated by Christ means adopting the Christian identity as one's primary identity, without destroying prior identities.

Last but not least, these theologians all view the church's nature—the ecclesial identity—as a theological concern, showing that Bediako's perception of Christian identity as theological in nature, an outworking of the Gospel, continues to be valid. Though identity in an apologetic or defensive sense may no longer be a major issue, the character of ecclesial identity is definitely of interest, demonstrating that identity concerns have shifted but not vanished from the landscape. Indeed, the appropriation of God's self-revelation has many implications for ecclesiology. Christian identity's relational character, linked to interdependent community, reflects the Trinitarian communion of God's own life at a human level. If the church fails to fully include the marginalized or make a place for each and every member, then it fails to accurately represent its divinely given identity and mission.

Again, the authors above do not present an apologetic for African identity, whether Christian or not; rather, they argue that African ecclesial identity must take a particular shape. While the authors presuppose primary engagement with their African contexts as the sites within which their ecclesiological proposals arise, they also presuppose that their insights reflect deeper and more universally Christian truths—ultimately, concerning the church's identity in the Triune God of loving communion. As a way of drawing together African ecclesiological insights and addressing those insights to other—not least European and North American—contexts, the final chapter takes up two primary tasks. First, it explores how African theologians might relate their cultural emphases in ecclesiology to other contexts in light of a Trinitarian theology of revelation. Second, it explores how recent interest in the social identity approach might resonate with and contribute additional language for the Christian communal identity that African theologians promote.

Chapter 6

ॐ

Christian Social Identity in Africa and Beyond

Having examined major theological emphases in Africa, theological insights on identity, biblical passages employed to support theological arguments about the nature of communal identity of God's people, and ecclesiological models and their prominent concerns, we are now positioned to observe the theological bases with which African ecclesiological claims can be shared with the church worldwide. After examining the theological bases for such sharing that appear among African theologians themselves, we then take the final step of introducing the social identity approach as a further means of communicating these ecclesiological insights. In particular, the social identity approach not only supports the African highlighting of relational components in identity, it also provides additional language to address African concerns over ethnocentrism and other divisions within God's people.

Theological Bases for Globalizing African Ecclesiology

What are the most common theological frameworks underlying African ecclesiologies' implications for other global contexts? One major foundation is God's Trinitarian self-revelation and its implications for YHWH's people: the Triune God is one, yet the three persons differentiate the way in which God is personal. YHWH invites humans to partake in the divine fellowship, abiding in Christ and with one another. So for instance the Trinity and pneumatology are Mbandi's theological support in favor of the importance of an ecclesiology of "integrative heterogeneity," a unity composed of both similarities and differences, "characterized by a mutual embracing and edification of one another, regardless of different socio-ethnic identities."[1] This unity does not obliterate distinction and differences. If God's people are not catholic, breaking down social barriers to form a new people, then they fail to represent God's plan of a varied universal assembly in the eschaton.[2]

YHWH is relational, eternally in community. Furthermore, the Triune God seeks to draw sinful humans into the very fellowship of the divine life, offering redemption and reconciliation, accomplished through Christ. "The new birth arises from a new relationship to the Christ in his Spirit and creates new relationships," a community created by the Spirit who "ensures the oneness of the church and endows each particular church with a resilience to bear witness to the Kingdom, breaking down thereby the artificial barriers erected by groups and people."[3] The Spirit of Christ brings new life, creating a new humanity united in Christ and embodying the reconciling power of the gospel: Ande refers here to Likambo Araba, the chief of Kumuru, who "reminded the church of its responsibility and opportunity to demonstrate to the nation the reconciling power of the gospel in a multiethnic society where ethnic groups suffer violence and discrimination."[4] The fact that humans are made in God's image also indicates that they are intended to be social—fellowship is healthy and necessary: it is not good for a person to be alone. Theologians in Africa draw on God's triune nature and intentions for humanity to argue that all people are intended for communal life. Indeed, "a Christian community in some way should reflect the Trinitarian communion which is its source and the ecclesial communion which is its sign."[5] Similarly, *Église-famille de Dieu: Esquisse d'ecclésiologie africaine* argues that "Church-Family of God is an icon of the Trinity in which the Holy Spirit is relationship of communion and love between the Father and the Son, the foundation of any relationship of communion and love," uniting people with God.[6]

God does not simply bring humans into relationship with the Trinity, but also with other people who are in Christ: the gospel is an earthly reconciling power.[7] God sent the Son to redeem the world, and the Spirit con-

1. Mbandi, *A Theology of the Unity*, viii.
2. Orobator, *From Crisis to Kairos*, 169, 170.
3. Uzukwu, *A Listening Church*, 49.
4. Ande, *Leadership and Authority*, 106, citing an interview with the chief on July 29, 2001.
5. Ibid., 122.
6. Bishwende, *Église-famille*, 7 n. 1, my translation. See also 14, 15, 19, 111, 165, 180.
7. Ande, *Leadership and Authority*, 106.

tinues this missional work of reconciliation and redemption among the new humanity that the Spirit creates and unites into one body in anticipation of the eschatological communion.[8] In the consummation, the isolation and destructive divisions caused by sin will be fully, finally reversed; at present, the unity among God's people should be analogous to Trinitarian unity and a foretaste of the perfect unity to come.[9] *Church as Family* too links the church's unity with its divinely given mission to announce the Kingdom.[10] In order to have unity, there must be reconciliation between the various parties. Reconciliation is a work of Christ and the Spirit, and is part of God's mission in which the church, animated by the Spirit, participates, as a facilitator and space for forgiveness.[11] It is specifically by the Spirit's power and motivation in overcoming "narrow divisions" such as ethnicity and kinship that God's people "witness to the coming of the Reign of God. . . . The metaphor of the church-family is connected to the church as the new Israel of God. Indeed it may be called the fulfillment of the prophecy of assembling of the nations on the mountains of the house of God devoid of divisions, humiliations, and violence."[12] African ecclesiologies may have a greater tendency than others to emphasize community, but this tendency is not merely a Christian reflection of a wider cultural trait: this emphasis is an instance of general revelation, the Triune God's self-witness through particular features of African cultures. Furthermore, this communal emphasis is validated by special revelation, by the Triune God's ultimate self-disclosure in the reconciling work of Jesus Christ by the Spirit's power.

Thus a second foundation for these African theological claims is general revelation, which means that a relational view of humanity is not just an African preference; instead, this view is an instance of divine revelation

---

8. Bishwende, *Église-famille*, 19, 20; for more on reconciliation as a key aspect of God's plan and God's people, see also 46, 62; Mbandi, *Theology of the Unity*, 153–62; Uzukwu, *Listening Church*, 106, 107.

9. Mbandi, *Theology of the Unity*, 136–37, 138, 139; see also ch. 5 of this book, exploring various models of ecclesial unity in response to ethnic diversity. *Listening Church* describes self-isolation as being destroyed by the Spirit and the gifts he bestows: the Spirit's gift(s) to a person "is a way of giving internal coherence to each Christian. It is a way of liberating each Christian from being closed with the self, so that he or she may be fully involved in the service of the community" (108–9).

10. Orobator, *The Church as Family*, 11, 45, 105–6, 124, 136, 162, 173. Orobator's *Crisis to Kairos* reaffirms the importance of the church's mission of proclaiming the Gospel of the Kingdom (14, 18, 59, 110, 111, 233, 243–44). Uzukwu's *Listening Church* also links the church's being and purpose to proclamation and thereby transformation of her context (8).

11. Bishwende, *Église-famille*, 62, 111, 165, 167, 168, 184; Orobator, *Crisis to Kairos*, 132, 141.

12. Uzukwu, *Listening Church*, 68.

at work. While Euro-American thinkers have emphasized the individual for years, the individual must not overshadow or obliterate the communal—and the personal-identity-in-community—emphases in the Bible. God's self-revelation occurs in two ways, frequently referred to as general and special revelation. General revelation affirms that God reveals some basic truths of God's nature and character in various forms tied to creation, making these truths potentially available to anyone, even in cultures not yet overtly shaped by the gospel. Theologies in Africa, drawing on this doctrine, frequently affirm that God is revealed in all cultures, including African cultures, hence also in ecclesiologies in Africa.[13] There are elements in African cultures which may be labeled general revelation, elements that reflect truths about God and are vital for ecclesiologies in Africa to redeem and incorporate.[14] *Listening Church* employs the inculturation approach, which examines "the totality of African culture, ancient and modern, as the context of theology. Inculturation theology is first and foremost a reaffirmation of African culture and identity, denied by Western colonialism and Christian missionary evangelism. Thus it cannot escape from being called a theology of protest."[15] What is being protested is the suggestion that African cultures have no positive traits, and that they are devoid of general revelation. Inculturation theology rejects these notions.

Even works that specifically avoid the approach of inculturation theology note that "care must be taken in using African categories to bring down to earth the reality and mystery of incarnation into the Body of

---

13. Bruce Hansen says that the comment that Christ is all and in all (in Col 3:11) summarizes Paul's "cosmic, eschatological vision in which Christ is reconciling all to himself. This coda implies that Christ is in particular cultures and their practices, gathering them into a renewed wholeness" ("*All of You Are One*," 188). See also Richardson, "Redemptive Analogy," 430-36.

14. Mulago's approach of the "stepping stones" or adaptation later gave way to an emphasis on inculturation, and inculturation theology in turn received critique for being too narrowly focused. Despite these changes and differences, the various streams of theology in Africa generally agree that for the Christian faith and the church to be fully embedded in and embodied by a particular culture, there must be a dialogue between Gospel and culture which realizes that God works in and through cultures, as seen in the Incarnation. This dialogue includes critique of culture, rejecting harmful elements in it, but it also insists that the Triune God is God of all people, and that those who love Christ, the Truth, will love God's truth wherever it is found (Ande, *Leadership and Authority*, 2, 167-68; Bishwende, *L'Écclésiologie trinitaire*, 17-18, 23, 44, 181-82; Mbandi, *Theology of the Unity*, 11-12, 15, 20, 43; Mulago, "Nécessité de l'adaptation," 19-40 (23, 33, 37, 38, 40); Orobator, *Crisis to Kairos*, 83, 84; idem, *Church as Family*, 23; Uzukwu, *Listening Church*, 5-6).

15. Uzukwu, *Listening Church*, 5.

Christ."[16] The unspoken assumption is that these African categories are being and must be used in theologies in Africa. Similarly, *Church as Family* points to inculturated liturgies as proof of authentic, mature worship among God's people in Africa: that ecclesiology, and Christianity as a whole, is rooted and healthy when it redeems and incorporates general revelation found in the local culture.[17] Drawing upon its own context and God's self-revelation there, the African church has both general revelation and the Spirit's presence to draw upon in formulating appropriate ecclesiologies. It is indeed God at work redeeming African cultures and working through theologies in Africa.

African cultures have long focused on community and the pursuit of life; YHWH too is relational and communal, and offers life in Christ's body to those who join God's people. The Christ also brings liberation, freeing Christians in Africa to be who God designed them to be, to celebrate their specific cultural strengths, and to participate as equals among God's people and bring their contribution into God's kingdom.[18] Besides loving God and bringing God their cultural wealth, Christians in Africa are also called to love and serve others, as Jesus makes abundantly clear. This is the other-focused, outward-facing aspect of the church that the African theologians earlier emphasized, in contrast to an inward-focused church that treats outsiders as lesser persons.

In line with such focus on imitating Christ, a third African foundation or framework for sharing its ecclesiological contributions moves beyond general revelation—which cannot conflict with special revelation—to examine the ultimate divine revelation in the Incarnation, affirming therefore that God does not come to destroy but to redeem and purify African

16. Ande, *Leadership and Authority*, 132.

17. Orobator, *Church as Family*, 23, 27, 36; idem, *Crisis to Kairos*, 15, 28, 83.

18. See chapter 3 above, with Mulago's call for the church in Africa to bring her gifts and particularities into God's kingdom, just as other peoples have done and will do (Mulago, "Nécessité de l'adaptation," 30–32, 38–39; "Christianisme et culture africaine," 324; "Le problème d'une théologie africaine," 119ff; and *Un Visage africain du christianisme*, 227). See also Bediako, *Theology and Identity*, 348, 371. Bediako highlights Mulago's claim that "Christ does not ask the African to divest himself of her personality in order to become his disciple. *But on the contrary the African who has become a disciple in the Kingdom is called to bring his 'Africanness' into that Kingdom to enrich it and to contribute to its varieties of beauty*" (*Theology and Identity*, 371, italics Bediako's, quoting Mulago, "Christianisme et culture africaine"). Bediako concludes his study of Mulago by noting that, "in specifically *theological* terms, what Mulago's work has consistently sought to argue is that there is in African tradition, a theology, a *natural* theology, the product of a *natural* revelation, which is the only valid and sure basis for an adequate Christian theological integration in modern Africa (375, Bediako's italics, based on Mulago, *Un Visage africain*).

cultures. Mulago's "Nécessité de l'adaptation missionaire chez les Bantu du Congo" provides but one instance of an African theologian appealing to the example of Jesus, the ultimate revelation of God, as the warrant for a focus on contextualizing the Gospel message: communicating God's revelation in ways that connect with the hearers, adapting the presentation and the resulting ecclesiology in a manner that seeks to redeem and work through local values to convey the Gospel.[19] This is the way God relates to people and communicates to them—by dwelling in their midst, becoming one of them; in turn, God's people ought to employ a similar approach to culture in their mission to share Christ's story.[20] Bediako too affirms that God works in and through cultures to express the Gospel message, transforming them; thus all theology engages cultures and reflects not only universal truths but also the particularities of the context in which it arose.[21] Special revelation is a crucial precedent for theologians in Africa, because it highlights that their emphasis on contextualization is simply an extension of God's own means of self-revelation.

Uzukwu appeals to inculturation theology's approach in part because it "acknowledges that the message of Jesus the Christ, which must always be carried and communicated culturally, has come to dwell among us. Thus it is deeply connected with the idea of incarnation."[22] The Incarnation demonstrates God's commitment to redeeming creation as a whole, including cultures. Since God's method is not to destroy but refine what is good and worthwhile, and to communicate in culturally appropriate ways, African theologians maintain they are not in any way aberrant in focusing on the importance of incarnation and of discovering aspects of African culture that can build up the Christian communal identity in that context. Further, if these elements are indeed divine revelation, then they are relevant for the church in all contexts, not just in Africa.

It has been frequently noted that community has traditionally been an important value in African cultures; hence many ecclesiologies compare the church to the clan or family. While the church as a community of solidarity is a prominent element in African ecclesiologies, ethnocentrism is a dangerous reality indicating that the character of such a community is vital. Some ecclesiologies reject familial language, for fear it may incorporate the harmful elements of a communal viewpoint. Regardless, these African

---

19. See also Mulago's *Un Visage africain*, 26ff, and his use of Revelation 21 to support his argument.

20. Mulago, "Nécessité de l'adaptation," 30–34.

21. E.g., Bediako, *Theology and Identity*, xv, 240, 273, 393, 431, 432, 434.

22. Uzukwu, *Listening Church*, 5.

theologians repeatedly emphasize God's intention of bringing God's people into a new community, which supersedes all others and incorporates them into itself. In other words, God creates a new humanity, offering a new identity and new community, which are permanent and which can withstand the pressure of the rapid changes in the African context. Yet it is not an altogether static identity that God offers, because what God's children will be, in the future, has not yet been revealed. There is still a dynamic element to this identity, an acknowledgement that adaptation and contextualization are ongoing processes in the community of God's people.

These, then, are three major doctrinal bases of African theology's argument about the Christian identity and its implications for global contexts beyond its own: the Trinity, general revelation, and special revelation, particularly the Incarnation.

As mentioned earlier, an additional form of argument would appeal more directly to passages of Scripture. From first to last, community, relationality, and interdependence run throughout the biblical narratives. When the Triune God creates the world and humanity, the first "lack" in creation is Adam's aloneness. This indication of interdependence can result in shared curses as a consequence of sin (Achan's family), but also shared blessings as a consequence of choosing to follow YHWH (Rahab's family). Like the divine community, so too the human community can and should integrate distinction and difference with interdependence and union. Rahab's ethnic identity remains, but is of less importance than her commitment to YHWH and YHWH's people. Ezekiel 18 shows that individuals bear responsibility for their actions; a communal emphasis does not erase this responsibility. The Apostle John reports the prayer of Jesus that his followers be one as the Son and the Father are one: unity is a key marker of God's people, and reflects the Triune God's unity. Paul employs body imagery to remind the Corinthians that diversity within God's people does not negate their unity, but rather results in valuing difference and interdependence among the members. Interdependence and union among God's people are not passing or temporary values, but as Paul specifically highlights, these are traits necessary for the fulfillment of God's plan.

Thus, these ecclesiologies display a pervasive concern with the African communal identity, and African theologians accordingly attend to Christian communal identity (ecclesiology). Theologians express the need for an identity that realizes the impact of communities of solidarity, an identity that can adapt to the rapid changes overtaking the continent, and values diversity. They add to this need that the church in Africa must reflect an identity formed by divine self-revelation: incorporating truths from local culture(s) and addressing local issues due to general revelation, while ultimately displaying the love of God.

However, the literature from Africa generally does not offer much definition of the term 'identity' amid all of the attention to its communal shape. Indeed, the pervasive emphasis on community in African literature underscores the need for identity language that deals with the group-influenced aspect of a person's identity, and therefore its multiplicity, fluidity, and potential internal conflicts. Identity language that simply focuses heavily upon the individual or downplays the important contributions of communities is insufficient and unequipped to address ethnic clashes. African ecclesiologies also question more specifically how to increase unity that lovingly values diversity, how to prioritize the Christian identity without losing other identities, and how to develop certain traits in the church so that it more accurately reflects God and the Gospel. While the African context helpfully highlights these crucial needs for reflection on identity and emphasis on community, room remains for more conceptual precision. Moreover, if Mulago gwa Cikala Musharhamina was correct that particularity and contextualizing are the necessary manifestations of Christianity's claim to universality, and Kwame Bediako was correct that the Gospel is simultaneously universal and particular, then making progress in this discussion would benefit the church elsewhere.[23]

African cultures were in the past community-oriented, and the communal identity provided by ethnicity was arguably often a person's most important social identity. As modernization continues to affect the continent, some of this communal focus has lessened. Yet the authors studied here affirm the importance of community in shaping identity, and point to biblical passages that support the value and role of belonging to God's diverse-yet-unified people. This identity transcends ethnic, national, gender, and church role divisions, and should be the foundational identity of individual Christians and the Christian community as a whole. The nature of God's people reflects God's self-revealed nature, in that God is relational and communal (triune).

Chapter 4 explores biblical passages that illuminate the nature of the Christian communal identity. Chapters 2, 3, and 5 demonstrate that identity concerns and questions of communal solidarity are prominent in African theology. It is undeniable that modernization, globalization, and outside (read: Euro-American) influences have affected African cultures, so that the communal structures of clan and tribe have, in many places, diminished in importance and/or changed in structure. Yet these developments have only

---

23. For example, see chapter 3, pp. 90–91, 96–97.

heightened the concern over identity and what part community might appropriately play in it. For Christian theology, such questions of identity and emphases on community meet in the realm of ecclesiology. Ecclesiology gives specific shape to the Christian communal identity, claiming that being a child of God (ecclesial identity) is a person's primary identity. Questions then arise: How do other identities—based on gender, ethnic group, etc.—relate to this primary identity? When a person's primary identity derives from being 'in Christ', what should their attitude be toward internal and external difference (alterity)?

The proposal here is that the social identity approach provides a potential resource for further discussion of ecclesial identity. Viewing humans sociologically and psychologically reinforces the cultural and theological position of African theologians that all humans are social creatures requiring relationships with other individuals and groups. These relationships shape a person's perception of their own identity, sometimes to the extent that one's membership in a particular group—for example, God's people—becomes one's primary self-identifier. When people highly value communal unity and identity, the well-being of the group often takes precedence, and the individual will sacrifice private or personal desires at times to achieve the group's goals.

On the other end of the individualist-collectivist spectrum, a more individualistic person would likely define themselves first and foremost not by group membership, but by personal accomplishments, and may prioritize their personal well-being over that of any group in which they voluntarily participate—yet they still are shaped by groups to which they belong. This may seem a truism, but elaborating on the implications of this focus will shed light on ecclesiological issues. So while Euro-American cultures may be less collectivist than African cultures, and African cultures can presumably more readily discern the influence and importance of community, the communal influence on identity is present in both settings: it is simply more easily noticed and intentionally appropriated in one than in the other. Insights from churches in Africa can then assist theology globally, particularly concerning how diversity plays a crucial role in comprising a genuine unity.

The Social Identity Approach

In his ecclesiology, Agbonkhianmeghe E. Orobator recommends that theologians should 'ground' theology by drawing on the social sciences.[24] Fol-

---

24. Orobator, *Church as Family*, 9, 13; idem, *Crisis to Kairos*, particularly 16, 23, 25–30, 45, 46, 49, 51. As mentioned, a recent work explicitly following Orobator's

lowing that recommendation, I recommend the social identity approach as a tool to better define and comprehend identity, providing a language for 'listening' to what African thinkers are saying.[25]

Surprisingly, identity discussions are more prevalent in recent decades. Richard Jenkins suggests that "popular concern about identity is, in large part perhaps, a reflection of the uncertainty produced by rapid change and cultural contact: our social maps no longer fit our social landscapes. We encounter others whose identity and nature are not clear to us. We are no longer even sure about ourselves; the future is no longer so predictable as it seems to have been for previous generations."[26]

Teresa Okure names globalization as a major force of change in today's world, one that attempts to forge a single universal or global culture at the expense of other cultures. Globalization, in her analysis, is driven by desire for power and money, and thus seeks homogeneity at the expense of the individual and particular. The impressive forces of globalization put weaker cultures at risk; Okure describes globalization's effect on Africa by playing off the phrase 'global village', concluding that "[globalization's] description as 'a global pillage' is particularly applicable to Africa."[27] She charges that globalization has forced negative changes upon African cultures, putting African cultural values and cultural identities at risk. Okure concludes that "each culture needs to know, identify and affirm itself before it can meaningfully enter into dialogue with another culture and not be absorbed by that other."[28] Kathryn Woodward agrees that "identities are contested," and "the cultural homogeneity promoted by global marketing could lead to the detachment of identity from community and place. Alternatively, it could also lead to resistance, which could strengthen and reaffirm some national and local identities or lead to the emergence of new identity positions."[29] Woodward notes that major disruptions and crises in societies, or globally, produce more identity crises.[30] How will national and local identities

---

methodological recommendation is Gregg A. Okesson's *Re-Imaging Modernity: A Contextualized Theological Study of Power and Humanity within Akamba Christianity in Kenya*.

25. Orobator, *Church as Family*, 31–32. Other theologians mention the importance of 'listening' in theology as well, such as Uzukwu, *Listening Church*, 137–38. For a philosopher's use of social identity concepts, see Appiah, *The Ethics of Identity*.

26. Jenkins, *Social Identity*, 9.

27. Okure, "Africa," 68.

28. Ibid., 73.

29. Woodward, "Concepts of Identity and Difference," 15, 16.

30. Ibid., 21. She notes that Ernesto Laclau refers to such crises as producing a sense of 'dislocation'.

in Africa be shaped by globalization? Identities previously marginalized by slavery and colonialism are now under further threat of annihilation or subjugation.

Henri Tajfel, the founder of social identity theory, concurs that these rapid changes in today's world push identity issues into prominence.

> We live in a world in which the processes of unification and diversification proceed apace, both of them faster than ever before. In some ways, large-scale human groups communicate with each other more than ever; know about each other more than ever; and have become increasingly interdependent. At the same time, there is a powerful trend, to be seen virtually all over the world, aiming at the preservation or the achievement of diversity, of one's own special characteristics and 'identity'.[31]

Globalization and other forces in the world prompt increasing reflection on identity, both personal and social. In sociological terms, personal identity refers to an individual's unique attributes, such as skills, achievements, or appearance, whereas social identity "refers to that part of a person's self-concept that derives from his or her group memberships."[32] Thus, where personal identity tends to place more emphasis on difference, social identity focuses more on (perceived) similarities of individuals within a group, and how group membership affects the individual's sense of self.[33] Such social categorization aids people in understanding and ordering their reality, and also orients the individual's self-perception and place in society.[34] A social identity can be assigned by others—as in giving a group a derogatory name—or chosen by the person exercising agency. Regardless, once a social identity is internalized, it affects a person's self: this 'ownership' or sense of belonging affects their identity, thoughts, and actions.[35]

---

31. Tajfel, "Introduction," 1–2.

32. Haslam, *Psychology in Organizations*, 22. Jenkins views the terms 'self' and 'identity' as inseparable and closely related; here too the terms are used interchangeably, as virtual synonyms, in order to indicate a focus on a person's self-perception: how they would describe their own identity (*Social Identity*, 29–30).

33. Haslam, *Psychology in Organizations*, 31.

34. Tajfel and Turner, "The Social Identity Theory," 283. The social identity approach includes social identity theory and self-categorization theory, which are closely related but distinct theories (Haslam, *Psychology in Organizations*, xi–xii, 43). In this work, social identity refers to both aspects of this approach (Haslam, *Psychology in Organizations*, 42, 43, 55, 56; Tajfel, "Social Categorization" 63; Tajfel and Turner, "The Social Identity Theory," 283; Turner, "Foreword" xi.

35. Cornelissen et al., "Social Identity," 5; Haslam, *Psychology in Organizations*, x, 26, 52.

To clarify, Tajfel emphasizes that social identity theory does not attempt to resolve or comprehensively define all issues of identity.[36] Likewise, the goal here is not to address all identity issues, but to express Christian social identity in Africa.

The social identity approach, integrating social identity theory and self-categorization theory, examines group membership and identity. This approach acknowledges the influence of social or communal identities on a person's identity, regardless of their culture, and examines the effects of claiming a particular social identity. Identity discussions in Africa concern social identities—What does it mean to be part of a group called 'African' and/or 'Christian', and how are the two identities related? If the Christian identity ought to be primary, what can be done to make it more salient? This question concerns the church universally, not just in Africa. The social identity approach recognizes both external influences and internal choice in claiming group membership, and also views identity as a complex, dynamic reality. In all these ways, the social identity approach coheres with and provides a resource for theology in Africa, specifically by articulating—or even just corroborating for skeptical Euro-American ears—what these ecclesiologies are trying to accomplish. Thus it can serve as a language with which African insights on community and identity can be more readily received and understood by non-African audiences.

One major contribution of the social identity approach has been hinted at above: it is well equipped to deal with the impact of globalization on identity, particularly concerning the relationship between the individual and communities.[37] Since this approach includes both the role and responsibility of the individual and a communal viewpoint,[38] it resonates with African and biblical values alike, within a vocabulary that can cross cultures. Respecting the influence of group membership and perceiving many positive effects from that, this approach is less likely to stigmatize or be

---

36. Tajfel, "Introduction," 19.

37. Social identity theory examines the causes and results of group membership on an individual's sense of self, as well as examining intergroup relations. Self-categorization theory studies the conditions in which a particular social identity becomes salient, and the consequences of that salience; Hornsey describes the difference as SIT focusing upon intergroup relations, whereas SCT focuses on intragroup relations (Hornsey, "Social Identity Theory," 205, 207, 208; Cornelissen et al., "Social Identity," 5; Haslam, *Psychology in Organizations*, xi–xii, 42, 49). For more detail, see Haslam, *Identity in Organizations*, 26–56.

38. Brown and Capozza, "Introduction," ix–x; Hornsey, "Social Identity Theory," 205.

condescending about collectivist tendencies while still remaining relevant in more individualistic cultures like those of North America and Europe.[39]

Because this approach views identity as always socially shaped, wherever a culture may be on the individualist-collectivist spectrum, this approach is able to avoid simply privileging any one culture. As Jenkins construes it, "The *individually unique* and the *collectively shared* can be understood as similar (if not exactly the same) in important respects; that each is routinely related to—or, better perhaps, entangled with—the other; that the processes by which they are produced, reproduced and changed are analogous; and that *both* are intrinsically social."[40] The difference between the two is one of emphasis or starting point. Even when their emphases differ, Jenkins argues, both personal and social identity have a social foundation: "Individual identity—embodied in selfhood—is not meaningful in isolation from the social world of other people. Individuals are unique and variable, but selfhood is thoroughly socially constructed: in the processes of primary and subsequent socialization, and in the ongoing processes of social interaction throughout their lives."[41] These identities have meaning within a group or society, and require some degree of validation from others.[42]

The recognition that identities are always social is a reminder that discussions about individualist or communalistic tendencies in a society must not fall into an either/or approach. If all identities have a social basis, and integrate both personal and group elements, then no society is entirely individualistic or communalistic. Rather, it is more accurate and helpful to view cultures on a spectrum, where the degree of emphasis may change, but both aspects (individual and group[s]) always remain present. Thus, to characterize African cultures as so communalistic that there is no recognition of the individual is false, and just as overly simplistic as representing European cultures as completely individualistic, with no regard for groups.[43] African

39. For example, see Shweder and Bourne, "Does the Concept?," 158–99 (particularly 169–70, 172–73, 190, 193–94).

40. Jenkins, *Social Identity*, 19–20, italics in original; Worchel et al., "A Multidimensional Model of Identity," 17.

41. Jenkins, *Social Identity*, 20.

42. Ibid., 21, 22, 49.

43. Shweder and Bourne, "Does the Concept?," specifically 158, 188–93. Shweder and Bourne examine the hypothesis that people with a more concrete, context-specific viewpoint (as found in the more collectivist culture in Orissa, India) cannot think in abstract terms and devalue the individual. They conclude that this is manifestly not the case, but it is a matter of the driving metaphor or values in a culture. In short, the people of Orissa are perfectly capable of thinking in such (Western) ways, but do not find it very valuable. The authors also enumerate the strengths and weaknesses of both ends of the spectrum.

cultures may be more communalistic, and if so, the social identity approach, with its focus on group membership, could help articulate this tendency in terms understandable to Europeans. The social identity approach rejects the above false dichotomy, and provides a more integrative, holistic approach—something of a shared language—for studying people and their identities amid a rapidly globalizing and homogenizing world.

A second contribution of the social identity approach is its view of humanly constructed identity as fluid and malleable; this perspective too attends to the concern of globalization's effect on African identities. So scholars in this field examine aspects of identity highly pertinent to this work, such as whether an identity is seen as secure and legitimate (and the way in which these factors influence how change is handled and how the self is perceived); how identities change and are formed by leaders; and what actions and attitudes promote unity and positive interdependence in merging groups or simply between groups, which is relevant beyond just ecclesiology.[44] Furthermore, the social identity approach values agency: it respects how people identify themselves, providing a viewpoint and vocabulary for that.[45] Previous chapters have shown that African thinkers desire to redefine 'Africa' in their own terms, and in ways that emphasize what is valuable in their cultures. Some works express concern over the effects of globalization, implying that identities are viewed as fluid. African theologies ponder the question of what Christian identity entails in current African contexts, again implying that identity is somewhat changeable in nature. Nana Akua Anyidoho affirms that identity is a perpetual challenge, whether it has been imposed or chosen, and Tinyiko Sam Maluleke agrees that "identity is a series of moving targets," an ongoing challenge that is inherent in the human condition.[46]

The third contribution of the social identity approach follows closely from the second: it specifically studies how shifting social identities relate to each other. This includes concerns such as muting the dangers of ethnocentrism without erasing ethnic identity, what might cause an individual to find one social identity more salient than another, and the relationship

---

44. Haslam, *Psychology in Organizations*, 36; Tajfel, "Introduction," 15; Cornelissen et al, "Social Identity," 1; Hornsey, "Social Identity Theory," 207, 214, and for an in-depth biblical example, Jack Barentsen's examination of how Paul shaped the identity of the churches in Corinth and Ephesus: *Emerging Leadership in the Pauline Mission: A Social Identity Perspective on Local Leadership Development in Corinth and Ephesus*.

45. Jenkins, *Social Identity*, 49.

46. Anyidoho, "Identity and Knowledge Production," 156, 161; Maluleke, "Identity and Integrity," 26, 29, 31, 39.

of previous or sub-group identities to a common, superordinate identity.[47] The social identity approach also may help Europeans and North Americans understand why ethnic identities continue to persist and at times cause intense clashes; because many regions in Africa have seen the negative aspects of ethnically prominent social identity, theologians there are now more attentive to the reconciling, unifying aspect of the Gospel. Indeed, Bediako and Mulago address the issue of social identity (though they do not explicitly employ the term) when examining how a person can integrate ethnic, Christian and African identities, or in other words, how their identity in Christ relates to and transforms—but does not disregard—other social identities. Social identity theory expresses why identity challenges perpetually arise for humans, suggests means to lessen or resolve identity conflicts, and indicates how a common superordinate identity can be made more salient.

The social identity approach notes that as a person moves from one context to another, such as from their job to a social event, which of the person's social identities is most relevant to them will vary. Social identities interact in various ways, sometimes in hierarchical layers (a particular section of a company, a certain branch of a family, a Sunday school group in a church). These are all examples of sub-groups within a larger group, where the sub-groups are "lower level social identities . . . nested as sub-groups in the higher level, superordinate identities."[48] Other social identities are not parts of the same hierarchy, or cut across various hierarchies if they do not fully overlap. The obligations of one social identity may conflict with another; these are cross-cutting social identities.[49] The nested sub-groups within a larger overarching superordinate identity may compete with each other as well.

The theologies treated in chapters 3 and 5 agree that the divinely given identity 'in Christ', due to its source, must be the primary identifier for all God's people. Other particulars—a person's relationships, societal roles, other group memberships, gender, ethnicity, and so forth—are not erased but *relativized* by the divinely given identity.[50] The God-given

---

47. Ros et al., "Comparative Identity," 94. They also note that how a sub-group acculturates to a larger/majority or more powerful group has significant consequences (89).

48. Barentsen, *Emerging Leadership*, 39.

49. Ibid.

50. For example, the work of Gaertner et al. suggests that degrading or reducing original group boundaries when a new common social identity is formed may or may not be desirable, depending on the situation. The authors suggest that in a large group, a single group identity may not be sufficient to fulfill a person's desire for both inclusion

identity more faithfully reflects God's creative purposes for humanity and his reconciliation of the broken relationships between humans, and in addition can provide continuity and stability amidst the temporal changes throughout the continent.

The ecclesiologies studied here indicate strengths and weaknesses of the church in Africa. One obvious weakness involves divisions based on ethnicity, gender, social standing, and ecclesial role. Yet these ecclesiologies affirm that belonging to God's people entails a welcoming stance toward those who are different or other. Repeatedly they urge God's people to incorporate these differences into the church, so that the divinely formed community will accurately reflect God's character and redemptive, reconciling plan. What will it take for God's people to realize that the divinely given identity transcends and transforms other identities, and for eccleisal identity to be properly marked by unity and love toward others?

African ecclesiologies emphasize that this divinely given, superordinate identity starts with encountering the nature of the Triune God, who exists as three distinct-yet-unified persons and welcomes humans into the joy of this divine fellowship. Indeed, the ecclesiologies tend to agree that Christian social identity incorporates and relativizes, but should rarely if ever destroy, distinctions among people. The divinely bestowed, superordinate identity is the foundation on which other identities are based, since other identifiers, such as roles and relationships, are finite and humanly formed. While other identities may only have relevance in a limited number of contexts, being 'in Christ' is applicable in every context and has an eternal basis. Hence, the church must take care to nurture this identity within every person and in the church's ethos as a whole. This social identity norms and shapes other identities, discerning how they relate to membership in

---

and distinctiveness, in which case original boundaries and identities can be maintained to some extent (Gaertner et al., "The Common Ingroup Identity Model," 134–36, 138, 144–46). The study specifically mentions cross-cultural and inter-ethnic settings, which are of particular concern to the church in Africa: "Racial and ethnic identity are fundamental aspects of individuals' self-concepts and esteem and thus are unlikely to be abandoned. We therefore also explored the effects of the dual identity (in which subgroup identities are maintained within the context of a superordinate identity) in the survey study of the intergroup attitudes in the multi-ethnic high school," discovering that students who "described themselves as *both* American and as a member of their racial or ethnic group has less bias toward other groups in that school than did those who described themselves only in terms of their subgroup identity. Also, the minority students who actually identified themselves using a dual identity reported lower levels of intergroup bias relative to those who only used their ethnic or racial group identity. These findings support the positive role of the dual identity" (144–45). As African theologians explore how to integrate people from various social groups into united wholes, dual identity is quite pertinent.

God's people. Each person must value the God-given distinctions within the community that make interdependence a requisite for the group's proper functioning. Due to (purposeful) differentiation in the community, each individual has a responsibility or role to fill for the others' sakes, contributions upon which they rely. When the social context of the individual and the community changes, certain aspects of identity must also be adjusted, but the basis for deciding which changes are valid and proper is the primary, superordinate social identity of 'in Christ.' African theologians draw attention to the continuing role of social identity, and highlight that persons bear various identities that can conflict with the Christian identity. They also make a strong case for the importance of solidarity, equality, and diversity as central marks of the ecclesial identity.

As Africans seek to reclaim and redefine their histories and cultures, identity questions inevitably arise. There exists a two-fold struggle for Christians: (1) having agency to positively define 'Africa' and 'Africans', as well as particular identities therein, and (2) expressing the primary Christian identity in a way which redeems and integrates cultural traits, addressing specific social issues. In this struggle the social identity approach helps to name some of the dynamics with which African theology in turn can illuminate a common human struggle.

As mentioned previously, the notion of identity intrinsically includes both difference and sameness with other individuals and groups.[51] Yet the attitude toward difference is crucial: Is it seen as a threat or a benefit?[52] Does the group with power become the standard of what is 'normal', pressuring those with less power to conform to the standard?[53] Regarding the value of such a shared superordinate identity, Marilynn B. Brewer highlights that it results in interdependence and recognition of common goals.[54] Cornelissen et al. agree that a common overarching identity results in increased efforts to coordinate behavior and seek agreement, particularly with regard to issues

---

51. Jenkins, *Social Identity*, 3–4. Within groups and organizations there is also recognition of similarities and distinctions or differences (127, 140).

52. Woodward, "Concepts of Identity and Difference," 9, 20–21, 30, 35–36.

53. Tajfel, "Introduction," 16. Because power dynamics within groups and among groups shift and change over time, it seems wise to acknowledge that identity likewise is shifting and negotiable, socially constructed (at least in large part), not a static, essentialist reality. For more on essentialist (fixed) versus non-essentialist views of identity, see Woodward, "Concepts of Identity and Difference," particularly 11, 12, 21, 24, 26, 28; Paul Gilroy's argument in favor of a non-territorial "identity in motion" in "Diaspora," 299–343 (esp. 307–11, 328, 329, 331, 334, 335, 336, 341); Jenkins, *Social Identity*, esp. 4–5, 20, 71, 102, 144.

54. Brewer, "Superordinate Goals," 120, 121, 123, 125, 129, 130, 131.

that are linked to the common identity.[55] Crisp and Hewstone and Ros et al. also note that a superordinate social identity moderates discrimination.[56] Furthermore, a superordinate identity does not require forsaking other social identities; rather, it integrates them under its umbrella. In fact, the research of Gaertner et al. shows that the superordinate identity is at times actually weakened if previous social identities are required to be forsaken.[57] Instead, it is preferable to develop a new combined identity that integrates, instead of simply assimilating or absorbing, the previous identities.[58] A dual identity, one with the superordinate identity as well as allegiance to an ethnic identity, actually proved to be better at dealing with other groups, and can lead to valuing differences instead of being threatened by them.[59] It appears from this study that a strong superordinate identity allows more other-focus and is less biased against alterity, which is a major concern of the African literature examined previously.[60]

Consider in this vein the frequent call of theologians across the African continent that the Christian identity must be superordinate: Eunice Kamaara refers to the practice of prioritizing ethnic or other social identities as "tantamount to idolatry," and urges African churches to "fight for Christian identity and unity that transcends all other identities."[61] Philomena Njeri Mwaura likewise refers to "conflicting identities" in Africa, particularly between ethnic, national, and Christian identities; her goal is to emphasize that Christian identity is most basic, and is marked by transformation, love, unity, and embrace of the 'other.'[62] Africa needs a secure Christian identity, she judges, one that does not eradicate but integrates old identities while transcending them, fostering a Christian identity that reconciles different

55. Cornelissen et al., "Social Identity," 5; Haslam, *Psychology in Organizations*, 53.

56. Crisp and Hewstone, "Multiple Categorization," 164; Ros, "Comparative Identity," 94.

57. Gaertner et al., "The Common Ingroup Identity Model," 134.

58. Ibid., 138. For more on amalgamation as seen in the NT, see Hansen, "*All of You Are One*," particularly 3, 4, 7, 38, 58–63, 65, 71, 73, 85, 86, 98–101, 125, 141, 183, 195, 198, 201, 202. Contra Daniel Boyarin and others, Hansen argues that Paul is not trying to erase all particularity among believers, nor is Paul saying that all believers are 'the same' in Christ. He notes the various ways in which Paul draws upon ethnic ideas to create a sense of social unity: referring to common (spiritual) ancestors, use of familial language, and laying out an ethos those in the group should display, as well as speaking of a common homeland; Hansen's argument seems to provide support for theologians describing the church as "family."

59. Gaertner et al., "The Common Ingroup Identity Model," 144, 145, 148.

60. Ibid., 146.

61. Kamaara, "Towards Christian National Identity," 141–42.

62. Mwaura, "Human Identity," 17, 19, 20, 22, 28.

identities without marginalizing or discriminating against those who are 'other'.[63] Teresa Okure too desires Christians in Africa to realize that the "mitochondrion" identity mark of Christians (the core or authentic identity) is mutual love, and that reconciliation with the 'other' is a large part of Christ-like love.[64]

Theologians desire to increase the salience of the Christian superordinate identity. Note then, in response, the discovery of the founder of the social identity approach, Henri Tajfel, that the relevance of a particular social identity would increase with (1) awareness of membership in the group, (2) the extent of positive and negative evaluations of that social identity, and (3) the extent of the individual's investment in the awareness of membership and evaluation of it.[65]

To provide a specific example of how the social identity approach aids ecclesiological discussions by providing the terminology needed to advance the theological claims being made, we can examine 1 Corinthians 12—a text often used in African ecclesiologies. African theologians frequently reference this text because it addresses the importance of solidarity with diversity among God's people: Paul describes God's people as a body, a unity of various parts working together to form a healthy whole. Paul desires that the Corinthian Christ-followers unify and realize the Christian identity is superordinate. On this point, Barentsen's work on 1 Corinthians 12 illustrates how the social identity approach can advance the discussion of Christian identity in Africa. He examines the methods Paul used to lead the Christians in Corinth and Ephesus. While some facets of leadership are tangential to the issue here, the examination of how Paul sought to shape the Christians' self-concept—their identity—is quite germane. Barentsen employs identity models that integrate both social (historical) and psychological (ideological) factors shaping these Christians, exploring the ethos Paul sought to develop within them.

Identity is defined as a "people's sense of who they are, as their subjective self-concept," which includes both personal aspects (what makes them different from others) and social aspects (groups the person belongs to, which shape this self-understanding).[66] Since there are a wide range of

---

63. Ibid., 26, 27, 29.

64. Okure, "Christian Identity," 176–77, 180; idem, "'The Ministry of Reconciliation,'" 111. For more on the relationship between ethnic identity and Christian identity, as well as the place of reconciliation and embrace of the 'other' as key to the Christian identity, from the perspective of a Mizo from northeastern India, see Pachuau, "Ethnic Identity," 49–63.

65. Tajfel, "Interindividual Behaviour," 28, 39.

66. Barentsen, *Emerging Leadership*, 38.

factors affecting a person's self-understanding, it is understandable that at times particular identities or loyalties will come into conflict with other aspects of identity; conflicting, unrelated loyalties Barentsen refers to as "cross-cutting social identities," in contrast with hierarchical identities (sub-groups within a larger, superordinate identity).[67] When identities and obligations collide—for example familial obligations clashing with work or religious demands—the individual must decide which social identity is more relevant in that situation.

Barentsen sketches the following scenario: a first-century world, where one's social identity is typically defined by kinship, ethnicity, trade, and religious belief, all of which were seen as predetermined matters. What drives him is the question of, "What happened [in the first-century world] when a new social identity was introduced, such as when Paul assembled people together in what he envisioned as a stable and enduring community of Christ-followers. How did this new social identity relate to pre-existing social identities? Which beliefs and values determined the group's identity as compared to" other social identities?[68]

As with many other scholarly works, *Emerging Leadership in the Pauline Mission* interprets 1 Corinthians as a 'problem-oriented' letter in which Paul addresses several major struggles causing division amongst the Corinthian Christians. For example, 1 Corinthians 1–4 deals with how subgroups within the church would relate to each other: Would they compete with other sub-groups, or coordinate their roles within the one superordinate group?[69] A second major problem is the way in which social status differentiations and loyalties are handled (1 Corinthians 5–10), and a third issue is disorder in the community's internal activities and identity narra-

---

67. Ibid., 39. Barentsen proposes that social identity theory can be particularly helpful to Western, individualist Bible scholars, because it focuses on analyzing and understanding groups and collectivist mindsets, which were prevalent in the NT Mediterranean world. It is also "particularly well suited to analyze intergroup relationships and intragroup differentiation, which played such an important part in the formation of Paul's churches and their leadership" (43). In short, this approach seeks to understand how these Christians understood their identity as Christ-followers, and how this commitment related to other aspects of their identity. To see a non-Pauline case for Christians sharing a common superordinate identity, see Coleman A. Baker's argument in *Identity, Memory, and Narrative in Early Christianity: Peter, Paul, and Recategorization in the Book of Acts*. Baker concludes that "the narrative of Acts attempts the recategorization of those on either side of the debate over non-Judean inclusion in the Christ movement into a common ingroup by presenting Peter and Paul as prototypical of a common superordinate identity" (199). If Baker's point is valid, it indicates that Paul was not alone in his approach to this issue.

68. Barentsen, *Emerging Leadership*, 44.

69. Ibid., 78.

tive (1 Corinthians 11–15).⁷⁰ Issues of social status, power, mutual concern, and unequal participation in the community are destroying their common identity. The Corinthian Christians appear to be either unsure how their Christian commitments relate to these issues, or they prioritize other values over Christian ones. Paul attempts to re-orient and re-order their values, but not in a way that eradicates all differences or denies their relevance. For example, in chapter 10, Paul discusses how to approach sacrificial meat, which can be eaten in certain circumstances but should be avoided in others; Barentsen thus concludes that Paul accepted social differentiations to a degree, "but he argued that mutual support, personal sacrifice, and winsomeness were relevant comparison dimensions for Christian social identity, not status and privilege."⁷¹ In other words, Christian social identity was not subordinate to previous social dualisms (Jew/Greek, male/female, etc.) but determined by particularly Christ-like behavioral traits.

In chapter 12, Paul highlights the importance of participation by every group member, and connects participation with the Triune Persons. Paul then discusses this unity and diversity within the Christian community, in such a way that differentiation (of gifts and of persons) within the group is not ruled out but preserved. Barentsen notes that from the standpoint of social identity, this is perfectly logical: equal participation of group members does not mean a lack of ordering or lack of unique roles for certain members within the group.⁷² From Paul's own analogy, as well as from the angle of the social identity approach, the idea of all members participating is not at odds with the idea of differentiation and ordering within a group. This correlation with social identity readings indicates that the community Paul enjoins in 1 Corinthians 12 befits how God has made social groups truly to be.⁷³

Based on his studies in 1 and 2 Corinthians and Ephesians, Barentsen avers that one reason social identity theory proves a useful heuristic is precisely its connection between socio-historical data and theological concepts, a weak point in NT studies in his estimation.⁷⁴ He also concludes that the concept of identity is a helpful angle from which to view discussions

70. Ibid., 80, 83.

71. Ibid., 96.

72. Ibid., 107–8.

73. It is not the goal here to argue about what type of structures Paul put in place, or desired to put in place. At this point the goal is only to establish further support for the argument that unity and diversity, equal participation and yet differentiation, are simultaneously possible within social groups. This argument has bearing on the ecclesiological arguments in the previous chapter.

74. Ibid., 322.

on unity and diversity in the NT because "the concept of identity revolves around sameness and difference."[75] He makes the case that

> Paul's extended argument in 1 Corinthians and Ephesians for the superordinate position of Christian social identity is not so much a plea for a universal theology that erases all local distinctions, but is rather a way to bind existing social and ethnic differences together in a higher level of unity without denying or erasing these differences. . . . . This provides a more sophisticated model for accommodating difference and sameness within the Christ-movement, allowing different subgroups to function unitedly by maintaining the superordinate nature of Christian social identity for all subgroups.[76]

Barentsen's argument coheres well with the evidence available, both from NT documents and social identity findings.

Early Christians understandably struggled with the issue of how their new Christian identity fit into, alongside, or above prior commitments and loyalties. Paul's body analogy in 1 Corinthians 12 underlines both the unity and diversity of Christ's body in regard to gifts and individuals. The baptismal formula in v. 13 emphasizes that unity in Christ 'trumps' all other loyalties and identities: it is more important than ethno-cultural group or social status. The reader can extrapolate and apply Paul's point on these two particular issues (Jew/Gentile, free/slave) to other areas of difference as well. God apparently delights in, and plans for, diversity within God's people in order for the whole community to function properly. God desires unity, not uniformity, among God's people. The social identity approach provides a broadly applicable grammar and framework for understanding the impact of communal identity and solidarity on a person's self-concept, and the ways in which social identities interact with each other. This approach can aid the church in all contexts to heighten the salience of the Christian identity as superordinate for all members of God's people, and to celebrate a diversity of social identities among God's people without threatening their unity.

Yet a series of caveats must carefully be offered. First, social identity theory can help to describe the Gospel's reconciling, and it fits with our relational nature by virtue of divine creation. But social identity theory does not enact, and cannot adequately describe, the fullness of this reconciling work in merely human terms, for reconciliation is God's gracious work in Christ by the Spirit. Second, therefore, social identity theory does not serve as European or academic legitimation for African concerns, even if it offers

---

75. Ibid., 321.
76. Ibid., 321, 322.

a measure of corroboration. Neither, third, does social identity theory provide European, academic, or general solutions to African problems from outside the gospel. Instead, the social identity approach offers a language that has begun to influence NT interpretation, with which African insights can be underscored for non-Africans, and African concerns can be named and pursued. Most especially, perhaps, social identity language suggests that Christian's identity (membership in God's people) can be superordinate, therefore reconciling conflictual ethnic or other identities, without eradicating those subordinate identities it seeks to relativize. There is, in short, sociological evidence that the aspiration of African ecclesiology is as true to the Triune Creator's world as the NT suggests.

Conclusions

The central claim of this work accordingly began to surface in chapter 2: Christian theology in Africa aspires to address concerns of inculturation and liberation, and promote life, in community. In so doing it remains centrally preoccupied with issues of identity, so that in a broad sense for Africa ecclesiology is first theology. A deeply contextualized Christianity will employ local colors, at the same time transforming them into something new with integrity. African theology needs to be nourishing and delightful, like a meal that encourages people to fellowship and celebrate as on a most holy occasion. It aspires to promote freedom from domination, to resist isolation of the self or ethnic group, and to make places without marginalization or social barriers, where all are equal.

Chapter 3 detailed the specifically Christian concern with communal identities in Africa. From a Christian theological perspective, Mulago gwa Cikala Musharhamina and Kwame Bediako argued that the Christian identity has a religious basis—being founded in Christ—and both universal and particular aspects, thanks to general revelation and the Incarnation. Mercy Amba Oduyoye affirmed this overall thrust, but offered a much more critical, nuanced perspective of the ways in which African and Christian identities fall short of God's intention, and how they must change to reflect the way of Jesus. All three agreed that other identities are relativized in light of the new identity in Christ, which integrates and transcends them all.

The treatment of Scripture in chapter 4 explored passages employed by African theologies, examining how these passages support their theological claims regarding the Christian identity, specifically the nature of its solidarity. Rahab's story highlights that the divinely given identity overrules ethnic identities, yet this communal identity does not erase individuality.

Ezekiel 18 indicates that individual responsibility and corporate solidarity co-exist within communal identity, while John 17 describes unity among God's people reflecting the unity of Father and Son. In 1 Corinthians 12, Paul argues that differences do not equal divisions, and are necessary for a healthy communal Christian identity. Galatians 3 explicitly relativizes other identities in light of the 'in Christ' identity, which supports the social identity approach concept of a 'superordinate identity' and the affirmation of African theologians that Christian identity should be primary.

Chapter 5 moves to ecclesiology in particular. African theologians examining the Christian community's identity note that it bears both divine and human traits. To accurately reflect the Triune God, it is clear that God's people must be relational, interdependent, and contain diversity in unity. The Trinity also highlights the importance of equality amidst difference, and an outward (or 'other') focus. From the human side, it becomes clear that God's people are shaped by their context, and have a dynamic identity, one which is still being transformed into the divine image. These theologians repeatedly emphasize that the Christian identity must adequately address diversity and alterity, as well as the past, present, and future of members of God's people. While other identities persist—such as ethnicity, gender, and church roles—they are relativized. At its essence, the Christian communal identity derives from the character of the Triune God.

Finally, this concluding chapter proposes that the social identity approach provides a complementary language for how such an ecclesial superordinate identity can be shaped and made more salient without eliminating prior ethnic or other identities, whether in Africa or elsewhere. In theological terms, this approach helps to describe what God in Christ by the Spirit makes possible. If the Christian social identity increases in salience and is treated as the superordinate identity, presumably Christians in Africa would have a dynamic yet secure identity from which to address ethnocentrism and other concerns over alterity, as well as a basis from which to develop a healthy African social identity in the face of globalization. Identity concerns are part of the human condition, as the African realities press upon us in particular ways. Identity concerns are also theological in nature, with the identity of God's people already determined in Christ yet not fully and finally realized until the eschaton. The Christian social identity is first and foremost based on the Triune God's self-revelation and historical acts seeking reconciliation between humanity and God and among humans. The Triune redemptive basis requires that Christian identity be marked by love, diversity in unity, and equality, among other traits. The social identity approach modestly offers some language with which to articulate these commitments, while honoring the particular African foci on some of their communal emphases.

In the words of John S. Mbiti, ultimately identity with and in Christ "makes nonsense of all other identities in that it claims the whole person and the whole cosmos as the property of Christ. Then, deriving from this Christocentric identity, the person is free to become whatever else he wishes, to be identified as an African, nationalist, neutralist, trade unionist or even beggar. That is the height to which Christianity in Africa must soar."[77] Indeed, it is the height to which Christian identity in all times and places is called: to be united to Christ, to imitate him, and to be transformed more and more into his image so that Christ will be all in all.

To recap, the representative theologians selected have established the theological nature of identity, showing that many theologians in Africa are still concerned with identity, and that this identity concern is specifically with communal or social identity. Yet it is important to note that identity discussions have shifted from apologetic in tone to examining the nature of Christian (communal/ecclesial) identity. Indeed, biblical material used by African theologians affirms the communal nature of humanity, and emphasizes God's relational nature as well as God's communal plans for humanity. However, aside from Nyamiti's *Contemporary Models of African Ecclesiology*, there are few works that survey and evaluate ecclesiologies in Africa, and none that I am aware of that examine their particular contributions to identity discussions.

Contemporary Models of African Ecclesiology's concern is with shortcomings in African ecclesiologies and providing magisterial teaching as a basis for analysis of said ecclesiologies. All of this serves as groundwork for Nyamiti's ecclesiology, so it does not explicitly link ecclesiology with other major concerns of African theology, such as identity. Seeking to round out areas of Nyamiti's survey, I have sought to show how concerns of African theology are addressed in ecclesiology. In particular, I highlight that identity concerns have shifted, but remain and are integrated into ecclesiological models. Exploring ecclesiology from the angle of communal identity provides a different perspective, one that has the potential ground identity on an enduring and a divine basis that provides stability amidst the sea tides of change and that integrates biblical and African emphases on the importance of one's community. Social identity language provides a grammar with which to examine a person's many loyalties and the conflicts these can cause, highlighting the relationship of ecclesiology to a person's other

---

77. Mbiti, *African Religions and Philosophy*, quoted in Maluleke, "Identity and Integrity," 38.

commitments, and doing so in a way that may be more understandable and relatable to non-Africans. Moreover, I am applying Bediako's insistence that identity concerns are, at heart, concerns of the Gospel. This being so, ecclesial identity links the Gospel, Christ, culture, and God's people together, and shows their ongoing dynamics in a way that includes both God's eternal designs and God's peoples' various particular contexts in which they must live out the Gospel message.

With regard to ecclesial identity, I have shown that ecclesiologies argue that the Christian identity must be characterized by a high degree of solidarity and a welcoming attitude toward the 'other', whether because of ecclesial role, gender, ethnic group, or some other trait. Christian identity is also eschatological in nature: it is not yet complete, and continues to change as it moves toward its fulfillment in the eschaton. Furthermore, the social identity approach is proposed as a specific means by which insights from African theologians can be extended to experts of other fields, as well as to non-African theologians. The social identity approach is useful because it explores how communities impact identity, how social identities interact, and what can be done to improve the salience of a particular social identity. It has the potential to offer the global church tools to increase the relevance of the Christian social identity. The goal in all this is that the church will be a faithful, credible witness to the transformative power of her Lord, who brings together individuals from all groups and nations, and unites them into a new people.

Bibliography

Achebe, Chinua. "The Nature of the Individual and His Fulfillment." In *The Colonial and the Neo-Colonial Encounters in Commonwealth Literature*, edited by H. H. Anniah Gowda, 205–15. Prasaranga: University of Mysore, 1983.

Adamo, D. T. "The Historical Development of Old Testament Interpretation in Africa." *Old Testament Essays* 16 (2003) 9–33.

Adewuya, J. Ayodeji. *Holiness and Community in 2 Cor 6:14–7:1: Paul's View of Communal Holiness in the Corinthian Correspondence*. Studies in Biblical Literature 40. New York: Peter Lang, 2001.

Adeyemo, Tokunboh, ed. *Africa Bible Commentary*. Grand Rapids: Zondervan, 2006.

———. *Salvation in African Tradition*. Nairobi: Evangel, 1979.

Adoukonou, B. "Construire l'église-famille de Dieu à partir du Sanctuaire Intérieur." In *Christianisme et Humanisme en Afrique*, 237–70. Paris: Karthala, 2003.

Aguilar, Mario I. "Postcolonial African Theology in Kabasele Lumbala." *Theological Studies* 63/2 (2002) 302–23.

Allen, Leslie C. *Ezekiel 1–19*. Word Biblical Commentary 28. Waco, TX: Word, 1994.

Ande, Titre. "African Christology: Hope for the Anglican Communion." *Journal of Anglican Studies* 7 (2009) 183–93.

———. *Leadership and Authority: Bula Matari and Life-Community Ecclesiology in Congo*. Regnum Studies in Mission. Oxford: Regnum, 2010.

Antonio, Edward P. "Inculturation and Postcolonial Discourse." In *Inculturation and Postcolonial Discourse in African Theology*, edited by Edward P. Antonio, 1–28. Society and Politics in Africa 14. New York: Peter Lang, 2006.

Anyidoho, Nana Akua. "Identity and Knowledge Production in the 4th Generation." In *Intellectuals and African Development: Pretension and Resistance in African Politics*, edited by Björn Beckman and Gbemisola Adeoti, 156–69. Africa in the New Millennium. Dakar, Senegal: Codesria, 2006.

Appiah, Kwame Anthony. *The Ethics of Identity*. Princeton, NJ: Princeton University Press, 2005.

———. *In My Father's House: Africa in the Philosophy of Culture*. New York: Oxford University Press, 1992.

Appiah, Simon Kofi. "The Quest of African Identity." *Exchange* 32 (2003) 54–65.

Appiah-Kubi, Francis. *Église, Famille De Dieu: Un Chemin Pour Les Églises d'Afrique*. Chrétiens en liberté: Questions disputées. Paris: Karthala, 2008.

Asamoah-Gyadu, J. Kwabena. "Bediako of Africa: A Late 20th Century Outstanding Theologian and Teacher." *Mission Studies* 26 (2009) 5–16.

———. "'The Evil You Have Done Can Ruin the Whole Clan': African Cosmology, Community, and Christianity in Achebe's *Things Fall Apart*." *Studies in World Christianity* 16 (2010) 46–62.

———. "Mission to 'Set the Captives Free': Healing, Deliverance, and Generational Curses in Ghanaian Pentecostalism." *International Review of Missions* 93 (October 2004) 389–406.

———. "Of 'Sour Grapes' and 'Children's Teeth': Inherited Guilt, Human Rights and Processes of Restoration in Ghanaian Pentecostalism." *Exchange* 33 (2004) 334–53.

Assenga, Peter. "The African Family Spirit: A Nexus of Justice, Peace and Reconciliation." *African Ecclesial Review* 51 (2009) 52–77.

Aune, David E. "Galatians 3:28 and the Problem of Equality in the Church and Society." *Supplements to Novum Testamentum* 136 (2010) 153–84.

Azuh, Michael C. "Corporate Personality in African Theology." MA thesis, Wheaton College, 1981.

Baker, Coleman A. *Identity, Memory, and Narrative in Early Christianity: Peter, Paul, and Recategorization in the Book of Acts*. Eugene, OR: Pickwick, 2011.

Balcomb, Anthony. "Review of *Leadership and Authority: 'Bula Matari' and Life-Community Ecclesiology in Congo*." *Journal of Theology for Southern Africa* 140 (2011) 91–92.

Barentsen, Jack. *Emerging Leadership in the Pauline Mission: A Social Identity Perspective on Local Leadership Development in Corinth and Ephesus*. Princeton Theological Monograph 168. Eugene, OR: Pickwick, 2011.

Barton, Stephen C. "Christian Community in the Light of the Gospel of John." In *Christology, Controversy, and Community: New Testament Essays in Honour of David R. Catchpole*, edited by David G. Horrell and Christopher M. Tuckett, 279–301. Supplements to Novum Testamentum 99. Leiden: Brill, 2000.

Bediako, Kwame. *Jesus and the Gospel in Africa: History and Experience*. Theology in Africa. Maryknoll, NY: Orbis, 2004.

———. *Theology and Identity: The Impact of Culture upon Christian Thought in the Second Century and in Modern Africa*. Regnum Studies in Mission. Oxford: Regnum, 1999.

Begg, Christopher. "The Ai-Achan Story (Joshua 7–8) according to Josephus." *Jian Dao Xue Kan* 16 (2001) 1–20.

Bird, Phyllis A. "The Harlot as Heroine: Narrative Art and Social Presupposition in Three Old Testament Texts." *Semeia* 46 (1989) 119–39.

Bishwende, Augustin Ramazani. *Ecclésiologie Africaine de Famille de Dieu: Annonce et Débat Avec Les Contemporains*. Études Africaines. Paris: L'Harmattan, 2007.

———. *Église-Famille de Dieu Dans La Mondialisation: Théologie D'une Nouvelle Voie Africaine D'évangélisation*. Paris: L'Harmattan, 2006.

———. *L'ecclésiologie Trinitaire Dans La Postmodernité et La Mondialisation*. Paris: L'Harmattan, 2008.

Bloch-Hoell, Nils E. "African Identity: European Invention or Genuine African Character?" *Mission Studies: Journal of the International Association for Mission Studies* 9 (1992) 98–107.

Block, Daniel I. *The Book of Ezekiel: Chapters 1–24*. Grand Rapids: Eerdmans, 1997.

Boesak, Allan Aubrey. *Farewell to Innocence: A Socio-Ethical Study on Black Theology and Black Power*. Maryknoll, NY: Orbis, 1977.
Bonganjalo, Goba. "Personnalite Collective En Israel et En Afrique." In *Chrétiens d'Afrique Du Sud Face À L'apartheid*, edited by Anne Marie Goguel and Pierre Buis, 177–88. Paris: L'Harmattan, 1978.
Boyarin, Daniel. *A Radical Jew: Paul and the Politics of Identity*. Contraversions 1. Berkeley: University of California Press, 1994.
Brewer, Marilynn B. "Superordinate Goals Versus Superordinate Identity as Bases of Intergroup Cooperation." In *Social Identity Processes: Trends in Theory and Research*, edited by Dora Capozza and Rupert Brown, 117–32. London: Sage, 2000.
Bruce, F. F. *The Gospel of John*. Grand Rapids: Eerdmans, 1983.
Buell, Denise Kimber, and Caroline Johnson Hodge. "The Politics of Interpretation: The Rhetoric of Race and Ethnicity in Paul." *Journal of Biblical Literature* 123 (2004) 235–51.
Bujo, Bénézet. *African Theology in Its Social Context*. Eugene, OR: Wipf & Stock, 2006.
———. "On the Way to an African Ecclesiology." In *The African Synod: Documents, Reflections, Perspectives*, edited by Maura Browne, 139–51. Maryknoll, NY: Orbis, 1996.
———. "Vincent Mulago: An Enthusiast of African Theology." In *African Theology in the 21st Century: The Contribution of the Pioneers*, edited by Juvénal Ilunga Muya and Bénézet Bujo, 1:13–38. Translated by Silvanu Borruso. Nairobi: Paulines Publications Africa, 2003.
Bujo, Bénézet, and Juvénal Muya Ilunga. *African Theology in the 21st Century: The Contribution of the Pioneers*. 3 vols. Nairobi: Paulines Publications Africa, 2003.
Butler, Trent C. *Joshua*. Word Biblical Commentary 7. Waco, TX: Word, 1983.
Cadier, Jean. "The Unity of the Church: An Exposition of John 17." Translated by Colette Preiss. *Interpretation* 11 (1957) 166–76.
Carney, J. J. "From Crisis to Kairos: The Mission of the Church in the Time of HIV/AIDS, Refugees and Poverty." *Mission Studies: Journal of the International Association for Mission Studies* 25 (2008) 311–12.
Chester, Leonard J. "'Reliable Leaders ... Qualified to Teach': The Story of the Theological College of Zimbabwe." *Brethren in Christ History and Life* 31 (2008) 356–74.
Clyburn, Scott. "Review of *Theology Brewed in an African Pot*." *Anglican Theological Review* 92 (2010) 583–84.
Conway, Martin. "Review of *Leadership and Authority*." *Transformation: An International Journal of Holistic Mission Studies* 28 (2011) 224–26.
Conzelmann, Hans. *1 Corinthians: A Commentary on the First Epistle to the Corinthians*. Translated by James W. Leitch. Hermeneia. Philadelphia: Fortress, 1975.
Cornelissen, Joep P., S. Alexander Haslam, and John M. T. Balmer. "Social Identity, Organizational Identity and Corporate Identity: Towards an Integrated Understanding of Processes, Patternings and Products." *British Journal of Management* 18, Supplement 1 (2007) S1–16.
Crisp, Richard J., and Miles Hewstone. "Multiple Categorization and Social Identity." In *Social Identity Processes: Trends in Theory and Research*, edited by Dora Capozza and Rupert Brown, 149–66. London: Sage, 2000.
Darr, Katheryn Pfisterer. "Proverb Performance and Transgenerational Retribution in Ezekiel 18." In *Ezekiel's Hierarchical World: Wrestling with a Tiered Reality*, edited

by Corrine L. Carvalho and Stephen L. Cook, 199–223. Symposium 31. Atlanta: Society of Biblical Literature, 2004.

Datiri, Dachollom. "1 Corinthians." In *Africa Bible Commentary*, edited by Tokunboh Adeyemo, 1377–98. Grand Rapids: Zondervan, 2006.

Dedji, Valentin. *Reconstruction and Renewal in African Christian Theology*. Theology of Reconstruction. Nairobi: Acton, 2003.

De Gruchy, John W. *Bonhoeffer and South Africa: Theology in Dialogue*. Grand Rapids: Eerdmans, 1984.

———. *The Church Struggle in South Africa*. Grand Rapids: Eerdmans, 1979.

———. *Liberating Reformed Theology: A South African Contribution to an Ecumenical Debate*. Grand Rapids: Eerdmans, 1991.

Dickson, Kwesi A. "The Old Testament and African Theology." *Ghana Bulletin of Theology* 4 (1973) 31–41.

Donders, Joseph G. "Review of *A Listening Church*." *Missiology* 27/1 (January 1999) 131–32.

Dube, Musa W. "Talitha Cum Hermeneutics of Liberation: Some African Women's Ways of Reading the Bible." In *The Bible and the Hermeneutics of Liberation*, edited by Alejandro F. Botta and Pablo R. Andiñach, 133–46. Semeia 59. Atlanta: Society of Biblical Literature, 2009.

Dwane, Sigqibo. "Christology in the Third World." *Journal of Theology for Southern Africa* 21 (1977) 3–12.

Dyrness, William A. *Learning about Theology from the Third World*. Grand Rapids: Academie, 1990.

Ehrensperger, Kathy, and J. Brian Tucker, eds. *Reading Paul in Context: Explorations in Identity Formation: Essays in Honour of William S. Campbell*. Library of New Testament Studies 428. London: T. & T. Clark, 2010.

Essamuah, Casely B. "Review of *Theology Brewed in an African Pot*." *Interpretation* 64 (2010) 211–12.

Eze, Emmanuel Chukwudi. *Achieving Our Humanity: The Idea of a Postracial Future*. New York: Routledge, 2001.

Ezeanya, Stephen N. "God, Spirits and the Spirit World." In *Biblical Revelation and African Beliefs*, edited by Kwesi A. Dickson and Paul Ellingworth, 30–46. Maryknoll, NY: Orbis, 1969.

Faculté de théologie catholique de Kinshasa. *Inculturation et libération en Afrique aujourd'hui: mélanges en l'honneur du Professeur Abbé Mulago gwa Cikala*. Kinshasa: Faculté de théologie, Facultés catholiques de Kinshasa, 1990.

Fee, Gordon D. *The First Epistle to the Corinthians*. New International Commentary on the New Testament. Grand Rapids: Eerdmans, 1987.

Ferdinando, Keith. "Christian Identity in the African Context: Reflections on Kwame Bediako's Theology and Identity." *Journal of the Evangelical Theological Society* 50 (2007) 121–43.

———. "The Legacy of Byang Kato." *International Bulletin of Missionary Research* 28/4 (2004) 169–74.

Furler, Peter. *Unified*. Franklin, TN: Essential Records, 2000.

Gaertner, Samuel L., et al. "The Common Ingroup Identity Model for Reducing Intergroup Bias: Progress and Challenges." In *Social Identity Processes: Trends in Theory and Research*, edited by Dora Capozza and Rupert Brown, 133–48. London: Sage, 2000.

Garland, David E. *1 Corinthians*. Baker Exegetical Commentary on the New Testament. Grand Rapids: Baker Academic, 2003.
Gehman, Richard J. *Doing African Christian Theology: An Evangelical Perspective*. Nairobi: Evangel, 1987.
Gilroy, Paul. "Diaspora and the Detours of Identity." In *Identity and Difference*, edited by Kathryn Woodward, 299–346. London: Sage, 1997.
Grenz, Stanley J., and John R. Franke. *Beyond Foundationalism: Shaping Theology in a Postmodern Context*. Louisville: Westminster John Knox Press, 2001.
Habtu, Tewoldemedhin. "Ezekiel." In *Africa Bible Commentary*, edited by Tokunboh Adeyemo, 933–88. Grand Rapids: Zondervan, 2006.
Hall, David R. *The Unity of the Corinthian Correspondence*. Journal for the Study of the Old Testament, Supplement Series 251. London: T. & T. Clark, 2003.
Hansen, Bruce. *"All of You Are One": The Social Vision of Galatians 3:28, 1 Corinthians 12:13 and Colossians 3:11*. Library of New Testament Studies 409. London: T. & T. Clark, 2010.
Haslam, S. Alexander. *Psychology in Organizations: The Social Identity Approach*. London: Sage, 2001.
Haslam, S. Alexander, and Naomi Ellemers. "Social Identity in Industrial and Organizational Psychology: Concepts, Controversies, and Contributions." *International Review of Industrial and Organizational Psychology* 20 (2005) 39–118.
Hays, Richard B. *First Corinthians*. Interpretation. Louisville: John Knox, 1997.
Heijke, Jan. "Review of *A Listening Church*." *Exchange* 27 (1998) 86–88.
Holter, Knut. "Old Testament Scholarship in Sub-Saharan Africa North of the Limpopo River." In *The Bible in Africa: Transactions, Trajectories, and Trends*, edited by Gerald O. West and Musa W. Dube, 54–71. Boston: Brill Academic, 2000.
Hornsey, Matthew J. "Social Identity Theory and Self-Categorization Theory: A Historical Review." *Social and Personality Psychology Compass* 2 (2008) 204–22.
Horrell, David G. *The Social Ethos of the Corinthian Correspondence: Interests and Ideology from 1 Corinthians to 1 Clement*. Studies of the New Testament and Its World. Edinburgh: T. & T. Clark, 1996.
Howard, David M., Jr. *Joshua*. New American Commentary 5. Nashville: Broadman & Holman, 1998.
Hutton, Rodney R. "Are the Parents Still Eating Sour Grapes? Jeremiah's Use of the *Māšāl* in Contrast to Ezekiel." *Catholic Biblical Quarterly* 71 (2009) 275–85.
Idowu, E. Bolaji. "God." In *Biblical Revelation and African Beliefs*, edited by Kwesi A. Dickson and Paul Ellingworth, 17–29. Maryknoll, NY: Orbis, 1969.
———. "Introduction." In *Biblical Revelation and African Beliefs*, edited by Kwesi A. Dickson and Paul Ellingworth, 9–16. Maryknoll, NY: Orbis, 1969.
Ilo, Stan Chu. *The Church and Development in Africa: Aid and Development from the Perspective of Catholic Social Ethics*. African Christian Studies 2. Eugene, OR: Pickwick, 2011.
Ilo, Stan Chu, Joseph Ogbonnaya, and Alex Ojacor, eds. *The Church as Salt and Light: Path to an African Ecclesiology of Abundant Life*. African Christian Studies 1. Eugene, OR: Pickwick, 2011.
Imasogie, Osadolor. *Guidelines for Christian Theology in Africa*. Theological Perspectives in Africa 5. Achimota, Ghana: Africa Christian, 1983.

Jacobs, Donald R. "Conversion and Culture: An Anthropological Perspective with Reference to East Africa." In *Gospel and Culture: The Papers of a Consultation on the Gospel and Culture*, edited by John Stott and Robert T. Coote, 186–91. William Carey Library Series on Applied Cultural Anthropology. Pasadena, CA: William Carey Library, 1979.

Jenkins, Richard. *Social Identity*. Key Ideas. London: Routledge, 1996.

Jenson, Robert W. *Canon and Creed*. Interpretation. Louisville: Westminster John Knox Press, 2010.

Joyce, Paul. *Divine Initiative and Human Response in Ezekiel*. Journal for the Study of the Old Testament, Supplement Series 51. Sheffield: JSOT, 1989.

———. "Ezekiel and Moral Transformation." In *Transforming Visions: Transformations of Text, Tradition, and Theology in Ezekiel*, edited by William A. Tooman and Michael A. Lyons, 139–58. Princeton Monograph 127. Eugene, OR: Pickwick, 2010.

———. "Individual Responsibility in Ezekiel 18?" In *Studia Biblica 1978: Papers on Old Testament and Related Themes*, edited by E. A. Livingstone, 185–96. Journal for the Study of the Old Testament Supplement 11. Sheffield: JSOT, 1979.

Kaiser, Walter C., Jr. *Toward Old Testament Ethics*. Grand Rapids: Academie, 1983.

Kamaara, Eunice K. "Towards Christian National Identity in Africa: A Historical Perspective to the Challenge of Ethnicity to the Church in Kenya." *Studies in World Christianity* 16 (2010) 126–44.

Kaminsky, Joel. *Corporate Responsibility in the Hebrew Bible*. Journal for the Study of the Old Testament Supplement 196. Sheffield: Sheffield Academic, 1995.

Kapolyo, Joe M. *The Human Condition: Christian Perspectives through African Eyes*. Christian Doctrine in Global Perspectives. Downers Grove, IL: InterVarsity, 2005.

Kato, Byang H. *Theological Pitfalls in Africa*. Kisumu, Kenya: Evangel, 1975.

Katongole, Emmanuel. *The Sacrifice of Africa: A Political Theology for Africa*. Eerdmans Ekkelsia. Grand Rapids: Eerdmans, 2011.

Keener, Craig S., and M. Daniel Carroll R., eds. *Global Voices: Reading the Bible in the Majority World*. Peabody, MA: Hendrickson, 2013.

Kibongi, R. Buana. "Priesthood." In *Biblical Revelation and African Beliefs*, edited by Kwesi A. Dickson and Paul Ellingworth, 47–56. Maryknoll, NY: Orbis, 1969.

Kilby, Karen. "Perichoresis and Projection: Problems with Social Doctrines of the Trinity." *New Blackfriars* 81 (2000) 432–45.

Kim, Yung Suk. *Christ's Body in Corinth: The Politics of a Metaphor*. Paul in Critical Contexts. Minneapolis: Fortress, 2008.

Kossé, Kuzuli. "Unity of Believers." In *Africa Bible Commentary*, edited by Tokunboh Adeyemo, 1288. Grand Rapids: Zondervan, 2006.

Köstenberger, Andreas J. *John*. Baker Exegetical Commentary on the New Testament. Grand Rapids: Baker Academic, 2004.

———. *A Theology of John's Gospel and Letters*. Biblical Theology of the New Testament. Grand Rapids: Zondervan, 2009.

Kuan, Kah-Jin Jeffrey, and Mai-Anh Le Tran. "Reading Race Reading Rahab: A 'Broad' Asian American Reading of a 'Broad' Other." In *Postcolonial Interventions: Essays in Honor of R. S. Sugirtharajah*, edited by Tat-Siong Benny Liew, 27–44. Sheffield: Sheffield Phoenix, 2009.

Kurewa, John. *Preaching and Cultural Identity: Proclaiming the Gospel in Africa*. Nashville: Abingdon, 2000.

Kwok, Pui-lan. "Mercy Amba Oduyoye and African Women's Theology." *Journal of Feminist Studies in Religion* 20/1 (2004) 7–22.

Lanoir, Corinne. "Rahab, traîtresse ou passeause?" *Foi et vie* 97 (1998) 33–39.

LeMarquand, Grant. *An Issue of Relevance: A Comparative Study of the Story of the Bleeding Woman (Mk 5:25–34; Mt 9:20–22; Lk 8:43–48) in North Atlantic and African Contexts*. Bible and Theology in Africa 5. New York: Peter Lang, 2004.

Letlhare, Bernice. "Corporate Personality in Botswana and Ancient Israel: A Religio-Cultural Comparison." In *The Bible in Africa: Transactions, Trajectories, and Trends*, edited by Gerald O. West and Musa W. Dube, 474–80. Boston: Brill Academic, 2000.

Lincoln, Andrew T. *Truth on Trial: The Lawsuit Motif in the Fourth Gospel*. Peabody, MA: Hendrickson, 2000.

Lindars, Barnabas. "Ezekiel and Individual Responsibility." *Vetus Testamentum* 15 (1965) 452–67.

Lo, Lung-Kwong. "'Neither Jew nor Greek' Galatians 3:28 Revisited." *Annali Di Storia Dell'esegesi* 27 (2010) 25–33.

Loba-Mkole, Jean-Claude. "Paul and Africa?" *HTS Teologiese Studies/Theological Studies* 67 (2011) 1–11. http://www.hts.org.za/index.php/HTS/article/viewFile/888/1479.

Magesa, Laurenti. *Anatomy of Inculturation: Transforming the Church in Africa*. Nairobi: Paulines Publications Africa, 2007.

Maina, Wilson Muoha. *Historical and Social Dimensions in African Christian Theology: A Contemporary Approach*. Eugene, OR: Wipf & Stock, 2009.

Malan, Gert J. "Does John 17:11b, 21–23 Refer to Church Unity?" *HTS Teologiese Studies/Theological Studies* 67 (November 4, 2011) 1–10. http://www.hts.org.za/index.php/HTS/article/viewFile/857/1502.

Maluleke, Tinyiko Sam. "Identity and Integrity in African Theology: A Critical Analysis." *Religion and Theology* 8 (2001) 26–41.

———. "In Search of 'The True Character of African Christian Identity': A Review of the Theology of Kwame Bediako." *Missionalia* 25 (1997) 210–19.

Manus, Chris Ukachukwu. "Galatians 3:28—A Study on Paul's Attitude Towards Ethnicity: Its Relevance for Contemporary Nigeria." *Ife Journal of Religions* 2 (1982) 18–26.

———. *Intercultural Hermeneutics in Africa: Methods and Approaches*. Nairobi: Acton, 2003.

Martin, Troy W. "The Covenant of Circumcision (Genesis 17:9–14) and the Situational Antitheses in Galatians 3:28." *Journal of Biblical Literature* 122 (2003) 111–25.

Matties, Gordon H. "Individual Responsibility in Community." In *Ezekiel 18 and the Rhetoric of Moral Discourse*, 113–58. Society of Biblical Literature Dissertation 126. Atlanta: Scholars, 1990.

———. "Reading Rahab's Story: Beyond the Moral of the Story (Joshua 2)." *Direction* 24 (1995) 57–70.

Mbaka, Geoffrey Njeru. "Self-Realization and Self-Esteem: A Preliminary Investigation of Young People in Nairobi Who Do Not Know Their Parentage." MA thesis, Nairobi Evangelical Graduate School of Theology, 2008.

Mbandi, Paul. *A Theology of the Unity of the Church in a Multi-Ethnic Context: Toward a Theological Understanding of the Unity of the Church in Relation to Ethnic Diversity*. Saarbrücken: Dr. Müller, 2010.

Mbenga, M. "Review of *Église Famille de Dieu Dans La Mondialisation. Théologie D'une Nouvelle Voie Africaine D'évangélisation* (2006) and *Ecclésiologie Africaine de Famille de Dieu. Annonce et Débat Avec Les Contemporains* (2007)." *Revue D'histoire et de Philosophie Religieuses* 88 (2008) 209–10.

Mbuvi, Andrew M. "Missionary Acts, Things Fall Apart: Modeling Mission in Acts 17:15–34 and a Concern for Dialogue in Chinua Achebe's *Things Fall Apart*." *Ex Auditu* 23 (2007) 140–56.

McConville, J. Gordon, and Stephen N. Williams. *Joshua*. Two Horizons Old Testament. Grand Rapids: Eerdmans, 2010.

Meeks, Wayne A. "The Image of the Androgyne: Some Uses of a Symbol in Earliest Christianity." *History of Religions* 13 (1974) 165–208.

Mehlman, Bernard H. "Rahab as a Model of Human Redemption." In *"Open Thou Mine Eyes . . .": Essays on Aggadah and Judaica Presented to Rabbi William G. Braude on His Eightieth Birthday and Dedicated to His Memory*, edited by Herman J. Blumberg, 193–207. Hoboken, NJ: KTAV, 1992.

Milgrom, Jacob. "Religious Conversion and the Revolt Model for the Formation of Israel." *Journal of Biblical Literature* 101 (1982) 169–76.

Mitchell, Margaret M. *Paul and the Rhetoric of Reconciliation: An Exegetical Investigation of the Language and Composition of 1 Corinthians*. Louisville: Westminster John Knox, 1993.

Mmassi, Gabriel. "Palaver: Church Leadership in Africa." *African Ecclesial Review* 52 (2010) 173–88.

Mol, Jurrien. *Collective and Individual Responsibility: A Description of Corporate Personality in Ezekiel 18 and 20*. Studia Semitica Neerlandica 53. Leiden: Brill, 2009.

Mudimbe, V. Y. *The Idea of Africa*. Bloomington: Indiana University Press, 1994.

———. *The Invention of Africa: Gnosis, Philosophy, and the Order of Knowledge*. Bloomington: Indiana University Press, 1988.

Mugambi, Jesse N. K. "Africa and the Old Testament." In *Interpreting the Old Testament in Africa Papers from the International Symposium on Africa and the Old Testament in Nairobi, October 1999*, edited by Mary N. Getui et al., 2:7–25. Bible and Theology in Africa. New York: Peter Lang, 2001.

———. "Okot p'Bitek." In *Critiques of Christianity in African Literature: With Particular Reference to the East African Context*, 80–98. Nairobi: East African Educational, 1992.

Mugambi, Jesse N. K., and Laurenti Magesa, eds. *The Church in African Christianity: Innovative Essays in Ecclesiology*. African Challenge. Nairobi: Initiatives, 1990.

Mulago gwa Cikala M., Vincent. "Christianisme et Culture Africaine: Apport Africain À La Théologie." In *Christianity in Tropical Africa: Studies Presented and Discussed at the Seventh International African Seminar, University of Ghana, April 1965*, edited by C. G. Baëta, 308–28. London: Oxford University Press, 1968.

———. "Dialectique existentielle des Bantu et sacramentalisme." In *Aspects de la culture noire*, 146–71. Recherches et débats, Nouv. sér. 24. Paris: A. Fayard, 1958.

———. "Mariage Africain et Mariage Chrétien: Perspectives Liturgico-Pastorales." *Revue Du Clergé Africain* 20 (1965) 547–64.

———. "Le Mariage Traditionnel Bantu." *Revue Du Clergé Africain* 26 (1971) 5–61.

———. "Nécessité de l'adaptation missionaire chez les Bantu du Congo." In *Des Prêtres noirs s'interrogent: cinquante ans après*, 19–40. Paris: Karthala; Présence africaine, 2006.

———. "Le nouveau ritual de la pénitence." In *Pêche, pénitence et réconciliation: Tradition chrétienne et culture africaine: Actes de la neuvième Semaine Theologique de Kinshasa (22–27 juillet 1974)*. Kinshasa: Faculté Théologique Catholique, 1980.

———. "Le Pacte du sang et la communion alimentaire, pierres d'attente de la communion eucharistique." In *Des Prêtres noirs s'interrogent: cinquante ans après*, 171–87. Paris: Karthala; Présence africaine, 2006.

———. "Le Problème D'une Théologie Africaine Revu À La Lumière de Vatican II." *Revue Du Clergé Africain* 24 (1969) 277–314.

———. "Projet de vie et itineraire." In *Interpellations et croissance de la foi: hommage au Prof. V. Mulago: actes de l'Atelier, Kinshasa 13–16 février 1991*, 25–26:25–31. Cahiers des religions africaines. Kinshasa: Facultés Catholiques de Kinshasa, 1992.

———. "Sauver La Vérité Des Sacrements Dans Nos Jeunes Chrétientés." *Revue Du Clergé Africain* 21 (1966) 274–91.

———. "Solidarité Africaine et Coresponsabilité Chrétienne À La Lumière de Vatican II." In *Foi Chrétienne et Langage Humain: Actes de La Septième Semaine Théologique de Kinshasa, 24–29 Juillet 1972*, 86–134. Kinshasa: Faculté de Théologie Catholique, 1978.

———. "Symbolisme dans les religions traditionnelles africaines et sacramentalisme." In *La Pertinence du christianisme en afrique, VIe semaine théologique organisée par la faculté de théologie de l'université nationale du Zaïre, Campus de Kinshasa, 19–23 juillet 1971*, 467–502. Mayidi, Republique du Zaïre: Revue du Clergé africain, 1972.

———. *Théologie africaine et problèmes connexes: au fil des années, 1956–1992*. Études africaines. Paris: L'Harmattan, 2007.

———. "La Théologie et Ses Responsabilités." In *Deuxième Congrès Des Ecrivains et Artistes Noirs*, 27-28:188–205. Rome: Présence africaine, 1959.

———. "Traditional African Religion and Christianity." In *African Traditional Religions in Contemporary Society*, edited by Jacob K. Olupona, 119–34. New York: International Religious Foundation, 1991.

———. *Un Visage africain du christianisme: l'union vitale bantu face à l'unité vitale ecclésiale*. Paris: Présence africaine, 1965.

———. "L'union Vitale Bantu." *Rhythmes Du Monde* 4 (1956) 133–41.

———. "Vital Participation: The Cohesive Principle of the Bantu Community." In *Biblical Revelation and African Beliefs*, edited by Kwesi A. Dickson and Paul Ellingworth, 137–58. New York: Orbis, 1969.

Muli, Alfred Muema. "The Contribution of African Theological Reflection to the Quest for Emancipation." MA thesis, Calvin Theological Seminary, 2003.

Murray, D. F. "The Rhetoric of Disputation: Re-Examination of a Prophetic Genre." *Journal for the Study of the Old Testament* 12 (1987) 95–121.

Mushete, Ngindu, ed. *Combats pour un christianisme africain: mélanges en l'honneur du professeur V. Mulago*. Bibliothèque du Centre d'études des religions africaines 6. Kinshasa: Faculté de théologie catholique, 1981.

———. "L'histoire de La Théologie En Afrique: De La Polémique À L'irénisme Critique." In *La Théologie Africaine S'interroge: Libération Ou Adaptation? Le Colloque d'Accra*, 30–48. Paris: L'Harmattan, 1979.

———. "Modernity in Africa." In *Trends in Mission: Toward the Third Millennium: Essays in Celebration of Twenty-Five Years of SEDOS*, edited by William Jenkinson and Helene O'Sullivan, 143–54. Maryknoll, NY: Orbis, 1991.
Mutunga, Stanley. "Africa's Urban Search for Identity." *Urban Mission* 16 (1998) 7–14.
Mveng, Engelbert. *L'Afrique dans l'Église: Paroles d'un croyant*. Paris: L'Harmattan, 1985.
———. "Un Visage africain du christianisme pour une ecclésiologie africaine." In *Combats pour un christianisme africain: mélanges en l'honneur du professeur V. Mulago*, edited by Ngindu Mushete, 133–35. Bibliothèque de centre d'études des religions africaines 6. Kinshasa: Faculté de théologie catholique, 1981.
Mwaura, Philomena Njeri. "Human Identity and the Gospel of Reconciliation: Agenda For Mission Studies and Praxis in the 21st Century: An African Reflection." *Mission Studies* 26 (2009) 17–30.
Ndlovu-Gatsheni, Sabelo J. "Africa for Africans or Africa for 'Natives' Only? 'New Nationalism' and Nativism in Zimbabwe and South Africa." *Africa Spectrum* 44 (2009) 61–78.
Ngewa, Samuel M. *Galatians*. Africa Bible Commentary. Grand Rapids: Hippo, 2010.
———. *The Gospel of John: A Commentary for Pastors, Teachers and Preachers*. Nairobi: Evangel, 2003.
Niang, Aliou Cissé. *Faith and Freedom in Galatia and Senegal: The Apostle Paul, Colonists and Sending Gods*. Biblical Interpretation 97. Leiden: Brill, 2009.
Njoroge, Nyambura J. "A New Way of Facilitating Leadership: Lessons from African Women Theologians." *Missiology: An International Review* 33/1 (January 2005) 29–46.
Noll, Mark A., and Carolyn Nystrom. *Clouds of Witnesses: Christian Voices from Africa and Asia*. Downers Grove, IL: InterVarsity, 2011.
Nottingham, William J. "Review of *Daughters of Anowa: African Women and Patriarchy*." *International Review of Mission* 94/372 (January 2005) 164–66.
Nwaigbo, Ferdinand. "Church-as-Family in the Rising Tide of Terrorism in Africa." *African Ecclesial Review* 48 (2006) 97–135.
Nyamiti, Charles. *Christ as Our Ancestor: Christology from an African Perspective*. Mambo Occasional Papers 11. Gweru: Mambo, 1984.
———. "The Church as Christ's Ancestral Mediation: An Essay on African Ecclesiology." In *The Church in African Christianity: Innovative Essays in Ecclesiology*, edited by J. N. K. Mugambi and Laurenti Magesa, 129–77. African Challenge. Nairobi: Initiatives, 1990.
———. *Some Contemporary Models of African Ecclesiology: A Critical Assessment in the Light of Biblical and Church Teaching*. Studies in African Christian Theology 3. Nairobi: Catholic University of East Africa Publications, 2007.
———. *The Way to Christian Theology for Africa*. Spearhead. Eldoret, Kenya: Gaba, 1975.
———. "Women from the Perspective of the Bible." *Orita* 2 (n.d.) 161–71.
Oduyoye, Mercy Amba. "The African Experience of God through the Eyes of an Akan Woman." *Cross Currents* 47/4 (Winter 1997–98) 493–504.
———. "The African Family as a Symbol of Ecumenism." *Ecumenical Review* 43/4 (October 1991) 465–78.

———. "Be a Woman, and Africa Will Be Strong." In *Inheriting Our Mothers' Gardens: Feminist Theology in Third World Perspective*, edited by Letty M. Russell et al., 35–53. Philadelphia: Westminster, 1988.

———. *Beads and Strands: Reflections of an African Woman on Christianity in Africa*. Theology in Africa. Maryknoll, NY: Orbis, 2004.

———. "Christianity and African Culture." *International Review of Mission* 84/332-33 (April 1995) 77–90.

———. "The Church of the Future, Its Mission and Theology: A View from Africa." *Theology Today* 52 (1996) 494–505.

———. "A Critique of Mbiti's View on Love and Marriage in Africa." In *Religious Plurality in Africa: Essays in Honour of John S. Mbiti*, edited by Jacob Obafẹmi Kẹhinde Olupọna and Sulayman S. Nyang, 341–65. Religion and Society 32. Berlin: Mouton de Gruyter, 1993.

———. *Daughters of Anowa: African Women and Patriarchy*. Maryknoll, NY: Orbis, 1995.

———. *Hearing and Knowing: Theological Reflections on Christianity in Africa*. Maryknoll, NY: Orbis, 1986.

———. "'In the Image of God . . .': A Theological Reflection from an African Perspective." *Bulletin de Théologie Africaine* 41 (1982) 41–53.

———. *Introducing African Women's Theology*. Introductions in Feminist Theology 6. Cleveland: Pilgrim, 2001.

———. "Naming the Woman: The Words of the Akan and the Words of the Bible." In *Parole de Dieu et langages des hommes: la rencontre de Yaoundé, Sept. 24-28 1980*, 81–97. Collection de théologie africaine 1. Yaoundé, Cameroon: Association œcumenique des theologiens africains, 1982.

———. "A New Community of Women and Men for Africa." *Media Development* 2 (1984) 25–28.

———. "The Search for a Two-Winged Theology." In *Talitha, Qumi! Proceedings of the Convocation of African Women Theologians, Trinity College, Legon-Accra, September 24-October 2, 1989*, edited by Mercy Amba Oduyoye and Rachel Angogo Kanyoro, 27–50. Ibadan: Daystar, 1990.

———. "The Story of a Circle." *The Ecumenical Review* 53/1 (2001) 97–100.

———. *Who Will Roll the Stone Away? The Ecumenical Decade of the Churches in Solidarity with Women*. Risk 47. Geneva: WCC, 1990.

Ogbonnaya, A. Okechukwu. *On Communitarian Divinity: An African Interpretation of the Trinity*. St. Paul, MN: Paragon, 1998.

Oginde, David. "Joshua." In *Africa Bible Commentary*, edited by Tokunboh Adeyemo, 255–94. Grand Rapids: Zondervan, 2006.

Okesson, Gregg A. *Re-Imaging Modernity: A Contextualised Theological Study of Power and Humanity within Akamba Christianity in Kenya*. American Society of Missiology 16. Eugene, OR: Pickwick, 2012.

Okure, Teresa. "Africa: Globalization and the Loss of Cultural Identity." In *Globalization and Its Victims*, edited by Jon Sobrino and Felix Wilfred, 67–74. London: SCM, 2001.

———. "Christian Identity and the Challenge of Authenticity: A View from Africa." In *Christian Identity II*, edited by Verein zur Förderung der Missionswissenschaft, 171–200. Mission Forum 3. Kriens, Switzerland: Brunner, 2007.

―――. "'I will open my mouth in parables' (Matt. 13:35): A Case for a Gospel-Based Biblical Hermeneutics." *New Testament Studies* 46 (2000) 445–63.

―――. *The Johannine Approach to Mission: A Contextual Study of John 4:1–42*. Vol. Reihe 31. WUNT 2. Tübingen: Mohr, 1988.

―――. "'The Ministry of Reconciliation' (2 Cor. 5:14–21): Paul's Key to the Problem of 'the Other' in Corinth." *Mission Studies* 23 (2006) 105–21.

Orobator, Agbonkhianmeghe E. *The Church as Family: African Ecclesiology in Its Social Context*. Hekima College Collection 5. Nairobi: Paulines Publications Africa, 2000.

―――. *From Crisis to Kairos: The Mission of the Church in the Time of HIV/AIDS, Refugees, and Poverty*. Nairobi: Paulines Publications Africa, 2005.

―――. *Theology Brewed in an African Pot*. Maryknoll, NY: Orbis, 2008.

Ott, Martin. "Auf Der Suche Nach Identität: Einige Anmerkungen Zum Stand Der Afrikanischen Theologie Aus Der Sicht Eines 'Gastarbeiters.'" *Zeitschrift Für Missionswissenschaft Und Religionswissenschaft* 86 (2002) 84–98.

Pachuau, Lalsangkima. "Ethnic Identity and the Gospel of Reconciliation." *Mission Studies* 26 (2009) 49–63.

Parratt, John. *Reinventing Christianity: African Theology Today*. Grand Rapids: Eerdmans, 1995.

―――. "Review of *Theology and Identity* and Emmanuel Martey's *African Theology: Inculturation and Liberation*." *International Review of Mission* 84 (1995) 171–72.

Penoukou, Efoe-Julien. "The Churches of Africa: Their Identity? Their Mission?" In *Trends in Mission: Toward the Third Millennium: Essays in Celebration of Twenty-Five Years of SEDOS*, edited by William Jenkinson and Helene O'Sullivan, 39–45. Maryknoll, NY: Orbis, 1991.

Phiri, Isabel Apawo. "Major Challenges for African Women Theologians in Theological Education (1989–2008)." *Studia Historiae Ecclesiasticae* 34/2 (2011) 63–81.

Pobee, John S. *Toward an African Theology*. Nashville: Abingdon, 1979.

Rah, Soong-Chan. *The Next Evangelicalism: Freeing the Church from Western Cultural Captivity*. Downers Grove, IL: InterVarsity, 2009.

Richardson, Don. "Redemptive Analogy." In *Perspectives on the World Christian Movement: A Reader*, edited by Ralph D. Winter et al., 430–36. Pasadena, CA: William Carey Library, 2009.

Robinson, Bernard P. "Rahab of Canaan—and Israel." *Scandinavian Journal of the Old Testament* 23 (2009) 257–73. doi:10.1080/09018320903303603.

Ros, María, Carmen Huici, and Angel Gómez. "Comparative Identity, Category Salience and Intergroup Relations." In *Social Identity Processes: Trends in Theory and Research*, edited by Dora Capozza and Rupert Brown, 81–95. London: Sage, 2000.

Rowlett, Lori L. *Joshua and the Rhetoric of Violence: A New Historicist Analysis*. Sheffield: Sheffield Academic, 1996.

Sanders, James A. "The Family in the Bible." *Biblical Theology Bulletin* 32 (2002) 117–28.

Sanneh, Lamin O. *Translating the Message: The Missionary Impact on Culture*. Maryknoll, NY: Orbis, 1989.

Sherwood, Aaron. "A Leader's Misleading and a Prostitute's Profession: A Re-Examination of Joshua 2." *Journal for the Study of the Old Testament* 31 (2006) 43–61.

Shweder, Richard A., and Edmund J. Bourne. "Does the Concept of the Person Vary Cross-Culturally?" In *Culture Theory: Essays on Mind, Self, and Emotion*, edited by Richard A. Shweder and Robert A. LeVine, 158-99. Cambridge: Cambridge University Press, 1984.

Stager, Lawrence E. "The Archaeology of the Family in Ancient Israel." *Bulletin of the American Schools of Oriental Research* 260 (1985) 1-35.

Stek, John H. "Rahab of Canaan and Israel: The Meaning of Joshua 2." *Calvin Theological Journal* 37 (2002) 28-48.

Stinton, Diane B. *Jesus of Africa: Voices of Contemporary African Christology*. Faith and Culture. Maryknoll, NY: Orbis, 2004.

Tajfel, Henri. "Interindividual Behaviour and Intergroup Behaviour." In *Differentiation between Social Groups: Studies in the Social Psychology of Intergroup Relations*, edited by Henri Tajfel, 27-60. European Monographs in Social Psychology 14. London: Academic, 1978.

———. "Introduction." In *Differentiation between Social Groups: Studies in the Social Psychology of Intergroup Relations*, edited by Henri Tajfel, 1-23. European Monographs in Social Psychology 14. London: Academic, 1978.

———. "Social Categorization, Social Identity and Social Comparison." In *Differentiation between Social Groups: Studies in the Social Psychology of Intergroup Relations*, edited by Henri Tajfel, 61-76. European Monographs in Social Psychology 14. London: Academic, 1978.

Tajfel, Henri, and John C. Turner. "The Social Identity Theory of Intergroup Behavior." In *Political Psychology: Key Readings*, edited by John T. Jost and Jim Sidanius, 276-93. Key Readings in Social Psychology. New York: Psychology Press, 2004.

Tempels, Placide. *Philosophie Bantu*. Introduction et révision de la traduction de A. Rubbens sur le "texte original" par A.J. Smet. Kinshasa: Département de Philosophie et Religions Africaines Faculté de Théologie Catholique, 1979.

Tennent, Timothy. *Theology in the Context of World Christianity: How the Global Church Is Influencing the Way We Think About and Discuss Theology*. Grand Rapids: Zondervan, 2007.

Thiselton, Anthony C. *The First Epistle to the Corinthians: A Commentary on the Greek Text*. New International Greek Testament Commentary. Grand Rapids: Eerdmans, 2000.

Tiénou, Tite. "Evangelical Theology in African Contexts." In *The Cambridge Companion to Evangelical Theology*, edited by Timothy Larsen and Daniel J. Treier, 213-24. Cambridge Companions to Religion. Cambridge: Cambridge University Press, 2007.

Toorn, Karel van der. *Family Religion in Babylonia, Syria, and Israel: Continuity and Changes in the Forms of Religious Life*. Studies in the History and Culture of the Ancient Near East 7. Leiden: Brill, 1996.

Toren, Benno van den. "Kwame Bediako's Christology in Its African Evangelical Context." *Exchange* 26 (1997) 218-32.

Turnbull, Colin M. *The Lonely African*. New York: Simon and Schuster, 1962.

Tutu, Desmond. *No Future Without Forgiveness*. New York: Doubleday, 1999.

Tutu, Desmond, and Mpho Tutu. *Made for Goodness: And Why This Makes All the Difference*. New York: HarperOne, 2010.

Ukpong, Justin S. "Inculturation Hermeneutics: An African Approach to Biblical Interpretation." In *The Bible in a World Context: An Experiment in Contextual*

Hermeneutics, edited by Walter Dietrich and Ulrich Luz, 17–32. Grand Rapids: Eerdmans, 2002.

———. "Jesus' Prayer for His Followers (Jn. 17) in Mission Perspective." *Africa Theological Journal* 18 (1989) 49–60.

Ukwuegbu, Bernard Onyebuchi. "Baptism 'Into Christ': Origin, Meaning and Implications for Christians Today." In *Celebrating the Sacramental World: Essays in Honour of Emeritus Professor Lambert J. Leijssen*, edited by Kekong Bisong and Mathai Kadavil, 129–53. Studies in Liturgy 24. Leuven: Peeters, 2010.

———. *The Emergence of Christian Identity in Paul's Letter to the Galatians: A Social-Scientific Investigation into the Root Causes for the Parting of the Way between Christianity and Judaism*. Arbeiten Zur Interkulturalität 4. Solingen, Germany: Borengässer Bonn, 2003.

———. "'Neither Jew nor Greek': The Church in Africa and the Quest for Self-Understanding in the Light of the Pauline Vision and Today's Context of Cultural Pluralism." *International Journal for the Study of the Christian Church* 8 (2008) 305–18.

Ungar, Sanford J. *Africa: The People and Politics of an Emerging Continent*. New York: Touchstone, 1986.

Uzukwu, Elochukwu E. *A Listening Church: Autonomy and Communion in African Churches*. Eugene, OR: Wipf & Stock, 2006.

———. "Trends in African Theology." *SEDOS Bulletin* (April 1994) 100–101.

———. "Trinity in Contemporary African Theology—Conversation with Augustin Ramazani, Bede Ukwuije, and Benoît Kungua." *Bulletin of Ecumenical Theology* 21 (2009) 23–40.

Uzukwu, Gesila Nneka. "Gal 3:28 and Its Alleged Relationship to Rabbinic Writings." *Biblica* 91 (2010) 370–92.

———. "The Oneness of the Believers: Studying Rom 16:1–16 in the Light of Gal 3:28." In *The Letter to the Romans*, edited by Udo Schnelle, 779–87. Bibliotheca Ephemeridum Theologicarum Lovaniensium 226. Leuven: Peeters, 2009.

Van der Merwe, D. G. "The Character of Unity Expected among the Disciples of Jesus, according to John 17:20–23." *Acta Patristica et Byzantina* 13 (2002) 224–54.

Vanhoozer, Kevin J. *Is There a Meaning In This Text? The Bible, the Reader, and the Morality of Literary Knowledge*. Grand Rapids: Zondervan, 1998.

———. "'One Rule to Rule Them All?' Theological Method in an Era of World Christianity." In *Globalizing Theology: Belief and Practice in an Era of World Christianity*, edited by Craig Ott and Harold A. Netland, 85–126. Grand Rapids: Baker Academic, 2006.

Van Wyk Smith, Malvern. *The First Ethiopians: The Image of Africa and Africans in the Early Mediterranean World*. Johannesburg: Wits University Press, 2009.

———. "'Waters Flowing from Darkness': The Two Ethiopias in the Early European Image of Africa." *Theoria: A Journal of Social and Political Theory* 68 (1986) 67–77.

Visser, Hans, and Gillian Bediako. "Introduction." In *Jesus and the Gospel in Africa: History and Experience*, by Kwame Bediako, xi–xvii. Theology in Africa. Maryknoll, NY: Orbis, 2004.

Volf, Miroslav. *Exclusion and Embrace: A Theological Exploration of Identity, Otherness, and Reconciliation*. Nashville: Abingdon, 1996.

Wagenaar, Hinne. "Theology, Identity and the Pre-Christian Past: A Critical Analysis of Dr. K. Bediako's Theology from a Frisian Perspective." *International Review of Mission* 88 (1999) 364–80.
Walls, Andrew F. "Kwame Bediako and Christian Scholarship in Africa." *International Bulletin of Missionary Research* 32 (2008) 188–93.
Watson, Francis. "Trinity and Community: A Reading of John 17." *International Journal of Systematic Theology* 1 (1999) 168–84.
Webster, John. "The Dogmatic Location of the Canon." *Neue Zeitschrift Für Systematische Theologie Und Religionsphilosophie* 43 (2001) 17–43.
———. "Principles of Systematic Theology." *International Journal of Systematic Theology* 11 (2009) 56–71.
Wild-Wood, Emma. *Migration and Christian Identity in Congo (DRC)*. Studies of Religion in Africa 35. Leiden: Brill, 2008.
Witherington, Ben, III. *Conflict and Community in Corinth: A Socio-Rhetorical Commentary on 1 and 2 Corinthians*. Grand Rapids: Eerdmans, 1995.
Woodward, Kathryn. "Concepts of Identity and Difference." In *Identity and Difference*, edited by Kathryn Woodward, 7–50. London: Sage, 1997.
Worchel, Stephen, et al. "A Multidimensional Model of Identity: Relating Individual and Group Identities to Intergroup Behaviour." In *Social Identity Processes: Trends in Theory and Research*, edited by Dora Capozza and Rupert Brown, 15–32. London: Sage, 2000.
Woudstra, Marten H. *The Book of Joshua*. New International Commentary on the Old Testament. Grand Rapids: Eerdmans, 1981.
Yamsat, Pandang. *An Exposition of First Corinthians for Today*. Koinonia Bible Commentary. Kaduna, Nigeria: Baraka, 2004.

www.ingramcontent.com/pod-product-compliance
Lightning Source LLC
Chambersburg PA
CBHW051053230426
43667CB00013B/2275